THE PRUDENT SPECULATOR
AL FRANK ON INVESTING

Al Frank

Dow Jones-Irwin
Homewood, Illinois 60430

This book is dedicated to my wife and partner, Victoria Baldwin, without whose encouragement, support, and help it would not have been written; and to my children, Phyllis, Lisa, and Jennifer, for whom it was written.

© **Al Frank, 1990**

Dow Jones-Irwin is a trademark of Dow Jones & Company, Inc.

All rights reserved. No part of this publication may be reproduced, stored in a retrieval system, or transmitted, in any form or by any means, electronic, mechanical, photocopying, recording, or otherwise, without the prior written permission of the publisher.

This publication is designed to provide accurate and authoritative information in regard to the subject matter covered. It is sold with the understanding that the publisher is not engaged in rendering legal, accounting, or other professional service. If legal advice or other expert assistance is required, the services of a competent professional person should be sought.

From a Declaration of Principles jointly adopted by a Committee of the American Bar Association and a Committee of Publishers.

Sponsoring editor: Amy Hollands
Project editor: Jane Lightell
Production manager: Ann Cassady
Jacket design: Renee Klyczek Nordstrom
Compositor: Carlisle Communications, Ltd.
Typeface: 11/13 Times Roman
Printer: Arcata/Kingsport

Library of Congress Cataloging-in-Publication Data
Frank, Al.
   The prudent speculator: Al Frank on investing / Al Frank.
    p.   cm.
   ISBN 1-55623-191-1
   1. Stocks. 2. Investments. 3. Speculation. I. Title.
HG4661.F69   1990
332.64'5—dc20

                       89–38724
                       CIP

Printed in the United States of America
1 2 3 4 5 6 7 8 9 0 K 6 5 4 3 2 1 0 9

CONTENTS

ACKNOWLEDGMENTS

I do not claim any original or creative thoughts for this book; it is made up of the ideas and commentary of others, sampled in a random fashion and cobbled together in an eclectic collection, which I hope is not too inconsistent or paradoxical. I also do not have a wonderful memory, so I can't truly acknowledge all those who have helped me, either in personal conversation or through their broadcast and printed words. For all those who see their insights on these pages without attribution, I thank you and ask your indulgence for any unintended slights.

I typed the several revisions of the manuscript myself, but did not hesitate to accept the suggestions, editing, and emendations of my wife, Vicki Baldwin, who is a very sharp editor in her own right. Vicki constantly questioned the use of jargon and complexities from the eye of a layman and strove to clarify the text. Phyllis E. Frank, C.P.A., my eldest daughter who now works with me, also read every page and helped to untangle my syntax as well as challenge propositions and conclusions.

I was helped by the knowledge and expertise of John Buckingham, our director of research, who emended some egregious calculations and dubious analytical concepts, as well as providing important data processing materials. The chapter on margin would not be as nearly accurate as it may be if it weren't for Mary McNally, who pointed out some blatant mistakes and tried to get me to conform to her knowledge of industry standards. Mike Moody volunteered to read the chapter on technical analysis and offered a more-balanced overview. Through our discussions over the years I have learned much from Gary J. Goodman, of G.J.G., Inc.

Naturally, I received many excellent suggestions and critiques from my editors, some of which found their way to print here. Notwithstanding, I claim any goofs or unclearness for myself.

A. F.

INTRODUCTION

DREAMED-OF REWARDS

The stock market may not return you undreamed-of rewards, because many beginners and long-time participants dream of fantastic and unrealistic rewards. However, if you are willing to get rich slowly, the market is the place to be to make or maintain a fortune. Few enterprises bring the great and systematic returns of a successful business. Real estate has been the source of many fortunes, usually over long periods of time. With the proper approach, attention, and long-term application, the stock market can hold its own with other traditional methods of making money on a grand scale. Happily, not much money is needed to start, and it can be done with a part-time commitment.

You can begin your stock portfolio with a few hundred dollars, building on it by making additional contributions and utilizing the gains from market appreciation. True, at this level it would take a long time to build a substantial equity, but most people have a long time or can start with more than a few hundred dollars. I have often been amazed by people in their 50's or 60's with good health who told me they were too old to undertake a three-to-five–year stock program, especially as their statistical life expectancies offered 20 to 30 years or more.

Let time work for you. As shown in Figure I–1, if you begin with $2,000, add $2,000 a year for 19 more years, and accomplish a 15 percent after-tax (or tax-sheltered) compounded annual return, your $40,000 cash contribution would become $237,620 in 20 years. That portfolio would appreciate $35,643 in its 21st year and could provide increasing income for many years thereafter.

If you were able to average a greater after-tax compounded annual return, or to take more risk by using leverage (margin), you might do much better. Just moving from 15 percent to 18 percent compounded annually for 20 years increases the total equity to $348,042—a 56 percent

Figure I-1

After-Tax plus $2,000 per Year Compounded Growth (Starting with $2,000, Plus Adding $2,000 Annually and Compounding at Various Rates)

Year	At 12%	Value	At 15%	Value	At 18%	Value	At 20%	Value	At 25%	Value
0		2,000.00		2,000.00		2,000.00		2,000.00		2,000.00
1	240.00	4,240.00	300.00	4,300.00	360.00	4,360.00	400.00	4,400.00	500.00	4,500.00
2	508.80	6,748.80	645.00	6,945.00	784.80	7,144.80	880.00	7,280.00	1,125.00	7,625.00
3	809.86	9,558.66	1,041.75	9,986.75	1,286.66	10,430.86	1,456.00	10,736.00	1,906.25	11,531.25
4	1,147.04	12,705.69	1,498.01	13,484.76	1,877.56	14,308.42	2,147.20	14,883.20	2,882.81	16,414.06
5	1,524.68	16,230.38	2,022.71	17,507.48	2,575.52	18,883.94	2,976.64	19,859.84	4,103.52	22,517.58
6	1,947.65	20,178.02	2,626.12	22,133.60	3,399.11	24,283.04	3,971.97	25,831.81	5,629.39	30,146.97
7	2,421.36	24,599.39	3,320.04	27,453.64	4,370.95	30,653.99	5,166.36	32,998.17	7,536.74	39,683.72
8	2,951.93	29,551.31	4,118.05	33,571.68	5,517.72	38,171.71	6,599.63	41,597.80	9,920.93	51,604.64
9	3,546.16	35,097.47	5,035.75	40,607.44	6,870.91	47,042.62	8,319.56	51,917.36	12,901.16	66,505.81
10	4,211.70	41,309.17	6,091.12	48,698.55	8,467.67	57,510.29	10,383.47	64,300.84	16,626.45	85,132.26
11	4,957.10	48,266.27	7,304.78	58,003.33	10,351.85	69,862.14	12,860.17	79,161.00	21,283.06	108,415.32
12	5,791.95	56,058.22	8,700.50	68,703.83	12,575.19	84,437.33	15,832.20	96,993.21	27,103.83	137,519.15
13	6,726.99	64,785.20	10,305.58	81,009.41	15,198.72	101,636.04	19,398.64	118,391.85	34,379.79	173,898.94
14	7,774.22	74,559.43	12,151.41	95,160.82	18,294.49	121,930.53	23,678.37	144,070.22	43,474.74	219,373.68
15	8,947.13	85,506.56	14,274.12	111,434.94	21,947.50	145,878.03	28,814.04	174,884.26	54,843.42	276,217.09
16	10,260.79	97,767.35	16,715.24	130,150.19	26,258.05	174,136.07	34,976.85	211,861.11	69,054.27	347,271.37
17	11,732.08	111,499.43	19,522.53	151,672.71	31,344.49	207,480.57	42,372.22	256,233.33	86,817.84	436,089.21
18	13,379.93	126,879.36	22,750.91	176,423.62	37,346.50	246,827.07	51,246.67	309,480.00	109,022.30	547,111.51
19	15,225.52	144,104.88	26,463.54	204,887.17	44,428.87	293,255.94	61,896.00	373,376.00	136,777.88	685,889.39
20	17,292.59	163,397.47	30,733.07	237,620.24	52,786.07	348,042.01	74,675.20	450,051.20	171,472.35	859,361.74
21	19,607.70	185,005.17	35,643.04	275,263.28	62,647.56	412,689.57	90,010.24	542,061.44	214,840.43	1,076,202.17
22	22,200.62	209,205.79	41,289.49	318,552.77	74,284.12	488,973.69	108,412.29	652,473.73	269,050.54	1,347,252.72
23	25,104.69	236,310.48	47,782.92	368,335.68	88,015.26	578,988.96	130,494.75	784,968.47	336,813.18	1,686,065.89
24	28,357.26	266,667.74	55,250.35	425,586.03	104,218.01	685,206.97	156,993.69	943,962.17	421,516.47	2,109,582.37
25	32,000.13	300,667.87	63,837.91	491,423.94	123,337.25	810,544.23	188,792.43	1,134,754.60	527,395.59	2,638,977.96

greater total return. Even more delicious would be a 20 percent compounded return, resulting in an equity of $450,051, or more than twice that of a 15 percent compounding.

Fantasizing to almost undreamed-of territory could include a 25 percent compounded annual gain, which would lead to $859,362 after 20 years. At this level, the dreamed-of portfolio would appreciate $214,840 in the 20th year alone, probably enough for most of us to live on, given the endemic inflation built into our economy. Even if $200,000 only bought one third as much in 20 years as it does now, it would be a nice financial cushion for the future.

A BIT OF BACKGROUND

Although my experience in the stock market is probably not unique, it is certainly out of the ordinary. None of my parents or extended family owned stocks, nor did I until I was 38 years old. I did not work for a bank or brokerage house, or take any finance courses in college. I happened upon the stock market due to a general interest in the world and because my Ph.D. sponsor was an active market player. Like so many people, I thought "the market" was only for "richies," not for a working class stiff like myself. Until I was almost 50 years old I never earned more than $25,000 a year, first as a printer and printshop owner, then as a teacher and assistant professor. The stock market changed all that.

I began with stocks late in 1968 by buying an occasional position with the few hundred dollars I'd managed to accumulate. By 1977, my interest in the market had increased enough for me to become a "professional" by registering as an investment advisor, managing small sums for a few friends and acquaintances, and starting a primitive stock advisory letter called *The Pinchpenny Speculator*. At the time, my career orientation was toward higher education, and I thought of my newsletter as an educational publication, as its original subtitle, "a fortnightly epistle on investing," suggested. The letter began as a journal of my experiences, learning, and decisions. It still is. The first letters were typed on a manual typewriter with 100 or so copies made at a local duplicating shop.

As my expertise and income increased, I moved on to an electric typewriter. I learned COBOL computer programming in night classes at Santa Monica College and generated computer analyses at school and at timesharing companies. After awhile, I changed my letter's name to *The*

Prudent Speculator, because too many people were confusing the former title with "penny stocks."

Still, investment advising was a part-time occupation for several years until I was discovered by *The Hulbert Financial Digest* (*HFD*). In 1983, *The Prudent Speculator* (*TPS*) was found to be the best-performing newsletter—of those monitored by *HFD*—in each of the four quarters and for the year overall. Publicity and subscriptions poured in, and life hasn't been the same since.

MY PUBLISHED CREDENTIALS

TPS Portfolio's gain for 1983, based on my actual *margined* portfolio, was 117.74 percent, quite exceptional for a common stock portfolio without emphasizing market timing, high-flying options, or futures contracts. Some would say that using margin—borrowed funds collateralized by stock equity—was pretty high flying, but I have always believed leverage is a reasonable businessperson's technique. I explain this belief in detail in Chapter 5, "The Myths and Magic of Margin."

More important than any one year's results, TPS Portfolio's long-term performance is exceptional, especially before the Crash of '87, but even after that event, including the traumatic losses incurred. For its first six years, beginning with $8,006 in cash (equity) value and some $16,200 worth of stocks, my actual TPS Portfolio was able to appreciate 1,379 percent, which works out to a 45.48 percent annualized rate of return from 3/11/77 through 12/31/83.

For the past 12 years TPS Portfolio managed a total net gain (accounting for trading commissions, margin expenses, dividends, but not taxes) of 1,773.85 percent, which is 27.08 percent compounded annually, including the carnage wrought by the Crash of '87. A replication of TPS Portfolio's audited performance report—conducted by Deloitte Haskins + Sells—is displayed in Figure I–2. Hindsight and reflection show in detail (see Chapter 6, "The Crash of '87") that I might have avoided much of the damage of that meltdown. Even having suffered through October–November of '87, TPS Portfolio still was able to outperform the major averages for over 12 years and to become the best-performing newsletter of those followed by *The Hulbert Financial Digest* for the past 9 years (since *HFD*'s inception).

FIGURE I–2
TPS Portfolio Audited Investment Performance

Year	Actual Margined TPS*	Hypothetical Unmargined TPS[†]	DJIA[‡]
1977[§]	+70.28%	+34.48%	−12.84%
1978	+25.00%	+19.17%	+2.81%
1979	+63.46%	+33.81%	+10.68%
1980	+15.69%	+16.99%	+22.13%
1981	−.74%	+17.28%	−3.65%
1982	+58.54%	+28.46%	+27.20%
1983	+117.74%	+45.44%	+26.06%
1984	−12.71%	+2.14%	+1.35%
1985	+50.72%	+23.41%	+33.62%
1986	+46.46%	+21.84%	+27.25%
1987	−55.65%	−23.78%	+5.55%
1988	+50.16%	+26.34%	+16.21%

Annualized Rates of Return for the 12-Year Period[§]

+27.06%*   +19.08%[†]   +12.14%[‡]

*Al Frank's actual margined portfolio (also known as TPS Portfolio); includes the effects of dividend income, margin interest, sales, purchases, cash additions, and withdrawals in computing the time-weighted percentage change in equity compounded quarterly.
[†]Al Frank's hypothetical cash portfolio, calculated as if TPS Portfolio were never margined; including effects of dividend income, sales and purchases, but of course not margin interest in computing the time-weighted change in market value, compounded quarterly.
[‡]Source: Lipper Analytical Securities Corporation, "Total Reinvested Percent Change," includes a full year for 1977; we have calculated the annualized rate of return.
[§]TPS Portfolio figures are for March 1977 through year-end, or approximately nine months, while DJIA figures are for the whole year of 1977.

As the justly required performance disclaimer says, past performance is no guarantee of future performance, and recommendations may not become profitable or equal past performance.

I have modified my approach to more heavily weigh the kinds of risks present in the summer of '87 in order to avoid suffering the repetition of a similar event. We plan never again to be heavily margined going into both an overbought and overvalued market such as occurred during August–September 1987. So, I feel some confidence in the long-range record of prudent speculating even while keeping in mind its singular big stumble and the potential for future devastating declines.

CAN A SUCCESSFUL STRATEGY
BE COMMUNICATED?

With this book I intend to stimulate thought and challenge reflection, resulting in clarifications and understandings that you may "know" but have not systematically considered. Such an encounter can lay the groundwork for further inquiry and action. I have worked hard to present accurate information to help you to integrate some dry and potentially overlooked facts into the matrix of your personal knowledge.

We will examine subtle, often commonplace errors or misleading ideas that have come to be expressed in cliches and slogans. We will challenge questionable dogma, false statements, and errors of reasoning that give rise to dubious assertions and unexamined half-truths. In these pages I am sharing valid, meaningful, and useful formulations. A good book on investing must be involved with semantics and psychology because, until we are in accord with an understanding of ourselves and our terms, there is diminished likelihood of understanding or consistently doing well in the stock market.

SEMANTICS IS MORE THAN JUST WORDPLAY

Right off, let us agree to a stipulated definition that all so-called investing in common stocks is a form of *speculation*. I believe it is important at the outset, throughout the pages of this book, and indeed in our everyday thinking about the stock market, to be aware and admit that when we trade stocks we are speculators. This is in keeping with classical definitions of that word and its cognates.

Consider the following entries in *The Random House College Dictionary* (Revised Edition, 1980):

> **speculate** **1.** to engage in thought or reflection; meditate. **2.** to indulge in conjectural thought. **3.** to engage in any business transaction involving considerable risk for the chance of large gains.

> **speculation** **1.** the contemplation or consideration of some subject. **2.** a single instance or process of consideration. **3.** a conclusion or opinion reached by such contemplation. **4.** conjectural consideration of a matter; conjecture or surmise. **5.** engagement in business transactions involving considerable risk for the chance of large gains.

speculative **1.** pertaining to or of the nature of speculation, contemplation, conjecture, or abstract reasoning. . . . **4.** of the nature of or involving commercial or financial speculation.

speculator **1.** a person who is engaged in commercial or financial speculation.

I submit that when we trade stocks we undertake a "business transaction involving considerable risk for the chance of large gains." Otherwise we would put our money into Treasury bills or insured certificates of deposit (CDs). Furthermore, the whole process of systematic and prudent stock speculation involves thought, reflection, contemplation, conjecture, surmise, and abstract reasoning. Why then is the word *speculator* an anathema to so many who find the word *investor* comfortable and satisfying? Because *invest* and *investment* carry connotations of gains and goods without great risks.

Note how the same dictionary defines these terms:

invest **1.** to put (money) to use, by purchase or expenditure, in something offering profitable returns, esp. interest or income. **2.** to spend; *to invest large sums in books*. **3.** to use, give, or devote (time, talent, etc.) as to achieve something; *he invested a lot of time in trying to help retarded children*. **4.** to furnish with power, authority, rank, etc.

investment **1.** the investing of money or capital for profitable returns. **2.** a particular instance or mode of investing money. **3.** money or capital invested. **4.** a property or right in which a person invests. **5.** a devoting, using, or giving of time, talent, emotional energy, etc., as to achieve something.

Nowhere in any of the definitions of *invest* or *investment* do the words *chance, risk* or *gain* occur. Oh no, investing is perceived as good and not dangerous because it offers "profitable returns," it offers "to achieve something." Perhaps we can trace the distrust of terms like *speculate* to their roots, which include *to see* (e.g., *spectacles*) and *to look out* (visually and mentally contemplating the distance and thereby the future?). Perception and conjecture are notoriously deceiving, especially compared to the comfortable connotation and psychic association with clothes, a *vest* or *vestment*, the root of *investment*.

But there is no investment—let alone stock market transaction—that does not carry with it chance and risk, and few stocks are bought without the thought of gain, usually large gains. Even allegedly safe "investments" carry several considerable risks. In early 1989 many "very safe" Triple A rated bonds (e.g., RJR Nabisco) lost some 20 percent of their market price in a few days after the announcement of a proposed leveraged buyout.

We know that common stocks can vary in price several percent on any given day and over the course of a year some will more than double in market price while others will lose a great portion or even all of their previous market price. We also know that real estate is not immune from serious depreciation and loss due to overbuilding or economic downturns.

It irritates me to see advertising, dressed in the most dignified tones, encouraging "investing" in the most risky and volatile of financial instruments, such as commodities, limited partnerships, futures, or collectibles. After years of trying to get people to use the appropriate word and thus think of themselves as speculators, I have obtained a reluctant acceptance by a very few and a turnoff by many who did not want to think of themselves as speculators or what they did with stocks as speculations. Still, I will keep rooting for this semantic honesty because it is so important to recognize that critical difference that will help in our outlook, thinking, and trading.

"A speculator is a man who observes the future and acts before it occurs," according to Bernard Baruch, as quoted by *tomorrow's stocks* (P.O. Box 6216, Scottsdale, AZ 85261), an excellent technical letter that pays attention to fundamentals also. While I like the image of Baruch and I love the sentiment expressed, I'm not sure how we can observe the future before it occurs. But I do think we can anticipate probable future events and speculate on them.

IS THIS APPROACH FOR YOU?

There are many excellent books on stock speculating available (even if their authors insist on using the word *investing*), but there is not—nor will there ever likely be—a definitive, all-satisfying book. Stock market participants vary too much in their experience and outlook to render any one approach appropriate for all. This is a case of reaching some of the people some of the time but never reaching all of the people all of the time.

I offer a relatively simple approach and system that has worked well for me for over 12 years of public practice. Because of the success of the method, many will find it appealing, yet few likely will pursue it completely because of preconceptions and personality.

Even those of you who decide the complete approach is not your cup of tea may pick up many useful pointers to modify and improve your speculative practices. All theoretical concepts are grounded in practice, and most of my daily activities have a theoretical basis. There is always the danger that some of my rationales are actually psychologically defensive rationalizations. At least rationalizations can be examined and are thus more productive than no reasoned bases at all.

FOUR CARDINAL PRINCIPLES

Here is my game plan. I buy undervalued stocks to be held until they are fully valued and then sold. If you think I've just said I buy low and sell high, that is very close to the main idea and you are almost correct. Alas, sometimes an undervalued stock becomes fully valued at a price lower than its original cost—due to its corporation's problems—at which time I find myself having bought high and perhaps selling low. Periodic losses are inescapable and part of the overall process. Generally losses are well overcome by gains, on average.

Our speculative method has four essential components. Each is clear on its own but is interrelated with the other three. The first is stock *selection,* arguably the easiest part of the system. Stock analysis, monitoring, and selection is usually the most time-consuming chore for prudent speculators. Stock analysis requires systematic updating and review but, depending upon how many stocks you would want to follow and how sophisticated a computer system you employ, could probably be handled in five to ten hours a week. It need not require daily involvement. Stock selection and valuation is reviewed in Chapter 2 and Appendix A.

Here is where some "summer speculators" get off the bandwagon. It sometimes takes years for an undervalued stock to become fully valued. Often a cheap stock becomes cheaper before its value is recognized only years later in the stock market. But this waiting game usually works in our favor. By the time many of our out-of-favor stocks do become recognized and priced fairly, their corporations have often grown even more valuable so that our initial estimated gains or goal prices are exceeded. Thus *patience* becomes one of the four cardinal principles of prudent speculating. Patience is a doubled-edge skill, useful both in waiting for a good speculation to come along and in holding it for an optimum gain. Evidence of the historical value of patience is detailed throughout this book.

Here is a complication. Common stocks—which represent equity ownership of corporations and *should* reflect the value of those corporations—often have a life of their own in the stock market. Stock prices are influenced by many noncorporate events such as the general economic cycle, interest rates, the money supply, rumors, Federal Reserve policy, and faith in the government. Stock markets can become overbought, and thereafter likely to sell off, or oversold and likely to rally. They also can become overvalued and likely to decline or undervalued and likely to advance. Each of these conditions can apply to the short, intermediate, and long term, requiring appropriate strategies and responses. *Risk management* which among other things considers the current condition of the market is dealt with in Chapter 4.

Here is a goody. Effective stock portfolio management balances stock diversification, market timing, dollar cost averaging, and risk management. *Diversification* is another of the four principles and is an integral part of stock portfolio management reviewed in Chapter 3. Several studies have shown that sufficient diversification, both among different stocks and over long periods of time, can reduce many of the risks involved in speculating.

Summarizing my four-fold approach is the acronym PASADARM, which stands for *Patience And Selection And Diversification And Risk Management*. Those *And*s are not present only as vowels. They are logically conjunctive, meaning that all elements are tied together and work together. To question which is more important—for example selection or diversification—is to miss the point. Sufficient diversification is a safety process to overcome the effect of those carefully selected stocks that unexpectedly go sour. Risk management coordinates each of the other three essentials as well as considering overbought or oversold and overvalued or undervalued markets. Note: *Diversification* and *Risk management* are cardinal principles.

TECHNICAL ANALYSIS VERSUS FUNDAMENTAL ANALYSIS

There are two principal schools of speculating, but the best practitioners of each school generally pay attention to what the other has to offer. I adhere to the school of fundamental analysis for stock selection and study the school of technical analysis for market timing. In a desert island scenario where we are only allowed one or the other, I would have to choose fundamental analysis for corporation (stock) selection. After the stocks' price fluctuations in the fickle market run their volatile course, the growing valuable corporations still will have great worth that the market sooner or later recognizes with higher prices.

But we do not live on a desert island, and we can integrate both methodologies. Interestingly enough, market timing—generally ascribed to technical analysis—can be achieved in large measure by keeping track of fundamental valuations. As stock and market valuations become too high on average—historically and in relation to other criteria such as interest rates—selloff signals are generated. This is brought out in detail in the chapter on the Crash of '87.

LUCK FAVORS THE WELL PREPARED

I have often been lucky in the stock market. That is, I have had some terrible luck and some wonderful luck. So many people approach the market in an adversarial attitude, as if the market is out there to entice them, frustrate them, and ultimately do them in. Of course, the market is indifferent. It has no will or agenda. Personifying or reifying the market— attributing to it human characteristics—is a great way to play mind games on yourself. I have for a long time felt, and experience has borne this out, that I had as much chance or more of enjoying good luck as suffering bad luck, especially if I attempted to understand much of what was ongoing, did my homework, and applied my game plan systematically.

That ancient book of Chinese wisdom—the *Tao Teh King* by Lao Tzu—tells us that it is not wise to go to extremes. How true that is in the stock market. On the other hand, it is wise to flow with nature and events, accepting them and adjusting to them. "Never fight the Fed (the Federal Reserve's interest rate and monetary policies) or the tape (the action of stock price trading)" is a Taoist-like idea, and sage advice. If you can develop that middle way and sufficiently prepare, much good fortune will likely follow from your efforts. You don't have to be a genius or certified public accountant, but you can't just throw the proverbial darts either and rely on blind luck.

The information and suggestions in this book should allow you to find sympathetic guidelines, or to modify your own, to achieve handsome gains in the stock market. Of course, I am still studying and learning, frequently amused at how many things I don't know, but aware that an encyclopaedic knowledge might be counterproductive. We have a manageable strategy that works and ain't broke, so we're not trying to fix it. But any speculative stock market methodology can be improved, adjusted, and modified, especially as the nature of the investment world changes over time.

In the past few years we have faced an explosion of new "derivative instruments" (e.g., new future contracts, indexes, and options on indexes), changed regulations, dominance by institutional trading, and the internationalization of markets. Still, "the fundamental things apply, as time goes by." Buy low and sell high, and do it before the other guy!

CHAPTER 1

PREMISES AND PRINCIPLES

So much information, so many possibilities, so many published "successful" methods and strategies for speculating with stocks. How is one to choose among the many approaches, especially as apparently successful strategists dismiss their competitors' methods as seriously flawed or completely missing the point? How can one apply even one of numerous systems when the skills involved seem to require a graduate degree in mathematics, accounting, social psychology, or individual psychology?

Ask yourself, "Does this system generally make sense to me?" Another important question is, "Has this system actually made superior profits investing real money in the stock market?" That the so-called experts put their own money where their mouths are can be an acid test. I could hardly believe my ears the first time I heard a famous newsletter writer intone that he did not buy the stocks he recommended because owning them might color his thinking and distort his objectivity.

It's very easy for a newsletter editor to say, "Sell all stocks!" because the market looks dangerous and we can always buy back later. It's quite another thing for prudent speculators to have to pay two extra brokerage commissions—getting out now and back in later—and to create tax consequences, then having to decide when to buy, often at higher prices than were received from bailing out. There are only a few newsletter writers and advisors who do buy stocks from the lists of stocks they recommend, as we do, albeit often there are more recommendable stocks than I can afford at a given time.

As anyone knows who has traded a system on paper and then traded that system in the marketplace, there is quite a difference, usually working against the performance of the actual versus the theoretical investing. If you understand a system's basics and you know it has worked for a meaningful 5-10–year period, you're much better off and more likely to find it useful than if you are merely impressed by authors' scholarly or entertaining explanations of why their approaches work.

In March 1977, I began publishing my stock advisory letter, *The Prudent Speculator* (*TPS*) (originally titled *The Pinchpenny Speculator*), showing my portfolio at the time to have $16,200 in stocks and $8,007 in equity. This portfolio, referred to as *TPS Portfolio,* has from the start been used as a real-time, actual model portfolio and is referred to throughout this book, its early history given in Chapter 7. The details show the results of my selections, strategies, and decisions, with winners and losers, in good times and bad, not only as "the record," but also as an actual example of the premises and principles I follow.

Audited statements of TPS Portfolio show a 27 percent compounded annual return—including the difficult losses endured during the Crash of '87—for the 11 years and nine months through December 31, 1988 (see Figure I–2). That compounded annual return is based on TPS Portfolio being heavily margined for the entire period. A hypothetical rendering of TPS Portfolio as a nonmargined account—that is, if all transactions were bought for 100 percent cash—results in an annualized rate of return of 19.08 percent, with 1987 as the only "down" year, depreciating 23.78 percent.

One condition that permitted me to gain those returns and become successful was starting in relative ignorance. I began with few preconceptions and quickly found a personally compatible approach that was manageable, comprehensible, and worked, most of the time. No matter how intelligent and effective a system might be, it probably will not be successful for you unless you understand it, believe in it, and are able to practice it systematically and with consistency.

BELIEF IS THE GROUND OF SPECULATION

Before working on this book, I used to think that patience was the most important quality a successful speculator needed. Without minimizing the essential ingredient of patience, I have come to realize that *belief* may be the most important characteristic for success in long-term, consistent, successful speculation. If we do not believe in what we are doing, how can we find the patience and perseverance to carry on when the process is often tedious, subject to unlimited mistakes and pitfalls, and cannot even avoid numerous losses?

Speculation is not a religion, but faith and belief surely are the individual's ground for participating in a system based upon future prospects that are in accord with present perceptions and past experiences. We do not need miracles in order to believe in the rewards of effective stock speculation. Historical and statistical probability are sufficient. Happily, there is incontrovertible evidence that common stocks provide the greatest return on equity of any kind of organized market speculation over long periods of time. Our first order of business then is to study the history of stock price performance over the past six decades and, in doing so, convince ourselves that the past is prologue to the future, albeit with unknown variations. (See Figure 1–1.)

THE MIRACLE OF COMPOUNDING

There is a miracle associated with speculation—the miracle of compounding. Many have commented upon the fantastic results of the consistent compounded annual growth of money or businesses. Warren Buffett, probably the greatest pure stock speculator in history, claimed in early 1986 that if you had invested $10,000 in the partnership he started in 1956 and maintained that investment through the years by moving on to Berkshire Hathaway after the partnership was disbanded in

FIGURE 1–1
Sixty-Three–Year Returns of Financial Instruments and Inflation
($1 invested year-end 1925 through year-end 1988)

Category of Investment	12/31/88 Value	Compounded Rate
Small Company Stocks	$1,478.14	12.3%
Common Stocks	406.45	10.0
Long-term Corporate Bonds	21.90	5.0
Long-term Government Bonds	14.64	4.4
Intermediate Government Bonds	18.98	4.8
U.S. Treasury Bills	8.93	3.5
Inflation		3.1

Source: Adapted from Ibbotson Associates, *Stocks, Bonds, Bills, and Inflation: 1989 Yearbook (SBBI)*. Chicago: Ibbotson Associates, Inc., 1989.

1969, you would have $15 million some 32 years later, a superlative return indeed.

Few of us would have had the money or the temperament to leave it untouched for four decades without wanting to use some or all of it for "emergencies" or foolishness. Ravages upon long-appreciated funds might also have been caused by Uncle Sam's participation in the annual gains (although with Buffett's practice of no dividends, tax consequences have been modest). Still, imagine setting up a trust fund of $10,000 at your child's birth and having it become worth $15 million 32 years later. Heck, how about seeing it grow to $867,000 after 20 years (using the same compounded rate), a nest egg for college and a capital start in adult life.

As truly handsome and exceptional as Mr. Buffett's record is, in actuality it is "only" some 25 percent or 26 percent compounded annually. Figure 1–2 is a brief compounded annual growth table to show how patience and perseverance could lead to independent wealth at various levels of performance. While these figures refer to the growth of an initial $100, you can compare beginning with $10,000 by just adding two zeros to the totals shown. For example, where an initial $100 becomes $146,977 after 40 years compounding at 20 percent per year, an initial $10,000 would become $14,697,700 if left to accumulate and compound for four decades and if not diminished by taxes or other expenses.

To be fair, outside a situation like Buffett's partnership and merely holding Berkshire Hathaway common shares, there would be trading commissions and income taxes along the way. However, these ongoing expenses might be less than you'd imagine, given long-term holding periods—where taxes are not incurred until a position is sold. It is also possible to keep your capital available to compound in tax-deferred programs such as pension, IRA, and Keogh accounts and to minimize commissions through negotiation with full-service or discount brokers.

Clearly, the miracle of compounding becomes greater with the passing years. This is an often overlooked but very important truth. For instance, a healthy (after costs, after taxes) 15 percent annualized rate of return for 20 years becomes $1,636.70 per $100 initial equity. Contrast that 1,536 percent gain with the next 20 years, after which the total return becomes a 26,686 percent gain of the initial $100 amount. While the first 20 years would bring $1,536.70, the second 20 years would bring some $25,249 more to the account per $100 invested.

FIGURE 1–2
Compound Annual Growth per Initial $100

Year	10%	12.5%	15%	17.5%	20%	22.5%	25%
1	110	113	115	119	120	123	125
2	121	127	132	138	144	150	156
3	133	142	152	162	173	184	195
4	146	160	175	191	207	225	244
5	161	180	201	224	249	276	305
6	177	203	231	263	299	338	382
7	195	228	266	309	358	414	477
8	214	256	306	363	430	507	596
9	236	289	352	427	516	621	745
10	259	325	405	502	619	761	931
11	285	365	465	589	743	932	1,164
12	314	411	535	693	892	1,142	1,455
13	345	462	615	814	1,070	1,399	1,819
14	380	520	708	956	1,284	1,714	2,274
15	418	585	814	1,124	1,541	2,099	2,842
16	460	658	936	1,320	1,849	2,571	3,553
17	505	741	1,076	1,551	2,219	3,150	4,441
18	556	833	1,238	1,823	2,662	3,859	5,551
19	612	937	1,423	2,142	3,195	4,727	6,939
20	673	1,055	1,637	2,516	3,834	5,791	8,674
21	740	1,186	1,882	2,957	4,601	7,094	10,842
22	814	1,335	2,165	3,474	5,521	8,690	13,553
23	895	1,501	2,489	4,082	6,625	10,645	16,941
24	985	1,689	2,863	4,796	7,950	13,040	21,176
25	1,084	1,900	3,292	5,636	9,540	15,974	26,470
26	1,192	2,138	3,786	6,622	11,448	19,568	33,087
27	1,311	2,405	4,354	7,781	13,737	23,970	41,359
28	1,442	2,706	5,007	9,142	16,485	29,364	51,699
29	1,586	3,044	5,758	10,742	19,781	35,971	64,624
30	1,745	3,424	6,621	12,622	23,738	44,064	80,779
31	1,919	3,852	7,614	14,831	28,485	53,978	100,974
32	2,111	4,334	8,757	17,427	34,182	66,123	126,218
33	2,323	4,876	10,070	20,476	41,019	81,001	157,772
34	2,555	5,485	11,581	24,060	49,222	99,226	197,215
35	2,810	6,171	13,318	28,270	59,067	121,552	246,519
36	3,091	6,942	15,315	33,217	70,880	148,902	308,149
37	3,400	7,810	17,613	39,030	85,056	182,404	385,186
38	3,740	8,786	20,254	45,861	102,068	223,445	481,483
39	4,115	9,884	23,293	53,886	122,481	273,721	601,853
40	4,526	11,120	26,786	63,316	146,977	335,308	752,316

KEEP IT SIMPLE, STUPID

KISS (Keep it simple, Stupid!) is an amusing acronym, particularly applicable to speculating with stocks. Being simple, in the best sense of that word, is one of the hardest things to do. Many believe that if a subject or a practice is too easy it must not be very valuable. We may be conditioned to believe, "No pain, no gain." In reality, pain may more often be counterproductive, destructive, and defeating than beneficial. Others may tend to complicate the process of speculating with psychological needs, perhaps feeling guilty for receiving such handsome rewards for so relatively little effort. Some people undoubtedly lose in the stock market in a subconscious effort to punish themselves, like compulsive or addicted gamblers. In such cases, one could easily confuse being simple with being stupid.

I recommend for developing and maintaining simplicity in stock speculation as well as life—and a book to come back to time and again—the *Tao Teh King* by Lao Tzu. There are many translations of this brief, 84-verse book of "the way," which represents the fourth century B.C. philosophy of Chinese taoism. Although there are many different and excellent translations, I am partial to the one subtitled "Interpreted as Nature and Intelligence" by Archie J. Bahm (N.Y.: The Ungar Publishing Company, 1986).

In verse 9 we are told, "Going to extremes is never best. . . . The way to success is this: having achieved your goal, be satisfied not to go further. For this is the way Nature operates." Fabulous advice for the successful speculator, both in the everyday decision making of taking profits and in avoiding dramatic dangers such as the Crash of '87. The more I read the *Tao Teh King*, the more I see applicable wisdom in its description of the intelligent person conforming to nature's ways. Other translations offer other language and emphases. I have found Baum's rendering very helpful and satisfying.

DESCRIPTIONS AND REALITIES

The opening lines of the *Tao Teh King* (in Bahm's translation) are

Nature can never be completely described, for such a description of Nature would have to duplicate Nature.

No name can fully express what it represents.

Words cannot express or describe completely what there is or what they are meant to represent. Still, we may name things or general ideas and try to infuse them with sufficient meaning to communicate and instruct. Be alert, however, to the partial nature of description and to the manifold ineffable details a concept may contain. So we begin with a few basic premises and principles—as few as feasible—and hope they are adequate.

THREE LITTLE WORDS: PRICE, VALUE, AND WORTH

The concept of *value* is a meaningful, measurable, and manageable idea that can be quantified and used to determine potential gains or losses in the prices of stocks. Value is a basic, nonradical, fundamentalist tenet. We can analyze within certain limits the probable value of a corporation and then compare that estimated value per share of common stock to its current market price. Chapter 2 (and Appendix A) reviews some of the basic measures commonly used to arrive at such estimates.

The importance of the premise of value is that since a share of stock represents a unit of ownership (equity) of a corporation, it is not just a piece of paper traded on some exchange but a claim on the physical and intangible assets of the corporation. A good analogy is to compare estimating the value of a corporation with estimating the value of a house or business property. While estimates of properties may vary significantly, nonetheless, the *value* of a house or business property is real, and therefore the borrowing of money (a mortgage or line of credit) against estimated values is permitted.

The term *value* can refer to several types of value. It is said that the ultimate value of a stock/corporation is its future earnings' stream. Where earnings are the principal consideration, earnings discount models are developed and computed in an effort to estimate the present value based upon future earnings. But one can also value a corporation strictly in terms of its assets, or merely on the basis of dividends it pays and is likely to pay over some future period. There are many other criteria of value, some of which are reviewed in Chapter 2 and Appendix A.

Value is my cornerstone of speculation. It is vital to understand the concept. We do not look at stocks but at corporations; we do not buy stocks but corporations, at least small fractions of them. While we would like to buy whole corporations or major portions of them if we could, we must content ourselves with a few or a few hundred shares of the corporation.

Warren Buffett, that paragon of value investing, has made and written many interesting, informative, and sage statements about stocks. He found it amazing that either a person gets the idea of value immediately or seems never to accept it completely. The idea that a company may be trading at a fraction of its clearly recognized value as a going concern in terms of its common shares seems so obvious. And yet, great numbers of market players could care less about the corporations with which they dabble through trading stocks, and they concentrate merely on the likelihood of a market or a stock going up or down because of its recent price and volume action.

"Occasionally, sensational businesses are given away," said Buffett on Adam Smith's *Money World* (6/20/88), citing the example of one of his core holdings. "In the mid '70s, the whole Washington Post Company was selling for $80 million at a time when the properties were worth not less than $400 million. The price was there for all to see." How does it happen that a great corporation can sell for only 20 percent of its appraised value? Buffett's explanation, ". . . people just didn't feel very enthusiastic about the world then."[1]

Seeming synonyms to *value* are the words *price* and *worth*. These three words should always be distinguished, for only at rare moments are they functionally equivalent, representing the same dollar amount. The *price* of a stock refers to that amount at which it is trading or has traded at a particular time, usually at a day's close. Rarely is the fluctuating price of a stock the same as its value. Like a pendulum, the price of a stock swings from one side (undervalue) through fair value to the other side (overvalue), spending most of the time out of sync with the stock's underlying value.

The erroneous statement that the current price of a stock is what it should be because of the action of the market's rational and informed participants is known as the *efficient market hypothesis*. An extension of this misguided notion is that there is no way to outperform the market's average except by taking additional risk. Because of the wide fluctuation

---

[1] Henry Emerson, ed., *Outstanding Investor Digest* (14 East 4th Street, Suite 501, New York, N.Y. 10012), 6/30/88, p 11.

of a stock's price and the price action of the stock market over long periods of time, I have come to believe that the market is rarely efficient, that it seldom fairly represents the fundamental values of the underlying corporations.

Worth is yet a third important description of a dollar amount associated with a stock. For a variety of reasons, a stock's objectively estimated fundamental value may not be the same as its worth to a shareholder. For example, I may determine that a stock's fundamental value approximates $30 per share while its current price is $25, but I would want to sell it at its current price because I am concerned that the market in general is about to suffer a severe selloff. In such a case, I would rather capture the $25 than take the chance of waiting for the fair value of $30. In this case, worth is less than value and equal to price.

In another example, I might find a stock valued at $30 trading for $33 and determine that, given the current conditions of a strongly uptrending stock in a rising market, I will take the reasonable chance of holding the stock for $35 or more, perhaps applying trailing stop loss limits (explained in Chapter 3). In this case, the stock's worth (to me) is greater than market price, which is greater than its estimated value.

You might think that I am fudging semantically when I say that a stock may be worth more to me than its fair or fundamental value. You may say, if it's worth holding for $35 per share, isn't that the stock's considered value? Shouldn't the stock's value include its extra potential considerations such as price momentum or the trend of the market? No, I don't think so. I believe it is very important to distinguish between a stock's estimated fundamental value and its context-dependent worth, which is the price I might find acceptable for selling that stock (for either more or less than its fundamental value) due to additional considerations. And, just as the fundamental value changes with changing corporate conditions, so a stock's worth would change with changing personal and market conditions.

There may be other nonspeculative considerations—such as taxes— that determine a stock's worth to be different from its value for its owner. Without getting too tricky or sophisticated, take the case of a stock that reaches its fair value near the end of the year. If I sell the stock before year-end, I will have to pay taxes on its gains by April 15, but if I can wait a few days to sell, I won't have to pay taxes until the following year, thus having the use of "taxes due" for almost 12 months. Say my profit would be $10,000 and my taxes would amount to about $4,000 (or more, adding

California's generous take to Uncle Sam's). If money costs me 10% annually, in this example I could save $400 in equivalent interest if I sell after 12/31, so the stock's worth to me is at least $400 more than its fundamental value. Other examples could include the costs and gains associated with hedged positions (more about that in Chapter 8).

A corollary to the premise of value is that "value will out," sooner or later. Unfortunately, fundamental value is not always realized, no matter how long a stock is held. Some corporations go bankrupt in such a manner that the market price of their stock is always undervalued until the final blow. Other corporations are merged or bought out at prices below their fair values. Happily, many corporations are bought out at prices well above their fair valuations, and those are the cases where one corporation is *worth* more to the acquiring entity than the target's fundamental value would indicate. Such worth may be found in the fit and synergy that a buyout is intended to produce or in some hidden or intangible assets not readily calculable in normally determining fundamental value.

My experience is that about 20 percent of the stocks I have carefully selected fail to make any profit, let alone reach their original estimated fair values. A few have lost 100 percent of their price, but many have lost lesser varying amounts to almost breaking even. The saving grace is that about 80 percent of the stocks have traded above their original cost prices, with many trading well above their original valuations. It is important to understand that fundamental value is not a static concept or one-time estimate; it changes whenever there is a significant change in a corporation's financials or whenever it seems appropriate to attribute higher or lower valuation ratios because of growth rates, trends, interest rates, and the general market level.

PATIENCE AND THE 50 PERCENT PRINCIPLE

A principal part of our strategy is to be patient in waiting for the fundamental value of a corporation to be recognized in its stock's price—the much-maligned buy-and-hold technique. The paradigm sell level is when the stock's price equals its fundamental value, which equals its unique worth. An alternative sell level is when *worth* incorporates *value* with perceived stock and market conditions.

Another aspect of the strategy of patience is to be patient in *waiting* for the fundamental value of a corporation to trade at 50 percent or less of market price before buying its stock. This 50 percent undervalued level is arbitrary but not capricious. Under certain circumstances it might be too rigid. However, in keeping to such a policy we have a strong tendency not to overpay for a stock, so as to diminish downside risk, and therefore to have the likelihood of relatively greater upside potential. As I've said and will repeat throughout this book, theory doesn't always work out in reality, but ours has worked out often enough to produce very lucrative long-term gains with stocks.

The 50 percent undervalued principle sometimes blocks us from acquiring stocks of excellent corporations that go on to have greater market price appreciations than many of the stocks that do qualify. Still, "rule utilitarianism" and systematic consistency argue in favor of keeping such a guideline. Rule utilitarianism is that philosophical notion that more is gained from the utility of following sound rules, which sometimes seem counterproductive, than in breaking them. Stopping at red stop lights at three o'clock in the morning (even when no cops or cars can be seen) to maintain a safety factor is an example of rule utilitarianism.

THE NEED FOR DIVERSIFICATION

Maintaining your analytic methodology, portfolio strategy, or steadfast patience even though some of your stocks or the market in general takes a tumble is an application of rule utilitarianism. When you believe in your system, in the long-term advancing nature of undervalued stocks and the market on average, then you can hold a stock through its recurring downward fluctuations in market price, even through as much as a 50 percent depreciation in price. In this regard Buffett has pointed out that, "You ignore that possibility at your own peril. In the history of almost every major company in this country, it has happened. You shouldn't own common stocks if a decrease in their value by 50 percent would cause you to feel stress."[2]

Even with careful selection, as previously mentioned, stocks do not always work out as anticipated. In fact, in a given 12-month period, 40 percent or more of my carefully selected stocks may be short-term

---

[2]Emerson, *Outstanding Investor Digest,* June 30, 1988, p. 9.

"losers". Many of the short-term losers turn around in two or three years and become handsome winners. What all this means is that, in addition to having patience, I want to be widely diversified with many different stocks in my portfolio. I want to have at least 20 and preferably 30 or more stocks in a portfolio so that when 5 or 10 of them underperform, that is offset by the good performance of the 15 or 20 others. Actual examples of these statistics and workings are detailed in Chapter 7.

THE INTERVENING STOCK MARKET

Speculating with common stocks is complicated in that stocks trade on the various stock exchanges and the over-the-counter market. We can think of the stock market—of course, there are many stock markets and many subsets of stocks within each—as an institution that has developed characteristics of its own, often independent of the stocks and corporations it represents.

I go along with the attitude attributed to Warren Buffett that we could just as well do without the markets as far as our approach to stocks is concerned. That is, we could buy the stocks we want today and, if the market ceased trading completely (or we went away on a very long vacation), we could come back three or four years from now to enjoy the fruits of our corporations' growth and profits.

Still, we do know that markets have fluctuating periods or advancing cycles and declining cycles. Markets can become overvalued in general and thereafter decline, after which they become undervalued and subsequently advance. Markets alternate between becoming overbought and thereafter selling off, after which they become oversold, which lays the foundation for the next rally. These swings from overbought and overvalued to oversold and undervalued are not neat, nor are the turning points easily predictable, if they are predictable at all. Market movements are further complicated by the nature of short-term, intermediate-term, and long-term fluctuations, which sometimes yield conflicting readings.

One could literally even ignore market swings as many great investors have. Consider Peter Lynch of Fidelity Magellan Fund fame. He says he attempts always to be fully invested, trading stocks for their long-term and short-term potential, regardless of alleged market states or conditions, which he asserts with becoming modesty and honesty that he is not smart enough to predict. The importance of Lynch's humility and strategy is backed up by his record. Over the recent 10-year span, the Fidelity Magellan Fund he has managed has gained a total return of $1,169.79 percent, the best long-term performance among thousands of mutual funds.[3]

MARKET TIMING

Other astute investors have pointed out in practice and in statistics how much better off one might be avoiding the market's great, periodic, and cyclic declines, thereafter becoming aggressive during the market's great, periodic, and cyclic advances. This subject is called *market timing,* and approaches to market timing are legion.

Some market timers time the markets for intraday movements of options and futures, while others are short-term stock profit-scalping timers who consider a few days to a few weeks sufficient exposure. Still others concentrate on the intermediate term of a few months to a year, perhaps concentrating upon telephone switching between equity mutual funds and money market funds. Many market participants are unaware that they are influenced by market gossip and faulty analysis, even though they decide from time to time to "get out" because of all the pessimism abroad. A few of us may be long-term timers, dealing with multi-year periods by adjusting our participation (invested) levels or by augmenting existing positions with shorter-term insurance hedging instruments, as reviewed in Chapter 8.

Among students of the stock market, a great debate rages about market timing, including whether it can be done effectively for more than one or two lucky guesses and whether it is productive for the average speculator to dabble in timing at all. As usual with stock market debates, there are extreme and rigid positions for the main camps, while a few individuals work for a commonsense pragmatic compromise that attempts to use the best ideas of the opposing extremes.

We should like to avoid much or most of the great market declines such as 1929–32, 1973–74, and—of vivid memory—September– November 1987. On the other hand, many of these declines set the stage for excellent market advances, which allowed the buy-and-hold speculator a chance to recover significantly in the bounce-back reactions. Recall

---

[3]Lipper Analytical Services, Inc., as published in *Barron's,* June 15, 1989.

that even in the Crash of '29 there was a 50 percent comeback rally early in 1930. Then, when most market players had given up by '32, there was a great 127 percent rally from February 1933 through February 1934. Again, in the depths of the depression, the Dow Jones Industrial Average managed a 127 percent gain in 32 months, from July 1934 into March 1937.

More recently, we see that the market has completely recovered from the Crash of '87 and its Meltdown Monday (October 19th) closing Dow Jones Industrial Average low of 1738.74. Its August 24, 1989, closing high of 2734.64 represents a gain of 57.28 percent. With the DJIA making all-time new highs, among the major indexes, only the Dow Jones Utilities have failed to make all-time nominal highs by September 1989.

How neat to have enjoyed most of the 43.6 percent Dow Jones Industrial Average (DJIA) gain registered between December 31, 1986 (1895.95) and the high at August 25, 1987 (2722.86), and yet thereafter to have avoided most of the 36.1 percent DJIA selloff through October 19th. How wonderful to have recognized the market's massive over-soldness and undervaluation at the close of trading on Monday (10/19) or after the opening on Tuesday (10/20) and to have returned to the market in time for the average 57.28 percent rise over the next 22 months. Whatever the market dynamics and our abilities to adjust to them, it seems clear that coping with major market moves should be considered, even if we can never catch all of their advances or avoid all of their declines.

We want to be aggressive in undervalued and oversold markets and defensive in overvalued and overbought markets. In between, we can pursue an optimistic policy based upon the historic upward bias to the market, hopefully augmented with good stock selection. The parameters for determining market undervaluations and overvaluations, as well as overbought and oversold criteria, are reviewed in Chapter 4.

PERFORMANCE, DOLLARS, AND PERCENTAGES

Although price, value, and worth are expressed in dollars and cents, performance is expressed in percentages, and those are the numbers on which to concentrate. If Berkshire Hathaway common shares close up $50, the reality is that we are witnesses to just over $\%_{10}$ percent advance, as the stock (at this writing) trades around $8,100 per share. But if a $2 stock advances a mere 1/8th—12.5 cents—then it has appreciated over 6% for the day. If we owned 10 shares of Berkshire Hathaway ($81,000 market value), they would have increased $500 in market value. But, an $81,000 position in a $2 stock up 1/8 would have increased $5,062.50 in market value. It's the percentages that matter, especially as portfolios are priced in terms of total market value.

Percentages can easily be used to mislead the unwary. For example, if a portfolio increases in price at 15 percent per year compounded, it will double in a little less than five years (see Figure 1–2). Some ignorant or unscrupulous merchandisers will take a five-year, 15 percent-compounded annual gain and claim that their return has been 20 percent per year. They will justify this figure by dividing the 100 percent gain by five years, resulting in "20 percent per year."

The deception is in improperly calling this "20 percent" (100 percent in five years) gain the "annualized rate of return" or "compounded annual gain" (which are equivalent statements). If the consumer is unaware of how the mathematics were manipulated, the performance could be construed incorrectly as the equivalent of a 148.8 percent total gain (instead of the 101.1 percent). For longer time periods, the deception becomes even greater. An annualized rate of return of 15 percent for 10 years provides a 304.6 percent gain. If you divide 304.6 percent by 10, you might think you gained "an average" 30.46 percent per year instead of the actual 15 percent compounded.

There are certain commonsense or intuitive understandings that a low-priced stock or a small market capitalization stock can advance faster and further than a high-priced stock or a large market capitalization stock. Market capitalization is the total dollar amount obtained by multiplying the number of shares outstanding times the price per share of a stock. If a corporation has one million shares outstanding trading at $5 per share, its market "cap" is $5 million.

There are elements of statistical probability in these intuitive notions about potential corporate growth and price appreciation, discussed at length in Chapter 2. It certainly seems easier for a $50 million dollar in sales corporation to grow faster than say IBM with its $50+ billion dollars in sales. For IBM to grow 20 percent a year, it has to create the equivalent of another $10 billion dollar of revenues; while for a $50 million corporation to grow 20 percent, it only has to gain another $10 million in sales.

Intuitively, it seems easier for a stock to advance from $5 to $10 than from $50 to $100. But such intuitions can be counterproductive if fundamental analysis shows the $50 stock to represent far more value than the $5 stock and thus to be far more likely to double in market price despite its higher current price. Again, we are interested in the percentages involved. We will not be misled by stock splits, where one share of an $80 stock becomes two shares of a $40 stock, causing no change in the stock's fundamental valuation (with all financial numbers halved). But we will notice that a $2 advance on our two shares of the $40 stock, which represents a 5 percent gain on the split shares, would have been only a 2.5 percent gain if the stock had not been split and were trading at $80 per share.

MARGIN OR LEVERAGE AND PYRAMIDING

Perhaps the subject of margin involves the greatest number of preconceptions and misconceptions of any term or subject involving stock speculation. *Margin* refers to the practice of borrowing money against the market value of a stock or stock portfolio. This is a somewhat complicated subject, reviewed in detail in Chapter 5, "The Myths and Magic of Margin." As part of "Premises and Principles," it is important to understand just what margin is, what can be done with it, what pitfalls to avoid, and how to protect oneself against abusing it and suffering the consequences.

Many people think that the stock market is risky enough, a crapshoot to begin with, and certainly no place to use borrowed funds for "investing" let alone speculating. Attitudes range from the proud boast, "I never borrow money, and certainly not for buying things I don't need!" to horror stories about how people were wiped out in 1929 (and ever since) because they used margin. If the use and effects of margin are approached in a rational way, employing margin need not be more dangerous than buying a house, where most people mortgage (borrow against the house) 75 percent to 80 percent or more of the house's market value in order to acquire it.

Obviously, one can overpay for a house and take out too large a mortgage that sometime later becomes overwhelming, especially in an economic downturn. Under such circumstances, one could lose the house, improvements, and down payment that went with it. But because some people are foolish or unfortunate is no reason to reject ever taking a mortgage. And where would modern business be without short-term borrowed funds to buy inventory and meet fluctuating cash flow and long-term borrowing to build or upgrade plant and purchase modern equipment for anticipated growth and improved returns on equity? Just as a thoughtful and prudent "businessperson's risk" is made in home buying or business expansion, so borrowing can be an effective tool for enhancing total return of an undervalued, diversified, long-term stock portfolio.

A simple example of the flexibility gained through the use of margin is being able to buy additional stocks without additional cash and without needing to sell currently held positions. Suppose I have an unmargined portfolio of 20 stocks with a market value of $100,000, and I believe that all the stocks I own are very undervalued. I do not want to sell any of my current positions, but I have found several other equally undervalued stocks that I would like to buy. If the market conditions seem propitious, I could go ahead and buy up to another $100,000 of stocks. I would then be 50 percent "margined," owning 50 percent of the market value of my portfolio and owing the other 50 percent. I would have $200,000 worth of stocks working for (or against) me. That much is clear.

Now suppose my $200,000 margined portfolio gains 10 percent in market price during the next few months, but all the stocks in it are still undervalued. Again I find a couple of great-looking bargains. With that 10 percent gain ($20,000), I can buy another $20,000 worth of stock without putting up additional cash. I am trying to pyramid my profits, which is to say, put them to work for me without cashing out (and creating tax consequences). More about pyramiding in Chapter 5.

Am I at greater risk after buying the additional $20,000 worth of stocks than I was before the 10 percent gain? No, because even after I buy the additional stock I am still in a 50 percent margined position. But look at the effect. I'm now controlling $220,000 worth of stock based upon my initial $100,000 of equity. If the portfolio continues to advance, I can continue to add stocks based on increasing borrowing or purchasing power. Of course, if the portfolio declines, the losses of original capital are magnified in proportion to the percentage the portfolio is margined and pyramided. A 10 percent loss on a $220,000 portfolio would represent a 22 percent loss of original equity. It's not a free ride.

Because I have not emphasized the very real risks of stock investing and the increased danger of stock investing with margin does not mean that these risks don't exist or that I am oblivious to them. For now, try to keep an open mind about the subject of margin, to be explored in several additional commentaries later in this book.

SUMMARY

Perhaps the most important characteristics of a successful stock speculator are belief and patience. If one understands the upward long-term bias of the stock market and has the patience to wait for bargains and then hold them for their fair values, a process that can take many years, the likelihood of handsome gains is great.

Stocks are measured in terms of their current price, their corporations' current and future estimated values, and their worth to the individual speculator based upon market, economic, tax, and other considerations. We want to buy stocks when they are bargains, when their market prices are at least 50 percent below their estimated present or near-future fundamental values. We want to sell stocks when they are fairly valued. Sometimes we will take less than full value if we are concerned about a serious market-wide decline. Sometimes we will hold out for a premium above fair valuation if stock and market trends and conditions appear propitious.

This process requires tremendous patience, both in waiting for undervalued stocks and even more so in holding onto stocks for their fair valuation. It is important to keep the basics clearly in mind and to be consistent and systematic in our methodology. Many of our stocks will fail to reach anticipated values while many will go on to outperform our most liberal estimates. Because some of the best-looking stocks will become losers, it is important to maintain a widely diversified portfolio. In such portfolios, the winning stocks tend to gain much more than the losing stocks lose for a positive average appreciation. Growth and value is a long-term proposition. Although there will be periods of disappointment, the overall gains will likely provide handsome returns.

We select stocks based on their corporations' fundamentals, and we purchase them based on their undervaluation in order to profit by selling them at or above full valuation. But we also consider the condition of the stock market in general. The stock market can be overvalued and overbought, thus likely to decline, or undervalued and oversold, thus likely to advance. Obviously, the stock market can be some combination of these criteria, so that our purchase or sale of stocks will be affected by our determinations of the stock market's condition and the significant likelihood of its advancing, declining, or maintaining a trading range.

After the system of stock selection, portfolio management, and market timing are well understood, total returns can be enhanced through the prudent use of margin or borrowing funds against the market value of portfolios in order to buy additional undervalued stocks, increase diversification, and take advantage of bargains in propitious markets. Not many speculators, investors or professionals really understand all the technicalities of margined portfolios, especially the underlying rational premises. We think we have a good handle on the topic as reviewed in Chapter 5.

CHAPTER 2

FUNDAMENTAL CORPORATE ANALYSIS

I can't decide whether thoughtful philosophers should make good stock marketeers, or successful investors and speculators should make good philosophers. For example, an important subject in philosophy is the problem of appearance versus reality. Common sense tells us that what we see, hear, or otherwise sense does not necessarily correspond to underlying or ultimate realities. We see individual stock prices jump up one day and drop down the next. We see the stock market do the same, and every day there are reasons given for what has happened. It's not that many of these reasons are untrue or miss the point entirely; it's just that they are neither necessary nor sufficient—they are not causal—to create the effect ascribed to them.

Many stock market participants often act like a huge population of lemmings who crowd this way or that, periodically rushing willy nilly into a euphoria near a market top or out of a crash near a market bottom. These behaviors are stimulated by emphasizing superficial appearances at the expense of recognizing significant underlying realities. Perhaps the worst single offending and misleading area of appearance is stock price, or at least our responses to it. If the price is going up, that's good; if it's going down, that's bad. While this accident or effect sometimes represents a strong underlying reality, often it doesn't. Often a stock's price is merely the temporary result of the lemmings rushing into or out of the stock for reasons that are independent of its, the market's, and the economy's underlying realities. One major reality, often masked by a stock's appearance (market action), is the underlying worth and growth of the corporation represented by its stock. If we can cut through the daily weather of storms and sunny days to get at the long-term climate of seasons and growth, we will obtain a much better understanding of what is actually going on and what is likely to happen in the future.

Cutting through the short-term ephemera is what a speculator attempts to do in looking out for the long-term likelihood of future events. The person who thinks as a speculator is a step ahead on the road to reality in recognizing the tenuous nature of guessing, estimating, or analyzing the outcomes of financial commitments. The speculator invests, but with a greater understanding and appreciation for the risks seeable and unforeseeable.

THE REALITY OF CORPORATE VALUE AND GROWTH

Fundamental analysis is usually called *stock analysis,* but of course it is really *corporation analysis.* In that semantic shift from talking about stocks instead of corporations lies the root of much erroneous thinking and emphasis among investors. Just as our outlooks and strategies are colored by our emphasis on the word *stock*—we say we deal in *stocks,* and we are in the *stock market*—so too what passes for fundamental corporate analysis may be overwhelmed and distorted by constantly referring to *stock analysis.*

One of the complications of investing is that stocks have a life of their own for long periods of time. Stocks, because they are traded in markets and on exchanges, have certain characteristics that are often independent of the corporations they represent. It is this pieces-of-paper and stock-market-dynamics independence that makes it doubly difficult to avoid mixing analysis of corporations with analysis of stocks as objects in the market. After all, who of us would really care how well a company is managed if we but had a way to pick stocks that almost always gained 20 percent to 25 percent or more a year?

Ironically, it is by evaluating businesses that we stand the best chance of finding stocks that may appreciate 20 percent to 25 percent a year, at least over a multi-year period.

One of the major themes of this book is that prudent stock investors deal in corporations. We are first and foremost prudent corporation speculators, those who inspect present worth and future growth probabilities. We buy and sell common stocks, but those stocks are equity positions in their corporations—we buy and sell small ownership parts of corporations. In that sense we literally buy into and sell out of the equivalent of limited partnerships,with most of the benefits and without many of the hassles (such as restricted entry and illiquid exit) limited partnerships involve.

A parallel to the corporation versus stock relationship may be seen in our health concerns about the causes of good health or illness versus their symptoms. That is, we can think of the corporation as the cause of the stock and the stock's price as a symptom of the corporation's perceived health or illness. There is an important area in medicine called *symptom management,* but the basis of a complete cure lies in understanding the causes of a disease and not in focusing on its symptoms. So too, the basis of speculating in common stocks lies in concentrating on the "health" and prognoses for corporations rather than on the apparent symptomatic price fluctuations of their stocks.

We can practice some effective stock management, especially since the stock market has a dynamic of its own, often independent of corporate reality. But if we could learn to think, "I deal in corporations; I am in the corporation market," then our focus and effectiveness would probably be improved immensely.

Technical analysis of stocks, on the other hand, tends to deal only with stocks, especially with the quantities of shares traded and their market price changes. You will not find much, if any, technical analysis of stocks in this book. You will find some technical market analysis, which is almost independent of individual stock criteria. I believe there are successful technicians who can ride the trends and scalp some profits. I also believe their successes are generally inferior to those of effective fundamentalists who buy value and growth—undervalued healthy corporations and unappreciated rapidly growing corporations—the shares of which reflect their values in increased market prices over the years.

I believe there are far more pure fundamentalists than pure technicians, although I imagine some technicians would dispute that observation. Technicians are proud of their basic premise, sometimes overweeningly so, that all they need to see is the trending price-volume action of a stock on a chart to determine whether it is a buy, sell, or hold.

Technicians and fundamentalists alike need not know, care, nor remember what a corporation does, but the fundamentalist's decisions are based on such staples as its balance sheets and income statements, its position vis à vis macro economic movements, or even impending or actual buyout announcements. On many occasions I've seen technical analysts strongly recommend a stock at its buyout price because they did not pay attention to fundamental news. Their charts merely showed the price rise on high volume, which automatically triggered a buy signal.

Many technicians also attend to corporate fundamentals, monetary conditions, interest-rate levels, and economic policy. Some fundamentalists also pay heed to technical indicators of specific stocks or, if not of individual stocks, then of the market in general or its subsets, such as industry groups or small capitalization companies. I also do not want to waste our attention on fruitless debates about the pros and cons of each approach. I still believe it worthwhile for us as students of stock speculation—by which I always mean corporate speculation—to become aware of major investment approaches to see if one or another (or a specific aspect in an otherwise incomprehensible or unwieldy system) has insights for our current approach. When doctrinaire technicians claim that all they need to know about a corporation is already reflected in the price/volume action of its stock, I believe they overstate their case and are flirting dangerously with fallacious after-the-fact reasoning (*post hoc, ergo propter hoc*).

DOWN AND DIRTY ANALYSIS MAY BE
GOOD ENOUGH

Fundamental corporate analysis—as practiced by professionals who have a vested interest in erudition and esoteric expertise—can be an exceedingly complex and time-consuming enterprise. Just think of all the accounting and auditing that goes on in a major corporation. Add to that the many projections made by the corporation's marketing department and the efforts by management for cost control and efficiencies in manufacture and distribution.

Not only might we want to know the past contributions of research and development projects, we might also be aware of current and anticipated funding as well as the possibility of any gang buster products in the pipeline. However, there is great danger of information overload, the syndrome of missing the forest by being preoccupied with the trees. There is also the problem that we are projecting or reinforcing uncertain future events on unrepeatable or questionable past events.

There are wonderful stories about clever company analysts counting the cars in the parking lot, visiting plants and offices at night (to see if extra shifts are working), and keeping tabs with the corporation's printers to see if orders for shipping cartons are on the increase. There are few if any stories about how such clever observations have sometimes proved misleading. If the corporation was on double shift, rapidly building up inventory and storing the excess at its retail outlets in all those cartons it ordered, while its sales were decreasing significantly, you would not recognize this by inspecting the plant, carton maker, and shipping dock, but you could notice it by reviewing the corporation's quarterly and annual financials.

On the other hand, I love the story told by Bernard Baruch in his autobiography, *My Own Story*, about sending an agent to check out a railroad in the Midwest. The agent walked along the tracks and noticed that a lot of coal was lying around the tracks. He wired back that the railroad was doing good business, on the observation that their coal cars were filled to overflowing as evidenced by the spilt coal. Another investor interested in the railroad had a detailed and handsome research report compiled and published, which required a few months of investigation and analysis. By then, Baruch had done his buying and was happy to sell out with a big gain after the good news was quantified and distributed.

THE SUPER SEVEN SELECTORS OR THE BIG THREE?

Well, you don't have to be a certified public accountant or an industrial spy at the loading docks in order to find undervalued stocks, which is to say corporations trading for less than their fair, intrinsic, fundamental (take your pick of adjectives) value in terms of their market prices. You can actually discover undervalued companies by checking out only three of the most fundamental measures of a corporation's value or by going further and including another four ratios. All these valuation figures are published public information, readily available for anyone to inspect. It's almost frightfully simple and aboveboard, perhaps a little (or a lot) boring compared to all the tales of insider information, corporate raiders, or market-maker manipulations one hears so much about.

In contemplating this chapter for some weeks, I questioned if only three indicators would be sufficient for effective stock picking or if I needed at least five or perhaps seven (at least for alliteration and luck) or even several more. I've wondered how much information and how many nuances there are that I might be taking for granted. There is a tradeoff between oversimplifying and overwhelming. There is also concern that with 20 years in studying corporations and the stock market, I have gained a number of intuitions and attitudes that are completely foreign to many if not most people likely to read this book and that are perhaps glossed over by myself.

The "big three" fundamental basics could be *price/earnings*, *price/revenues*, and *price/book value* ratios. With these alone, I think we could find all the undervalued stocks we could use. Of course, we would want to work out criterion levels and a gestalt (whole versus parts) relationship among the ratios. For instance, if the book value and revenues were deeply discounted, we might not be very concerned about the current price/earnings ratio. Further, we might look at the five-to-seven–year trends of these ratios as support for a probable continuation of them into the next few years.

P/ε

$P/\rho e \vee$

$P/b.\vee.$

From another point of view—and I hope this doesn't frustrate or confuse you—the big three could be *price/cash flow*, *return on equity*, and *market capitalization*. I think if one were limited to only three criteria there would be a strong likelihood of finding all the undervalued stocks we could use with these other three criteria as substitutes for those in the paragraph above, with similar caveats and considerations as above. As this and the next chapter unfold, I hope you'll see why I believe such minimalist analytic criteria would be sufficient for effective stock picking.

$P/c.f.$

ρoe

$c4p.$

I honestly believe that one would do better speculating with too little information than with too much. (Do I mean that? Yes.) Also, one would do well to explore intuition and nonanalytical powers, so genuinely discussed in Bennett W. Goodspeed's *The Tao-Jones Averages*, wherein Taoism and right-brained thinking are reviewed in hopes of moving toward a whole-brained approach to life as well as investing. Remember, information is not knowledge, and knowledge is not wisdom. That is not to say that wisdom is not necessarily an outcome of information and knowledge; wisdom is an integration and distillation that often involves a letting go of what passes for information and factual knowledge.

For my part, I have tried to latch on to the "big picture" statistical assumptions and outcomes. Since I do not believe that we can have certain knowledge of the future—perhaps that admission is a first small step toward wisdom—it doesn't bother me that the stock market is uncertain and unpredictable, at least when it comes to great precision.

So many people have told me they do not like investing in stocks and the stock market because they have so little control over what goes on and the outcomes. Often, these same people crow about how great real estate is because of its tangibility and accessibility. They have convinced themselves they have economic control with real estate. After all, it's real, isn't it? In the past few years, talk to any number of midwestern farmers or Texans about how much control they have (had) over their real estate. These same appearances of control versus the reality of unexpected trends in interest rates and bond prices should be recognized by each reader in an effort to accept the speculative but okay nature of investing.

Since I believe that I operate in an economic system that will continue pretty much in its present form, then past patterns will likely be repeated in a similar if imprecise manner in the future. Thus, if the stock market has advanced—managed a total return of 10 percent per annum on average—for over 63 years, I suppose that it will continue to do so for an appreciable while longer. I take it that this positive sum game in stocks is a reflection of the positive sum earnings of their corporations over the years.

Along the road to investment success, there may be any number of variations; the big picture is made up of many little pictures. There are periods when some kinds of corporations fare better than others, only later to be eclipsed themselves. If I can find a sufficient number of diversified, undervalued companies, while avoiding fully or overvalued businesses, perhaps I can capture twice the gains of the historical averages. Perhaps I can also find techniques to anticipate patterns of corporate growth and regression, as well as predictive indications of market manias and depressions, and thus better historical averages by minimizing long-term market declines and maximizing long-term market advances.

At any rate, I believe it is good common sense to go with the flow, to find economic values that are underpriced in the marketplace. By persevering in this quest, albeit with many corporate stumbles and market misfortunes, we should be able to enjoy the fruits of our analytic and intuitive skills.

In this chapter I will review seven criteria for picking an undervalued corporation—even though you might want to settle on only three of these criteria, as noted above. If several of these fundamental financial criteria indicate significant to serious undervaluedness, the stock under analysis is a bargain and likely to outperform the general market over the next three to five years. I must admit that I haven't run a study on all the stocks I recommended over the past 12 years that were mainly considered in terms of these criteria because the number of permutations is too great to find a single, neat formula. In many cases, one must make a judgment call when some criteria are screamingly undervalued and others are not. Rarely is a corporation's stock perfectly undervalued by each and every measure.

Not necessarily in order of importance—because different fundamentals are more important for some corporations than for others—the seven selection criteria I will concentrate on are

1. Price to earnings (P/E).
2. Price to sales or revenues (P/R).
3. Price to book value (P/BV).
4. Price to cash flow (P/CF).
5. Return on equity or net worth (ROE).
6. Market capitalization (market cap).
7. Return on assets (ROA).

You may be shocked or disappointed not to see *dividend yield*, *current ratio*, *debt to equity*, or *price to net working capital*, among other widely followed criteria, listed above. These and other ratios, fundamentals, and considerations are reviewed in Appendix A. For now, let us agree to have a "willing suspension of disbelief" that the Super Seven Selectors are sufficient (if not all necessary) for superior stock selection.

What we are doing is called *screening*. We review a large number of corporations' financials—such as the over 4,700 entries on the StockPak II floppy disks that are published monthly by Standard & Poor's—looking for those configurations that meet our basic criteria. With StockPak II discs you can easily program your computer to select for any of a large number of criteria, including sets of several criteria. If we find too many stocks meeting one set of fundamentals, say P/E 10 or less, price per share less than two times book value per share, and revenues per share equal to or less than price per share, we can raise our criteria. The next pass-through might select stocks in the data base at P/E 9 or less, 1.5 times book value or less, or .75 or less revenues to price. These passes can be made in a few minutes, after which the results can be printed out and individual stocks can be inspected for additional available fundamental information.

Х ||

StockPak II is available to the public through Standard & Poor's, 25 Broadway, New York, N.Y. 10004, (212) 208–8581. Recently you could obtain the full service (a monthly mailing of two discs: New York Stock Exchange plus American Stock Exchange, and Over-the-Counter I and II) for $1,180 per year. You can also get individual discs (for most popular personal computers), including a Composite service of over 1,500 stocks (one disc per month) for $295 per year.

Essentially, this initial filtering of the undervalued wheat from its fairly or overvalued chaff usually provides us with too great a selection of bargain stocks. However, from this first "harvest" we may obtain a hundred or more candidates that are then analyzed further for superior total configurations of these or other criteria. We also test further for dubious or undesirable characteristics, usually found by perusing quarterly and annual reports as well as checking out trends and projections, or perhaps just noticing high debt ratios.

THE MOST WIDELY FOLLOWED, P/E IS STILL IMPORTANT

The price/earnings ratio, P/E, is probably the most quoted fundamental indicator. Some analysts downgrade relying on current (most recent reported) earnings as being too subject to accounting choices and changes. P/E is simply the current price of a share of stock divided by the "current" after-tax earnings per share. P/E can be confusing or misleading. Current earnings usually refer to the most-recently reported year's after-tax earnings, so they might be called *this year's, last year's,* or preferably *trailing* (the past four quarters or past 12 months of) earnings. Even the "current" trailing annual earnings will be somewhat out-of-date, usually published two or three months after the year-end close, or referring in many publications to what happened up to 12 months ago or longer. From now on, I will use *earnings* to refer to trailing four-quarters' (or *current*) earnings.

Earnings are generally reported quarterly, often with a several week delay. Even so, we would want to update earnings with each quarter's reported earnings, and refer to *the recent 12-months* earnings or *the last four quarters' reported earnings* rather than waiting for (or using) the fiscal year's earnings only. Of course, we are long-term speculators, more interested in corporate growth and valuations over the years than with quarterly jumps and stumbles. We prefer to "smooth out" quarters of volatile earnings for the long-term trend. We do not want to buy a stock because of one quarter's "earnings explosion" only to have to sell it (or another) stock a few months later solely because of one quarter's "earnings disappointment."

Interpreting earnings can be devilishly tricky due to the potential for arbitrary and self-serving accounting decisions and practices. Writeoffs and writedowns; changes in reserves; changes in valuing inventory from last-in, first-out (LIFO) to first-in, first-out (FIFO), or vice versa; and other adjustments can play havoc with reported earnings, especially when comparing them to prior (or projected) years as well as to another company, industry, or market-wide earnings-ratio averages.

Earnings are also subject to "dilution," such as when there are convertible bonds or convertible preferred stocks, warrants, or options outstanding. Usually earnings are reported in two ways, as primary after-tax earnings and as fully diluted after-tax earnings. Fully diluted earnings take into account the potential increase in common shares if all convertible instruments were changed into shares of common. Fully diluted earnings can be misleading as warrants expire or convertible instruments are retired. Many corporations do not have fully diluted earnings because they have no convertible instruments outstanding, but when they do, we use fully diluted earnings. Otherwise, primary earnings are the figures we use.

There are also special one-time "extraordinary" earnings, such as occur from the sale of a major asset, which do not occur in the normal course of business. Because of their nonrecurring nature we factor out extraordinary earnings, at least as far as earnings trends and projections are concerned. Likewise, there are extraordinary losses, which may distort the earnings picture for a period of time. Extraordinary gains and losses are more exceptional than normal; however, they can be recognized in even a simple analysis. In the case of fully-diluted earnings, you would want to guard against both comparing these numbers against undiluted numbers as well as inconsistently adjusting criterion P/E levels.

In spite of the various snares, I found that one can almost ignore the potential accounting pitfalls, which are masked by the simple P/E number, especially since this (or any) one criterion by itself does not a corporate analysis or selection make. Also, there is that wonderful statistical idea that if the quality of earnings in one corporation is overstated, the likelihood is that the quality of earnings in another corporation is understated. In a large group of analyzed corporations, the average of their P/Es probably reflects a relatively fair assessment of their earnings valuation in the stock markets on average, despite individual company accounting variations.

Sometimes higher average P/Es represent higher quality of earnings and more consistent growth patterns, "the market's" judgment as to the quality of the underlying company itself. Pharmaceutical companies traditionally sport relatively high average P/Es, while auto companies struggle with relatively low average P/Es. Some of these traditional levels are based on historical precedent, perceptions of the cyclical nature of a business, and the perceived potential for sustained high profit margins given the economic outlook.

In general, a high relative P/E is at least a danger signal that the market is rewarding a company its great confidence but will tolerate no faltering in that company's progress and profits. In the jargon, the stock with a very high relative P/E may have limited upside but large downside price vulnerability.

The P/E can be interpreted in several ways. P/E tells us what investors are willing to pay per $1 of earnings for a particular corporation at a particular time. For example, if a corporation has earned $1 per share in trailing (after-tax) earnings and its shares are trading for $10 each, then it is trading for 10 times earnings or P/E 10. In this example, stock buyers are willing to pay 10 times earnings and thus to receive a 10 percent *earnings return* on their investment. Another term for an undervalued corporation (and its stock) is an *out-of-favor* corporation (or stock). The P/Es of out-of-favor corporations are relatively low for any number of different reasons but often because investors do not believe these corporate earnings are as valuable as those of other corporations whose stocks reflect their popularity with higher P/Es.

Some investors emphasize buying high P/E stocks of large and well-known or popular corporations for a variety of reasons such as perceived economic strength and investment visibility. Many studies have shown that low P/E stocks tend to outperform high P/E stocks over longer periods of time. I am indebted to the 4/7/89 edition of *Market Logic* for featuring a wonderful research report, "Earnings Yields, Market Values, and Stock Returns," by J. Jaffe, D. B. Keim, and R. Westerfield (published in *The Journal of Finance* [Vol. 44, no. 1]), which concludes "that both [P/E ratio and market capitalization selection indicators] have independent forecasting value, and that investors can improve their odds of success in the market by using both."

I noted in *TPS 253* (4/13/89) that this study is particularly strong in its use of 36 full years—from 1951 through 1986—of broadly based data using nearly all common stocks listed on the New York and American stock exchanges. Each year (from March 31 through the following March 31) stocks were sorted into five equal-sized categories, for both P/Es and market values. Confirming previous studies, the study shows that low P/E stocks significantly outperformed high P/E stocks, while demonstrating that both categories experienced similar degrees of price volatility. "This means that investors did not have to assume greater risk to achieve the greater returns of the low P/E stocks." Figure 2–1 shows the performance of the various groups.

There are a few caveats. The researchers found that the predictive value of P/Es worked better in the 1970s and '80s than in the 1950s and '60s, while the market cap effect was equally predictive through the 36-year period. However, the researchers found that nearly all the advantage achieved by small stocks was attributable to the single month of January—"the January Effect."

The clear admonition to buy low and sell high is easily understood by everyone. Difficulties arise when we try to quantify what is low and what is high, especially relative to P/Es. Not only are these relative terms, but they represent different levels for different corporations during different economic and market conditions.

Categorical guidelines or rules such as "Never buy a stock for more than 10 times earnings!" or "Only buy stocks in the lowest 20 percent of P/Es!" may have a substantial degree of merit but may also be counterproductive when they keep us away from a stock that rarely if ever

FIGURE 2–1
Annual Returns by P/E Ratio and Market Capitalization Selection

P/E Groups	Annual Returns	Market Cap Groups	Annual Returns
Lowest 20%	19.1%	Smallest 20%	19.4%
Next lowest 20%	17.3	Next smallest 20%	15.5
Middle 20%	13.9	Middle 20%	14.8
Next highest 20%	12.9	Next highest 20%	14.5
Highest 20%	13.9	Highest 20%	13.1

trades under 10 times earnings or less, yet has other severely undervalued corporate criteria. Many undervalued and great growth corporations tend to trade on average (or for brief periods) for one and one half to twice that. If we are so mechanical as to exclude all stocks trading at greater than P/E 10, we may well miss many wonderful opportunities based on assets, growth, or turnaround potential.

THREE GUIDELINES FOR P/E NORMS

The three guidelines I have in mind, which are appropriate for analysis of all fundamental criteria are

1. Historic ranges of individual stock.
2. Industry and market averages, past and present.
3. Comparisons with other fundamental ratios.

I am going to spend considerable time reviewing P/E considerations because these considerations are often applicable and appropriate for considering other fundamental criteria. In the name of reducing redundancy, these considerations won't be repeated for every criterion. There are at least three uncomplicated guidelines for determining what is high and low as far as P/Es—and many other fundamental criteria—are concerned. We can first look to the stock under analysis and determine what its historical range and average(s) have been. This number can be found in several publications, such as *Value Line Investment Survey* and *Standard and Poor's Stock Reports*, or easily calculated from annual reports that show the P/E range per year for several years. Even this specific approach may not provide much precision because of the tendency for stocks to trade in a wide P/E range annually and over the years.

Still, for example, taking the Dow Jones Industrial Average (DJIA) as a proxy for the market—a much-abused liberty because the DJIA 30 stocks often do not reflect the thousands of secondary stocks—an industry, or a typically large capitalization stock, we can determine (or accept published calculations) that the DJIA has traded between 5 and 22+ times earnings over many years, with a multi-year average of about P/E 14. We can see that when the DJIA is trading between P/E 5 to 10 it is in a low range, and when the DJIA is trading between P/E 18 to 23 it is in a high range. We can extend this review to say that a DJIA-type (blue chip) stock is generally undervalued below P/E 10 and overvalued above P/E 18, at least in terms of this one criterion and its historical levels.

The rather crude analysis of DJIA-type stock P/Es actually fits in with a relative rule of thumb, at least for DJIA-type (large industrial) corporations. If such stocks trade 30 percent or more below their P/E norm (average), they are undervalued, and if they trade more than 30 percent above their P/E norm, they are overvalued. *Fair valuation* is defined as the average P/E, or a reasonable area, say 5 percent, above and below the average. For example, if the stock of a hypothetical corporation, International Widgets Inc. (IWI), has a P/E norm of 12, then IWI is into undervalued territory at 8.4 or less times earnings and overvalued at 15.6 or more times earnings.

Notice that the P/E spread from undervalued to overvalued in this example is 7.2 times earnings, but we would like to buy a stock in anticipation of its doubling in market value, which might seem to require going from P/E 8.4 to P/E 16.8. Ah, but that doubling of the P/E would only be necessary if the earnings remained absolutely constant, which they rarely do! What often happens is that between buying an International Widgets Inc. at 8.4 times earnings and seeing it subsequently trading for 15.6 times earnings, its earnings have increased, sometimes dramatically. In such a case the actual market price has more than doubled in the process, often without coming close to a double of the initial low P/E ratio.

One of the tables I often construct at investment seminars is the potential P/E growth table. For purposes of simplification, let's assume that we've found an out-of-favor corporation whose stock is trading for five times $2 per share earnings, or $10 per share. The P/E norm for the past 10 or so years has been determined to be 10. Our analysis shows that this corporation has the potential to grow at 15 percent per year (or more) for the next several years. What might happen to its stock in the marketplace, given these assumptions? Remember, at 15 percent per year compounded quantities double in 5 years.

Figure 2–2 illustrates what could happen. Suppose we bought a stock at $10 because its earnings were $2 per share (thus P/E 5) and

FIGURE 2–2

P/E Potential Growth Table   (Price per Share Equals Earnings Times P/E)

Years (Earnings)	P/E 5	P/E 7.5	P/E 10	P/E 12.5	P/E 15	P/E 17.5	P/E 20
0 ($2)	**$10**	$15	$20	$ 25	$ 30	$ 35	$ 40
5 ($4)	20	30	**40**	50	60	70	80
10 ($8)	40	60	80	100	**120**	140	160

because we thought it should be trading at $20, at its "average" P/E 10. If, while we are waiting for our fair price, the corporation grows at 15 percent per year, then in five years it would probably earn $4 per share. If its stock advanced apace, that is, to 10 times earnings because the company showed a good growth rate for five years and the market valuations in general approached average P/Es, the shares would trade for $40, not merely doubling but quadrupling—a 300 percent gain in five years or 31.95 percent compounded annually.

Then, if the corporation continued to grow at the strong but not phenomenal rate of 15 percent per year, in another five years it would probably earn $8 per share. With this lucrative, solid growth rate over a decade, and if the bullish market itself rose to high but not necessarily record valuation levels, the stock would probably trade at 15 times its $8 earnings or $120—an 1,100 percent gain in 10 years—or 28.2 percent compounded annually. Of course, the market could go crazy after awhile and trade at 20 times earnings on average, carrying our stock along with it.

Ah, the deception of numbers. If you would have asked me what I would rather have, a 300 percent profit in 5 years or an 1,100 percent profit in 10 years, I would have immediately chosen the 1,100 percent. But I would have chosen "only" a 28.2 percent gain compounded for 10 years versus a 31.95 percent compounded annual gain for five years. It would have been better, in theory, to have gone from $10 to $40 twice (in two successive 5-year periods) than hold still 10 years for the $120. After reaching $40 in 5 years, that amount would have to become $160 (another 4 times the then original capital of $40) in another 5 years in order to maintain the 31.95 percent compounding for 10 years.

I say *in theory* because in practice, we would have to pay taxes on the first position if the gains were realized after five years. If our tax liability came to 33 percent of the $30 profit, we would then have $20 left after taxes plus the original $10, or $30 overall to reinvest. Then a four-fold increase would bring us back to $120 again, after the second five years. In California or another high tax state, we might also have to pay another 9 percent or more in tax, leaving us with less than $30 to reinvest for the second five years. Although this topic is reviewed a bit in the chapter on margin and also mentioned in Chapter 4 (on Stock portfolio management), I reemphasize that a major benefit of long-term speculating is in minimizing tax "attrition" as well as excessive trading commissions.

By the way, I hope you don't think the kinds of observations in the above paragraphs are merely a superficial playing with numbers. It is just such details, arithmetic, and awareness that can make the difference between a systematic, long-term accumulation of assets instead of a hit-or-miss grasping at good-sounding numbers that actually fall short upon closer examination of what you thought they meant.

A SECOND P/E GUIDELINE: INDUSTRY AND MARKET AVERAGES

Instead of determining the fair or normative P/E from historical analysis of a corporation's (stock's) average P/E, we can make comparisons with industry or sector averages, as well as market-wide averages. Again, these comparisons also may be fruitful for other fundamental criteria. I tend to avoid industry averages because of the variability of individual corporations within an industry. The sample number of corporations in an industry may be too small for statistical significance or the corporation being analyzed may not be comparable to the "average" corporation in that industry. You could check to see how other companies are trading, but then you would have to calculate several of their norms and note any significant differences among corporations, a potential tempest-in-a-teapot exercise in analysis.

More promising, especially for down-and-dirty comparisons, are market-wide or major index P/E average or current ratios. Having such a guideline, we would want to remember it applies to long-term averages or moderate levels associated with "normal" market periods. For example, the Standard & Poor's 500 Index (S&P 500) of 500 stocks, mainly taken from the New York Stock Exchange, had a P/E of over 22 in late August 1987 (at the S&P 500's all-time high) but was trading for less than 11 in mid-November 1988.

Market or major index P/Es are relational to many other considerations such as the current early, middle, or late position in a rising or falling market cycle, the interest-rate levels, and the money supply levels. As you become aware of and work with individual stock P/Es and market or major index P/Es, you will likely develop a feel for what is relatively high or low at any given period.

Given that the S&P 500 Index average P/E for the past 63 years is around 14, the S&P 500 was very historically overvalued at 22 P/E and somewhat undervalued at 11 P/E. If you blindly compared our hypothetical International Widgets Inc.'s (IWI's) P/E to the S&P 500 P/E at these extremes, without invoking the long-term P/E average, you might conclude that in late August 1987, IWI's P/E could be 22 (or even 30 percent higher) before being overvalued and would be undervalued at 15.4 (30 percent below 22), which would be a terribly distorted and misleading criterion levels.

On the other hand, if IWI's P/E was 7.7 in November 1988, you could say it was trading at a 30 percent discount to the S&P 500's current P/E, or a 45 percent discount to the S&P 500's long-time average P/E. This might be an interesting and useful comparison, especially if IWI typically traded at the S&P 500's varying P/E or at a premium to it. Likewise, comparisons could be made to the Dow Jones Industrial Average's current and average P/E, as well as to broader and perhaps more representative indexes such as the New York Stock Exchange Composite Index or the Value Line Composite Index. If the stock under analysis was a transportation or utility issue, it could be compared to those indexes' P/Es and likewise to appropriate subsets in the over-the-counter market or the American Stock Exchange.

A THIRD P/E GUIDELINE: COMPARISON WITH ASSOCIATED RATIOS

Estimating a fair or normal P/E for any given stock may involve the interrelationships of other fundamental and economic criteria. A rule of thumb suggests that a stock's P/E ratio can be the same number as its corporation's return on equity (ROE), sometimes called return on net worth. That is, if IWI's ROE is 15 percent, IWI could be fairly valued—at least in terms of its earnings' criterion—if its P/E was 15.

This rule of thumb might get you into trouble if you invoke it for extreme readings. If IWI's ROE jumped to 30 percent, I doubt that I would want to pay 30 times earnings (P/E 30) for its stock. On the other side, if IWI's ROE came in at 5 percent, I still might want to buy its stock at 5 times earnings (P/E), especially if I could buy IWI for 20 percent (one fifth) of its equity. If I could buy IWI at 20 percent of equity, with only a 5 percent ROE, I would be getting a 25 percent *return on* (my) *investment* dollars in the stock. More about this relationship under the topic of book value, later in this chapter.

Some important criteria could be included in our estimating fair P/E levels, for those investors who wish to take a more academic or analytical approach than I believe is necessary. I mention a few of these criteria not to overwhelm the average reader but rather to satisfy the more technical types. These criteria include inflation levels (actual and perceived) and Federal Reserve Board (a.k.a. the Fed, or FRB) policies, including money supply growth, free bank reserves, and interest rates. In normal times—the term *normal times* may be an oxymoron—a P/E norm (for either a stock, an industry, or the market overall) would exist in relation to "normal" interest rates as well as to other historically average monetary conditions.

Ostensibly, as interest rates advance, the cost of doing business increases and the likelihood of increasing profits diminishes. Perhaps a P/E of 14 would be fair for IWI when the 30-year "long" Treasury bond trades to yield 8 percent or the 91-day T-bill yields 5 percent. With the long T-bond at 9 percent, and 3-month T-bills at 8 percent, perhaps an IWI P/E of 12 would be fair (assuming equivalent "levels" of monetary criteria). When the long bond yields 6 percent and the 91-day T-bill yields 4 percent, perhaps a P/E of 16 would be fair—*fair* meaning a fairly or fully valued, average criterion level under those conditions—and so forth for other configurations of the interest yield curve.

Again, I almost question the review of these relatively esoteric considerations, for they are probably more than our analysis requires. Such considerations as Fed policy and inflation are certainly important background information to be utilized intuitively, if not systematically, in fundamental analysis. Fortunately, many other valuation criteria already factor in and reflect this panoply of potential economic and monetary considerations that affect the analysis of fair P/Es, so again, one can almost set them aside in a down-and-dirty-but-sufficient analysis of corporate valuations for stock speculation.

To the degree that we can generally ignore stock market and macro economic considerations as we doggedly persevere in the systematic *purchase of undervalued stocks in a widely diversified portfolio to be held for long-term appreciation* and in the subsequent sale of fully valued stocks, we can pay as much or as little attention as we like to other than elementary corporate fundamental analysis.

P/E LEVELS ARE RELATIVE AND CHANGING

It would be nice, as mentioned before, to say, "Only buy stocks that are trading for less than 10 times earnings or 30 percent below their 10-year average P/Es.'' I cannot do that. Some stocks at some times are fully valued at P/E 9 or less, while others may be significantly undervalued at P/E 12 or more. Then there are the cases where a stock doesn't have a P/E because it has recorded deficit earnings (normally negative P/Es are not used), or its P/E is ridiculously high because of a sharp drop in earnings or explosive rise in market price.

I arrive at a stock's P/E norm based upon its average P/E for a number of years, often weighting the most recent years more heavily, considering its ROE, and integrating general market and major index P/Es. Obviously, no P/E norm is carved in stone and all are subject to revision as corporate fundamentals fluctuate and long-term market conditions change. The P/E norm should reflect a P/E attributable to the stock in a "normal" market, adjusted for current and likely conditions. I will review some actual examples of determining a P/E norm in Appendix A, detailing three specific stocks' analyses, based on my method of using fundamental criteria.

FOR SOME, BOOK VALUE IS THE DOMINANT CRITERION

Book value is generally defined as assets less liabilities. Again, the criterion seems simple enough, but soon one finds that neither all assets nor all liabilities are created equal. As *book value (BV)* is an accounting term, all sorts of accounting options and decisions go into the rendering of the final figure. There often arises the question of so-called intangibles, such as goodwill, patents, trademarks, and names. I am going to short-circuit the very large amount of gross and subtle analysis that can go into determining the elements of book value and the adjustments that could be made.

In general, I accept the book values stated in annual reports, *Barron's*, *Forbes*, various Standard & Poor's reports and publications, *Value Line Investment Survey*, and other financial publications. In a few cases where the book values may be severely overstated or understated, that condition is frequently highlighted in the above-mentioned sources.

I take it that most corporations' book values generally understate what their replacement cost values would be. Such replacement cost (or whole business) values are usually made dramatically clear during corporate mergers and acquisitions, where some multiple of book value is almost always paid for the target company. Again, invoking my statistical attitude, within a large number of analyzed corporations, errors of overstated book values in some will be balanced by understated book values in others.

A small review of price/book value (P/BV) ratios will show that different companies within the same industry will trade with a wide range of values. Also, different industries will exhibit different average book-value–to–share price ratios. There is no magic criterion or absolute guideline for an undervalued or overvalued P/BV. Truly, in fundamental analysis everything is relative, especially to each corporation but also to the current general market level, which itself is fluctuating and relative to general economic and monetary conditions.

We know that the Dow Jones Industrial Average (DJIA) of 30 large capitalization "industrial" stocks, for example, has traded at a P/BV ranging from slightly below 1.0 at market lows to over 2.7 during 1987, but generally around 2.2 at market highs. Yet individual DJIA stocks show the extremes that are masked by their average, just as the wide range of P/BVs for individual secondary stocks is masked by their overall average. For instance, in March 1989, General Motors traded for a P/BV of 0.86 while Merck's P/BV was 8.84, and many more analysts were recommending Merck than General Motors.

I have been quoted in a national publication as saying that I buy stocks when they are trading at 50 percent of their book value, with the implication that 50 percent of book value is my limit. Other conditions being amenable, I would love to buy the stocks of corporations trading at a 50 percent or greater discount from their book values. Still, I am frequently happy to pay more than twice book value if other fundamental criteria indicate extreme undervaluation.

Interestingly, the 30 percent principle that can be applied as a trading criterion for P/Es—buy stocks 30 percent below their P/E norm and sell them 30 percent above—applies almost equally as well to P/BVs. If our hypothetical IWI normally (on average over a multi-year period) trades around 1.5 times its book value, then when it is trading for 105 percent of its BV it is "cheap" or undervalued on this criterion, and when it trades at 195 percent of its BV it is "dear" or fully valued.

If you had reviewed corporate fundamentals during the winter of 1974, you could have found a large number of solid corporations trading for 20 percent to 50 percent of their tangible book values. In long-term (bear) market lows, you might buy corporations for "20 cents on the dollar'' and thereafter hold them until they are trading for ''$2 on the dollar,'' that is, for two times their BVs. Although it can stagger the imagination and be difficult to take advantage of at the time, one can easily understand how in a depressed stock market great companies are auctioned at half or less than half of their net asset value because people are afraid that the bad times can only get worse, or shareholders are forced to liquidate in order to raise cash to meet current obligations.

There is a curious economic pattern that occurs during both enthusiastic or fearful conditions—the vicious stock market cycle version of the self-fulfilling prophecy. The *self-fulfilling prophecy* refers to events occurring because we believe they are going to happen, and we curiously effect such outcomes. Suppose that interest rates are rising and money is getting scarce. The average person (or competent chief financial officer) who is considering borrowing funds in the near future will think, ''I'd better make that loan today (or as soon as possible) because tomorrow (or next month) I will have to pay a higher interest rate or there might not be any funds available at all.'' Thus, numerous lemmings—many of whom may not even need a loan for quite a while—create a ''run'' on the system, depleting the available funds and forcing up interest rates, just the phenomenon they prophesied would happen.

Okay, suppose the stock market is rising based on rational reasons of improved corporate earnings and the early phase of a growing business cycle, such as happened in 1988–89. After a while of this market advance, the average market player—who has been out of the market or underinvested waiting for the bear market that was supposed to follow the Crash of '87 to occur—may well think, ''I'd better get in on the good times before they get even further away from me.'' As the ranks of these reborn bulls grow, the prices of stocks are bid up in an effort to obtain these stocks before their prices go even higher.

The self-fulfilling ''melt-up'' trend might continue until a ''blow off'' top occurs and the downward trend reversal sets in. Then, after a while, the negative self-fulfilling trend becomes dominant and drives prices down to ridiculous levels, as the market cycle is completed, only to begin the advancing cycle all over again.

For long spells, perhaps 40 percent of the time, the stock market stays in a trading range, neither rallying out of sight nor crashing to the ground. These relatively dull periods are generally good times to accumulate undervalued corporations, because stocks trading for less than book value after a big market-wide decline can take years to be revalued upward to their historic norms. As the market averages increase, based on the increasing valuations of individual stocks, the criteria for what is undervalued or overvalued become modified to reflect current conditions.

In 1974, I was looking for industrial corporations trading for 50 percent or less than their book values. By 1982, I was looking for industrial and service corporations trading for less than their book values. In 1989, I am satisfied to find undervalued corporations that are trading for less than 150 percent of book values, especially when those book values are understated and several other fundamentals indicate significant undervaluation.

I have been asked how I feel about the "future value" of companies trading at 150 percent of book value. After all, isn't our basic principle to buy stocks at 50 cents on the dollar or 50 percent of what we think they are worth? Actually, I am interested in acquiring companies—or small fractions of them as represented by some shares of their stock—for 50 percent or less of what I believe they will probably trade for in the next three to five years. In many cases we don't have to wait that long; in other cases no amount of time brings profits.

Even if a corporation is currently trading at 150 percent of its book value, that book value may be significantly understated, especially in terms of replacement costs or as a going business value. Then too, over the next few years the corporation may double in value, continue to trade at 150 percent of book value or more, and thus double or more in its market price.

A LOT OF NICE THINGS CAN HAPPEN
WITH REVENUES

A corporation may have much room for improvement and many problems, but if its sales or revenues are adequate or growing it is more likely improvements can be made and problems solved than if revenues are inadequate and diminishing. I learned about the importance of the Price/Revenues ratio from Ken Fisher in his book *Super Stocks*. Ken called it the *Price/Sales Ratio (PSR)* and spelled out many of its peculiarities, especially as it applies differently to different types and sizes of businesses. He also reviewed many wise observations, keeping up with his family tradition—his father, Philip A. Fisher, wrote the classic *Common Stocks & Uncommon Profits*.

Like all stock price valuation criteria that show what marketeers are willing to pay for a corporation's fundamentals, the P/SR or as we call it, the price/revenue ratio (P/R) shows what it costs—in terms of the current price of a share of stock—to buy $1 of corporate sales or revenues. This is not unlike the P/E ratio, which shows what investors are willing to spend to buy $1 of earnings. Like the P/E, the P/R also indicates a stock's perceived worth or popularity, that is, how the investing public values a corporation. If our hypothetical International Widgits Inc. (IWI) trades for a P/R of 1.0, that means the price of a share of IWI is the same as one share's worth of its revenues. If IWI's P/R were 0.5, that would mean "the market" is willing to pay 50 percent of IWI's revenues to own IWI shares—50 percent of the per share revenues equals the per share price.

Clearly, most of the caveats and considerations of how to determine a fair ratio or norm and consequently undervalued/overvalued criteria for a corporation's P/E or P/BV apply similarly to its P/R. That is, each corporation has its historical average P/R, which can be compared to P/Rs of similar companies, its industry group, major market averages, or even the market as a whole. Certain averages, which are displayed in Figure 2–3, have been worked out by Ken Fisher, but beware the fixed guideline, especially when it involves the gross categorizing of corporations. For examples, The Singer Corporation no longer manufactures sewing machines, and many people were unclear about Stop & Shop Companies, categorizing it only as a supermarket.

The historical precedents of superior market appreciation for low P/R stocks are most encouraging, even as they are for low P/E and low P/BV stocks.

Ken Fisher claims The Popularity Monitor numbers are empirically derived and that in each case the PSR doubles between steps in popularity. He writes in *Super Stocks*, "The absolute scale of PSR/popularity seems consistent—as stocks rise from obscurity to high regard. I have no explanation for this and report it merely as an interesting observation, worthy of further consideration." (P. 234) Often in fundamental or technical analysis, certain relationships are predictive and work, although their discoveries were accidental and empirical with no satisfying rationale or theory to account for them. At such times the profound maxim, "If it works, use it; if it ain't broke, don't fix it!" applies.

FIGURE 2–3
The Popularity Monitor

	Stocks Are		
If Companies Are	Very Unpopular, with PSRs Less than	Accepted, with PSRs over	Very Popular with PSRs over
Small, growth oriented, of technology type	0.75	1.50	3.00
Multibillion-dollar–sales sized or without growth attributes	0.20	0.40	0.80
Inherently thin margined, such as supermarkets	0.03	0.06	0.12

Source: Adapted from *Super Stocks*, by Kenneth L. Fisher (Homewood, IL: Jones-Irwin), 1984, see pp. 36–7.

I would take Fisher's PSR/popularity numbers at face value as a general (or at least starting) guideline for under-, fair-, and overvaluation, subject to possible adjustment for unique conditions of individual corporations. When a giant industrial company is trading at cycle lows, at 20 percent of sales or less (price per share to revenues per share), it is both very unpopular and very undervalued according to this criterion. Then, when it trades at 40 percent of sales or so, it is "accepted" and in the range of fairly valued. Finally, when it trades at a very popular 80 percent of sales or greater, it is overvalued.

By itself, such a simplistic categorization might be misleading, and we would take some care by checking historical price/revenue ratios to see if a corporation under analysis approximated these categories. Often, several measures of popularity/valuation will be consonant with each other, reinforcing a general picture. Obviously, not all undervalued stocks are unpopular, just as not all unpopular stocks are undervalued. As the logicians might say, there is no necessary bisymmetrical relationship between these two attributes. That is, we shouldn't confuse the appearance of popularity with the reality of overvalue, and likewise the appearance of unpopularity does not necessarily imply undervalue. Nonetheless, the popularity and valuation attributes frequently reflect each other in many other fundamental criteria as well as P/Rs.

As is true of so many guidelines for fundamental (or technical) criteria, we must guard against being too slavish to any given element. If International Widgits Inc. were a retailing company with a market value of less than $200 million, we might not want to call its stock undervalued if its P/R were 0.5. If a review revealed that 10 percent of IWI's revenue came from royalties on its patents and 35 percent of IWI's revenue came from the manufacture of exotic (high technology) electronics equipment—which it also sold in its retail outlets—then we would be wrong to assign IWI strictly to the retailing industry and look for a retailing P/R level without accounting for IWI's manufacturing, niche, and growth potentials.

Often, if not usually, the guides for fundamental criteria are imprecise—not to mention that the criteria can fluctuate significantly over the reported quarters and years—and should not be applied too rigorously. We are looking for a recognizable picture of a corporation that is undervalued in general or on average. Any given criterion may indicate overvaluedness, either temporarily or systemically. Nonetheless, the weight of combined evaluative indicators will range along a spectrum from very undervalued to very overvalued, and depending perhaps upon economic and market conditions—and the requirements of our portfolio management strategies—we would choose *sufficiently* undervalued stocks to accumulate and *approximately fully* valued stocks to sell.

CASH FLOW IS USUALLY MORE IMPORTANT THAN EARNINGS

Earnings, ultimately, is the name of the game in corporate speculating. Corporations are begun and run ostensibly to earn profits for their shareholders. This notion can get lost in a complex society and stock market where special interest groups—other than the corporation's shareholders—believe the company exists for them and their interests. We see more and more entrenched managements that run public corporations as if they were private partnerships.

In this era of laissez-faire regulation and willful indifference to antitrust laws on the books, many managements have worked against their shareholders to take "their" companies private or to sell out to "white knights" in order to maintain their jobs and obtain golden parachute termination and retirement benefits. To add injury to insult, rogue managements have used the leveraged buy out (LBO) to accomplish their desires, essentially basing the purchase of the corporation on its own assets—assets belonging to its shareholders. Sometimes managements have deliberately failed to maximize earnings, lowering the analyzed value of their corporations in order to grab them on the cheap, only to subsequently institute necessary reforms that bring on profitability and reemergence as a public corporation with windfall profits for the pirates.

Because speculating in corporations involves many factors other than earnings, at least for substantial periods of time, the aware speculator will consider value and growth potentials over recent earnings disappointments and periodic glitches in rising earnings trends. Also seriously considered will be fundamentals that may reflect a more accurate picture of the health of a corporation than does a period of fluctuating or down earnings. Cash flow is one of the measures that may be more stable than earnings, and as such may be more important in determining undervalued corporations than P/Es.

Cash flow is generally defined in accounting terms as the net income of a corporation before the deduction of book charges such as depreciation and amortization. As depreciation and amortization charges—merely allocations of the cost of an asset over its useful life—are not actual cash outlays, they do not penalize the use of current income or the cash available for conducting business operations, expansion, debt repayment, and investment in other enterprises.

Cash flow is another tricky accounting subject. If the principal item, depreciation, which is based upon original cost and "useful life," is insufficient to cover the asset's replacement costs, then earnings are probably overstated and the business may be facing (or developing) financial difficulties in maintaining and renewing its plant and equipment. On the other hand, if plant and equipment have appreciated in value over the years and are worth more than their depreciated value on the books, then earnings were probably understated, and there are "hidden" asset values.

Yet again, as with other fundamental criteria, P/CF ratios are relative to their corporation's historic average as well as to comparisons with other corporations, market averages, and especially rule-of-thumb ratios. P/CF numbers act similarly to P/Es except P/Es are higher, because cash flow is net earnings plus tax-reducing depreciation and amortization charges. If International Widgets Inc. (IWI) trades for ten times cash flow on average—currently $10 per share, with a cash flow of $1 per share—that would be its fair cash flow value. Then, invoking the 30 percent over or under criterion, when IWI trades for P/CF 7 (7 times cash flow) it would be just undervalued, and at P/CF 13 it would be just overvalued.

Often we can find corporations trading for almost half their average P/CF, which is a strong indication of undervaluation. If IWI traded at P/CF 5, that would mean at $10 per share it was generating $2 per share in cash flow, which yields a handsome 20 percent *return on cash*. As each integer of P/CF comes down, the return on cash expands greatly. At P/CF 4 the return on cash is 25 percent, and at P/CF 3 the return on cash is 33.3 percent. Of course, we are not to confuse these "returns on cash" with earnings returns.

Andrew Tobias in *Money Angles* agrees that cash flow is worth reckoning:

> In many respects more important than earnings, this is the simpleminded measure of how much cash is pouring in or draining out. Real estate operations always report bad earnings (because of the depreciation they claim, for tax purposes, on their properties), but the cash just rolls in bigger and bigger each year (because the properties actually *app*reciate and the rents get raised).[1]

An analyst would want to be aware of the cause(s) of any significant changes in cash flow, such as a massive rebuilding or replacement program, that would lead to greater depreciation deductions but would also eat up available cash, perhaps requiring massive borrowing and a burdensome interest and debt repayment.

Not all fundamental analysts think highly of cash flow as a measure of a corporation's worth. Benjamin Graham and his coauthors, writing in *The Interpretation of Financial Statements*, find fault with cash flow when it is presented on a per share basis, thus implying "that it represents the 'true earnings' of the business. Such an inference would be completely wrong." Of course, we shall not confuse cash flow with earnings, just as we do not confuse extraordinary earnings with operating earnings or with fully diluted earnings. We take to heart old Ben Graham's carefulness and conservative ways, and consider his admonition.

> In our view the average investor would do well to ignore the cash-flow figure, as it is more likely to mislead than to enlighten him. Security analysts should study these figures mainly to determine whether the

---

[1] A. Tobias, *Money Angles* (New York: Avon, 1985), pp. 200.

amortization charges need revision as being either too high or too low from the comparative standpoint.[2]

What many corporate pickers look for is free cash flow, or the money a corporation has available to work with. Technically, this is the cash flow surplus left after capital expenditures and other required costs necessary to support the business and anticipated revenues. Free cash flow is usually highest for corporations that have large depreciation expenses, which are tax deductible, but do not need to replace the equipment being depreciated, such as the aforementioned real estate companies, leasing corporations with equipment that outlives its depreciated "useful life," or pipeline companies and even utilities whose major capital expenditures are behind them.

For our purpose, which is to find that handful of valuation criteria that will help us select undervalued corporations without becoming accountants or wheeler-dealers, we can throw plain, old P/CF into the pot and see if it confirms our other criteria. Of course, we do not need to ignore information about free cash flow if we stumble over it in our research.

Each of the Big Three or Super Seven selection criteria can be fraught with questions of quality and appropriateness. What is the quality of earnings, the quality of assets that make up book value, or the appropriateness (quality) of cash flow? can be important questions. Still, by finding several gross or general criteria that reaffirm each other—and perhaps a few other safety checks like the amount of debt a corporation carries—the likelihood of picking a winning stock is good.

MARKET CAPITALIZATION: DAVIDS DO BETTER THAN GOLIATHS

If you like irony, then the stock market is the place for you. After all the learned analysis, the hours spent hunched over financial reports keeping track of corporations by interviewing officers, customers, vendors, and the competition, it turns out that small capitalization stocks outperform large capitalization stocks by significant and important percentages over long periods of time. From data reviewed in Figure 2–1 comparing P/Es and market capitalizations, we see that for the past 36 years small caps

---

[2]B. Graham and C. McGoldrick, *The Interpretation of Financial Statements*, 3 rev. ed. (New York: Harper & Row, 1987), p. 67.

stocks—defined as the smallest 20 percent of market capitalization—gained 19.4 percent annual returns compared to only 13.1 percent for the largest 20 percent of market capitalization.

Confirming evidence, if more subdued, using somewhat different stock populations, comes from Ibbotson Associates, who conclude that small company stocks have averaged 12.3 percent total return per year for the past 63 years. In the same period, large capitalization stocks, as represented by the S&P 500 have averaged 10.0 percent total return per year. More about Ibbotson's analyses below.

Many authors and researchers have reported on this phenomenon in books, journals, and investment newsletters. For a detailed analysis you might want to peruse Gerald Perritt's scholarly yet readable book *Small Stocks, Big Profits*. Perritt takes a serious academic view that shows how "the small firm effect" has produced superior results without a commensurate increase in risk. Efficient market theorists insist that investment returns are proportionate to risks taken, and thus "explain" how some investors outperform the market averages because they take greater risks.

I don't want to get involved with grand academic theories in this book, as I have considerable intuitive problems with so-called standard measures of risk, especially when risk is cast in terms of price or market volatility alone. The subject of risk in investing is much larger than most investors I've met have ever considered. Some kinds of risk are reviewed in Chapter 8, "Potpourri."

One of the best sources of documented results for long-term investment returns is the book *Stocks, Bonds, Bills, and Inflation: 1989 Yearbook*, (*SBBI*) published by Ibbotson Associates (8 South Michigan Avenue, Suite 707, Chicago, Ill. 60603, (312) 263–3434, $85). In Chapter 7, "Twelve Years and Counting," I have based several comparison results on *SBBI* figures. Especially interesting are the comparisons between the total returns of "Common Stocks, represented by the Standard and Poor's 500 Stock Composite Index (S&P 500)" and "Small Company Stocks, represented by the fifth capitalization quintile of stocks on the NYSE for 1926–81 and the performance of the Dimensional Fund Advisors (DFA) Small Company Fund thereafter."

Beginning with 1.00 at 12/31/25, an index of S&P total returns closed 1988 at 459.86, which works out to a 10.0 percent compounded annual growth rate, while small company stocks closed 1988 at 1,478.14 for a compound annual growth rate of 12.3 percent. In addition to showing that small company stocks outperformed S&P 500 stocks by 23 percent per year on average for 63 years, that difference between 10.0 percent and 12.3 percent for 63 years results in over three times the greater gain for small companies over big companies.

You might wonder if 63-year comparisons make much sense since few of us will be investing or speculating for six decades, besides which there is no guarantee that the next 60 years will echo the past three score. Fair enough, but I find it both comforting and encouraging to see that through all those years of wars, depressions, recessions, economic booms, technological and informational revolutions, governments, scandals, and what not, large capitalization stocks have advanced 6.9 percent above the 63-year average 3.1 percent annual inflation rate, while small cap stocks managed a 9.2 percent after-inflation annual growth.

True, there were multi-year periods when stocks in general suffered losses or when large cap stocks did better than small cap stocks. But the long-term comparisons between the returns on equities and interest-bearing instruments such as "safe" Treasury bills (average 3.5 percent, for a real return of 0.5 percent) and long-term government bonds (average 4.4 percent, for a real return about 1.3 percent) can be astounding, especially considering the ravages of the post–World War II inflation, which reached a peak of 13.3 percent in 1979. "On a month-by-month basis, the peak inflation rate was a breathtaking 24.0 percent, stated in annualized terms, in August, 1973." (*SBBI*, p. 28)

I can't remember when I first heard that "bonds are a form of legalized confiscation," but the long-term numbers sure support that bitter assertion. After factoring in the costs of taxes and inflation-reducing purchasing power, the long-term bill and bond holder—as well as the bank passbook and CD holder—except for brief transition periods, have been committed to a policy of systematic diminishment of future buying power.

THE BOTTOM LINE: RETURN ON EQUITY

For some value investors, the bottom line is *return on equity* (ROE), also called *return on net worth* (or even *return on net asset value*), and which for practical purposes could be called *return on book value* when common stock represents all shareholder equity. Now we're talking about how much a corporation earns after taxes in terms of its owners' (shareholders') equity. This ROE percentage represents several important considerations, such as how well (profitably) management has run the business and how fast it is growing. Like every other financial figure, it can be compared to prior years, other companies, and market averages.

If common stocks tend to generate a total return of about 10 percent per year, then it might seem that the average bottom line for corporations would be a 10 percent ROE. This crude analysis involves some major assumptions, such as stocks generally trade at their equity per share amount. In that case, shareholders would obtain the same return on a cost basis as the corporations earned on equity. As we have seen, shares rarely trade at equity per share. The market is almost always overvaluing or undervaluing corporations according to this criterion.

The phenomenon of inefficient market pricing or not fairly valuing stocks most of the time is what creates the great opportunities and permits the speculator's or investor's great gains and losses to occur. It is the backward-looking, trend-projecting, and herd (mob) instinct of a majority of market analysts and participants that fails to account for the individual case and tends to fight "the last war." This typical attitude toward the stock market is another misleading form of the self-fulfilling prophecy.

When conditions have been favorable, analysts tend to raise their estimations of profits and returns, a tendency that sooner or later leads to excess. Conversely, when conditions have been negative, estimates are generally reduced, often swinging too much toward underestimation, until conditions appear better and are in a firmly established uptrend.

Corporations' returns on equity range from negative to high percentages. A young emerging growth company might show a 50 percent or greater ROE, at least for a few years, although such growth rates are not sustainable or that company would soon dominate all commerce. Experience has shown me that a 15 percent ROE is a solid return for moderate-size industrial companies; it could be used as a base guideline with the understanding that other fundamental factors may be more important in determining an undervalued stock than ROE. As there is variability of price/revenues among corporations, so too there is a wide spread of ROE among corporations, and often within a corporation over the years.

With ROE, we would generally like to see higher percentages, say 20 percent rather than 10 percent, unlike the lower ratios that spell undervaluedness in P/E, P/BV, and P/CF. However, there are interesting relationships of undervaluedness with relatively low ROEs. As previously pointed out in relation to the price/revenue ratio, if International Widgits Inc. (IWI) is registering a 10 percent ROE—which I would consider puny as a return on equity—then I could still do well if IWI were trading at only 50 percent of its equity. In such a case, though IWI managed only 10 percent ROE, I would be getting a 20 percent return on *my invested* (equity) capital, since I would be buying ROE for 50 cents on the dollar.

Sometimes relatively low measures of profitability can be a mask hiding a severely undervalued corporation. Sooner or later almost all corporations have bad years or special conditions that make them look bad in terms of earnings and ROE. In 1988, for the first time in its history, American Telephone and Telegraph reported a loss as it took a huge writedown for obsolete analog equipment that was being replaced by state-of-the-art digital equipment. Obviously the ROE for American Telephone for 1988 would register its stock price as hopelessly overvalued if taken out of context. Clearly, the long history of a steady and substantial ROE—in this case restricted by regulatory commissions—augured well for a resumption after the special writedown. In fact, AT&T's stock quickly recovered in anticipation of even higher future ROEs given the relaxed regulatory processes underway, where instead of limiting returns, the utility (and manufacturing) company will have its rates limited and will probably be able to increase its returns.

Again, we want to keep our analysis as simple as is reasonable, perhaps limited to a few hours work a week perusing readily available public sources of information. When we check out ROE, compare it with historical trend and rule-of-thumb levels, and check the *return on investment* of capital (what we have to pay for the equity in return on equity), we have done all we need to do with this selection criterion.

RETURN ON ASSETS, OR HOW THE CORPORATION MANAGES ITS LEVERAGE

A companion criterion to ROE is *return on assets* (ROA). This is an especially revealing number in corporations that have a lot of assets compared to their equity, such as banks, savings and loans, insurance companies, and some highly leveraged industrial or service outfits.

Imagine a corporation—let's call it International Assets Inc. (IAI)—that has $10 million in equity but manages $200 million in assets. Try as it might, IAI is able to earn an (after-tax) ROA of only 1 percent, or $2 million, apparently not a very good return. On the other hand, IAI also reports a 20 percent ROE because it earned those $2 million on its $10 million equity base. Reporting such results, IAI could be a savings and loan, a bank, or a financial management company.

In looking at ROE and ROA, we would want to notice not only their absolute percentages but if there were any improvement (increasing percentages) over the past few years. Two corporations might have the same ROEs and ROAs at the same moment, but one may represent a rising trend and the other a declining trend. Though the trends might easily reverse in the future, between the two I would prefer the company with apparently improving returns, indicating likely improving management of equity and assets. On the other hand, I might look to see if the rising trend were at the expense of other criteria, such as if it coincided with a diminishment in maintenance and replacement spending or with big cuts in research and development spending, which might hamper the company in the future.

Or, we might simply be content to see that we found a corporation that is undervalued on several criteria and meets our ROE or ROA minimums. "Let well enough alone" is often good speculative advice. You may think that I am ambivalent or cavalier when, after mentioning some potential danger signal, I write not to worry, the minimum criteria will lead us to the promised stocks, which will pay for our passage in the promised land. My experience is that no matter how carefully I analyze corporations, about 20 percent or more of the time my stock selections don't work out over the years—with as many as 40 percent or more of them appearing unprofitable in their first year after selection. Some selections that I think are golden turn out to be dross, while others that barely made the cut become big winners.

NOT ALL VALUATION CRITERIA APPLY TO ALL CORPORATIONS

Most of the selection criteria in this chapter apply to industrial, manufacturing, natural resource, and service industries. Financial institutions such as banks, savings and loans, insurance companies, brokerages, and financial services companies may be analyzed with several of the selection criteria already reviewed, but not with all of them. For instance, cash-flow analysis or price/revenue analysis, for that matter, are not appropriate for financial companies. For financial corporations, other criteria may supplant or augment those—like current ratios or return on sales—which are also not appropriate.

For savings and loan (S&L) analysis, we would want to emphasize four other criteria. The ratio (percentage) of common shareholder equity (or net worth) to total assets measures the financial strength of an S&Ls capital base, with 6 percent or more considered good. Average financial strength of net worth is 5 percent–6 percent, with 3 percent–4 percent below average, and below 3 percent considered poor. Another important S&L ratio is net interest income to total general and administrative expense, which indicates whether interest income can meet expenses without requiring other, nonrecurring income.

The ratio of nonperforming assets to total loans is one of the best tangible indications of effectiveness in sustaining loan quality as delinquent loans and foreclosed properties impact negatively both earnings and management's time. Currently nonperforming assets have been averaging well over 2 percent of total loans for both banks and S&Ls, so look for the ratio below 2 percent, with below 1 percent being outstanding. Finally, we can check out the "gap" as a percentage of total assets, which refers to the maturities (repricing) of assets and liabilities, which reflects balance sheet and interest rate vulnerability.

I might well have skipped S&L analysis, as some stock pickers do by avoiding the industry because of long-time negative publicity, but over the years many S&L stocks have appreciated handsomely. It is in just such out-of-favor and depressed (undervalued) stocks that great returns can be gleaned, given good selection and patience. After the current travails have passed, the strong and well-managed S&Ls will emerge profitable and valuable, as they did after the high interest rates of the early '70s.

I want to alert readers that financial companies may require different fundamental criteria than those used for industrial corporations. For detailed reviews of S&L analysis, I suggest you study S&L annual reports, such as those of FirstFed Financial of California (FED) and Boston Bancorp (SBOS), but especially the 1988 annual report of Golden West Financial (GDW), which explains in understandable English and tables the nuances of the items mentioned above as well as other crucial fundamentals.

AN ICONOCLASTIC CLANG

While working on this chapter, I had the good fortune to read an interview of Walter J. Schloss and his son Edwin by Henry Emerson, editor of the *Outstanding Investor Digest*, published 3/6/89. Walter J. Schloss Associates has racked up a gross annual return from 1956 through 1988 of 21.6 percent, compared to the S&P Total Return of 9.8 percent per annum for the same period. Walter Schloss had worked with Ben Graham and Warren Buffett in 1954–55. Buffett has lauded Schloss as one of the "Super-Investors of Graham and Doddsville." Of the many wonderful stories relating to Schloss's experiences and developed investing wisdom, I was particularly fascinated with his reminiscence about Ben Graham, often called the father of fundamental analysis.

After commenting on Graham's interest in ideas and new ways of doing things and his renaissance nature, Walter Schloss said,

> Then, he discovered he could make good money by just buying stocks at 2/3rds of their working capital. My job was really finding those working capital stocks and then recommending which ones we should buy.
>
> After he found out he could make money this way, he kind of lost interest. It seemed like a good game. If he were alive today and couldn't find working capital stocks, he'd very likely be looking around for something else.

There are innumerable stock selection schemes, some using only two criteria or even one as mentioned above. I sometimes wonder as I read of them if I haven't spent years in unnecessary computation and research. Then too, I read romantic, commonsense research reports that are based on anecdotal analyses of future events, as if a good idea and a sharp entrepreneur are all an investor needs to know. Somewhere between the oversimplified and the overcomplicated lies a middle path, but the ideal is probably closer to the simpler approaches.

SUMMARY

I believe that what is important in stock speculation is to find significantly overlooked or out-of-favor corporations, buy their undervalued stocks, and continue holding them until stock market participants recognize their fundamental values and growth potential by bidding up their prices in accumulating them. This is my formulation of the cliche, "Buy low, sell high" slogan, except that I would modify it to "Buy low, sell fully valued."

The criteria for *low*, *high*, and *fully valued* are not fixed; they are relative to the present and future prospects of the corporations as well as stock market dynamics, the economic business cycle, and governmental policies. Still, we have a long history of fundamental valuation criteria that can be employed as meaningful, if imprecise, guidelines to select relatively undervalued stocks for purchase. These same criteria tell us when our stocks are fully valued and probably should be sold.

There is no limit to the amount of inquiry and effort analysts can expend toward evaluating a corporation, but it is not necessary to go into great or subtle detail. A selection of gross measures is usually sufficient to make such evaluations and selections for successful stock speculation.

In this chapter we have looked at seven fundamental criteria: price/earnings, price/cash flow, price/revenues, price/book value, return on equity, return on assets, and market capitalization. We have considered that, even with only three well-selected criteria, a sufficient "down-and-dirty" analysis could be made.

It would be neat if we could give specific guidelines for these criteria, but such a set could be counterproductive as it unnecessarily excluded undervalued stock selections due to one criterion or another. The important idea is that these criteria are relative and reinforcing of each other rather than any one being sufficient or necessary. At the risk of being counterproductive, I will list below gross average levels to look for in considering buy candidates.

1. *Price/earnings.* Normally stocks trading below 10 times earnings or below 30 percent of their P/E norm (average P/E), an item reviewed in Appendix A.

2. *Price/revenues.* Normally stocks trading near their out-of-favor levels or below their accepted PSR levels (see Figure 2–3).

3. *Price/book value.* Normally stocks trading below their book value per share or below 30 percent of their book value norm, reviewed in Appendix A.

4. *Price/cash flow.* Normally stocks trading at less than six times cash flow or below 30 percent of their cash flow norm, also reviewed in Appendix A.

5. *Return on equity.* Normally stocks trading at 15 percent return on equity or better, return 15% or better on cost of shares.

6. *Market capitalization.* Normally stocks with a market capitalization of less than $200 million (computed as shares outstanding times price per share). While the small company effect is important, I am still more concerned with bargains in value and growth of any market capitalization stock, especially as a mix can aid in diversification for those periods when large cap stocks outperform small cap stocks.

7. *Return on assets.*Normally stocks trading for an ROA compara-ble to their historical ROA, although lower ROAs in stocks found to be otherwise undervalued may indicate room for improvement. Especially check out the trend of this component, in addition to all the others.

One of the humbling realities of corporate analysis is that so much can go wrong with a corporation, even after extremely stringent criteria have been met or followed. Also, so much can go wrong with stocks independent of their corporations as the marketplace becomes ebullient or depressed. I have found it counterproductive to spend too much time on analysis, especially when experience shows that stock selection is perhaps about 25 percent of the battle for effective speculation. Once you have "sufficient" information, accept it, go with it, and go on to the next chore, because you will never find perfection in this process.

In order to avoid personal frustration from this reality that we can't always win, I take a statistical and accepting attitude, consistent with my actual experience. Some 20 percent to 25 percent of my selections have been losers—an acceptable number in terms of long-term holdings and superior long-term annual returns—over market cycles of three to five years.

To cope with the reality of stocks that don't work out well, I call for widely diversified portfolios for the systematic risk reduction they provide (see details in Chapter 3, "Stock Portfolio Management"). Still, if you have the time and feel the need to do more than this chapter calls for, you can consider additional criteria that are reviewed in Appendix A, wherein actual stock examples are noted.

CHAPTER 3

STOCK PORTFOLIO MANAGEMENT

The word *portfolio* is used in many activities and has several dictionary definitions. Derived from the Latin and Italian words *to carry* and *leaf* or *sheet*, portfolios are portable cases for carrying loose papers, prints, government documents, and even stock certificates. Nowadays, hardly anyone carries securities around; they are usually left with stockbrokers (most of whom use The Depository Trust Company) or put in a safe deposit vault. Still, it's rather romantic to speak of one's stock portfolio as if there were a briefcase, chock-a-block full of fabulous stock certificates, ready at a moment's notice to be carried off and exchanged for vast sums of cash.

Stock portfolio management (hereafter "portfolio management") refers to much more than keeping track of one's stock positions or the safekeeping of one's stock certificates. It includes coordinating and monitoring our speculative strategies with guidelines for buy, hold, and sell decisions. Corporate analysis discovers undervalued stocks worth buying and also tells us when they are fully valued and have thus become sell candidates. Market timing tells us about dangerous periods, when we should not accumulate more stocks but rather become defensive, and lower-risk periods, when we might aggressively add to our portfolios if we can afford it. But portfolio management tells us how much to buy or sell and which stocks to choose in order to balance and diversify our portfolios—our collection of stocks.

As with most "services" connected with Wall Street, purveyors of advice think up enticing marketing names for the most pedestrian of tasks. One doesn't decide to buy or sell, one develops an *asset allocation model* with complicated formulas and percentages, which translate into

"Now's a good time to buy (or sell) some more." But *asset allocation* is getting to be old hat, so now we hear of *tactical asset allocation*, and charging to the front is *cash asset/liability management*. All this stuff is supposed to make you believe that the advice-givers have achieved a new height in scientific investment portfolio management, and therefore you should put your assets in their care. While people have been allocating assets since the beginning of time and it is vital to have a systematic discipline, just buying a fancy approach doesn't mean you are assured effective results.

For almost all of us, there is not nearly enough money or credit available to buy all the bargain stocks that fundamental analysis uncovers, especially at market lows. A constant, persistent question faces the investor daily: How exposed to the stock market should I be, and how should that exposure be managed among the many positions I have accumulated or want to obtain? Furthermore, there are techniques for enhancing or hedging the portfolio—taking various forms of "insurance" against sharp market drops—other than just buying and selling stocks. We will start with some of the basics and see how the simple decisions tend to get a bit more complicated with the passage of time, the growth of portfolios, and stock market events.

PASADARM

Our overall speculative watchword or mantra is PASADARM, an acronym of the first letters of the words *P*atience *A*nd *S*election *A*nd *D*iversification *A*nd *R*isk *M*anagement. Each element is as important as any other one, and they work together to form a total speculative approach, so the conjunctive *And* is logically meaningful.

Our slogan used to be PASAD. I had considered risk management embedded in the fulfillment of the three other basic principles, patience, selection, and diversification. The trauma of the Crash of '87 convinced me that even more emphasis needed to be paid to the management of risk, especially market risk. Now, undervalued and fully valued stocks are reviewed in the context of overbought and overvalued markets as well as oversold and undervalued markets.

Speculative or investment patience includes waiting for the right corporation at the right price before buying, then owning it years (if necessary) while it reaches its fair price before selling. Selection includes fundamental analysis in order to discover bargains—stocks trading at no more than 50% of their estimated present or probable three-to-five–year market price—so as not to overpay and also to minimize the risk of deep price declines. Diversification includes the spreading of risks both over many corporations, often in different industries and sectors of the economy, as well as over time, which turns out to be a more important consideration than the number of stocks held.

With the Crash of '87, I was shocked that the risk management principles built into patience, selection, and diversification did not provide enough protection. It became apparent that even with the original PASAD I would have to expand and systematically review risk management considerations, adding that area as a basic and separate principle. Of course, all the elements of PASADARM are interrelated. If one element seems independent or exclusive, we should remember that it is definitely interdependent with and inclusive of the others.

PATIENCE—THE UNLIKELY QUALITY

How can we learn to be patient when for most of our lives we are conditioned to be impatient? When ethos pervades that "time is money," the implication is that we had better not waste time unless we are willing to lose money, and that everything we do or don't do will either cost us or gain us, depending on how quickly we do it. Reflection might be okay for philosophers, and meditation is acceptable for those outside the mainstream, but for the rest of us it seems there are jobs to be done, stock trades to be won, and no time to waste.

"Whom do you trust?" could be another theme for our times, with the most common answer being, "No one!" If we can't trust anyone, and by extension can't trust our institutions, how can we be patient with them? Too many stock market investors believe, "We must get ours, and get out, while the getting is good or suffer the consequences."

Is my perception accurate of a rise in organized gambling—not to mention state-run lotteries—over the past few years? Perhaps the age of affluence, with its emphasis on winners and losers with the score kept in terms of dollars, has led to these excesses. Gambling is an enterprise of impatience. Place your bet and in a few seconds, hours, or days you will know whether you are a winner or a loser. Are the calculated risks of lotteries computed and published? Yes. Are they paid much attention to by participants? Hardly ever. Chicago futures and options vie with Las Vegas and Atlantic City cards and dice as the gaming capitals of the world, especially since the advent of so-called derivative instruments, which are often little more than bets on whether a stock, collection of stocks, or the stock market is going to advance or decline in a brief period of time.

The psychology of impatience is a fascinating subject involving anxiety, self-esteem, and conditioned behavior patterns. Students in elementary school will often blurt out a known wrong answer because the teacher is impatient and thus the students perceive it as more important to say something stupid than to keep thinking a moment while being the focus of attention of an impatient class. How many of us in our ordinary conversations continue this practice of responding rapidly if haphazardly, often making statements about situations we know little about in an effort to facilitate social intercourse and allay another's impatience or anxiety? Yes, there are two problems here—speaking of that which we know not and speaking without thinking—but I think they are both aspects of our lifelong conditioned impatience.

In order to manage impatience, we have societal structures that require systematic participation in extended-time enterprises. Of course, some of these, like the 60-minute football game and the 48-minute basketball game, are compromises, as are the tie-breakers and three-set championships in tennis. How many spectators want to watch a tennis set go to 20–22 games or a match last over five hours these days?

As with the 30-minute TV program and the two-week vacation, so too with the stock market, do most people want near-instant gratification. For a few investors, very short-term day trading meets their tolerance for patience. They scalp a few eighths here and there, getting lucky or unlucky, but go home at night or on the weekend without the anxiety of what might happen to their investments or the market on the next trading day's opening. For other traders, *intermediate term* refers to a few days while *long term* means a week or two. For some investors, owning a stock for one year is the height of folly. These kinds of folk tend to watch the market whenever they can or eagerly await the first available newspaper edition with closing stock quotes to see how they've done or would have done if . . .

The best way to teach speculative patience is by successful examples. The only way to learn speculative patience is to practice it systematically. Of course, the stock market is full of examples, and almost any reasonable-sounding thesis can be proved by a plethora of one set of examples or another. Still, there are the long-term records of famous value and growth speculators—who usually call themselves *investors*—as well as the highly convincing long-term statistics that are scattered throughout this book.

TIME DIVERSIFICATION

A subject that seems as appropriate under the rubric *patience* as it does in the section on diversification or the discussion of risk is *time diversification*. Time diversification is rarely commented on. That is surprising, considering its importance may be greater than stock diversification. The *Market Logic* edition of September 21, 1984, reports on a study published in the *Journal of Portfolio Management* (Vol. 6, no. 3) quantifying risk reduction through time diversification compared to stock diversification. Apparently, "time diversification is at least as important as stock diversification when it comes to reducing risk."

Testing portfolios varying in size from 1 to 100 stocks, with holding periods from six months to six years, "[The researchers] concluded that a 1-stock 'portfolio' held for one year was less risky than a 100-stock portfolio held for a single six-month period." The authors also found that holding a 10-stock portfolio for four years was one third as risky as holding a 100-stock portfolio for one year.

There is a commonsense rationale for these statistical probabilities supporting the importance of time diversification. For any relatively brief period the market can have a selloff that carries most stocks down without regard to each of their corporation's fundamentals. This kind of price fluctuation is called *market* or *systematic* risk. But over longer time periods, the aphorism, "Value will out" tends to work. We can get a taste of how time diversification has worked in reality by glancing at the 12 years of quarterly results of The Prudent Speculator Portfolio (see Figure 3–1).

First let's look at the actual margined account where we note that 17 of the past 48 quarters (35.4 percent of the time) have been down. This is in keeping with the generalization that the market declines about one third of the time. In the 47 6-month periods, 13 or 27.7 percent of them were down; but for the 45 12-month periods, only 11 or 24.4 percent of them were down—a distinct trend showing the effects of time (long-term)

FIGURE 3–1
Results of Time Diversification in TPS Portfolio

		TPS ACTUAL MARGIN ACCOUNT							TPS HYPOTHETICAL NON-MARGIN ACCOUNT						
Per.	Quarters	Qtrlv%	6-Mos.	12-Mos.	24-Mos.	30-Mos.	48-Mos.	60-Mos.	Qtrlv%	6-Mos.	12-Mos.	24-Mos.	30-Mos.	48-Mos.	60-Mos.
1	2ND	53.97							25.68						
2	3RD	-11.94	42.03						-5.33	20.35					
3	4TH	25.59	13.65						13.03	7.70					
4	1ST-78	7.11	32.70	74.73					4.49	17.52	37.87				
5	2ND	22.46	29.57	43.22					11.55	16.04	23.74				
6	3RD	32.28	54.74	87.44					15.45	27.00	44.52				
7	4TH	-27.95	4.33	33.90					-11.45	4.00	20.04				
8	1ST-79	42.26	14.31	69.05	191.33				18.19	6.74	33.74	99.35			
9	2ND	4.97	47.23	51.56	196.53				4.04	22.23	26.23	101.23			
10	3RD	13.60	18.57	32.88	201.45	162.35			8.08	12.12	18.86	105.65	83.73		
11	4TH	-3.64	9.96	57.19	178.71	104.74			.68	8.76	30.99	96.89	58.73		
12	1ST-80	-37.58	-41.22	-22.65	107.92	79.10			-13.58	-12.90	-.78	67.95	50.48		
13	2ND	45.43	7.85	17.81	61.03	98.94			17.19	3.61	12.37	44.56	54.64		
14	3RD	45.83	91.26	50.04	147.96	137.66			19.09	36.28	23.38	76.84	69.24		
15	4TH	-12.60	33.23	41.08	166.88	102.60			-3.00	16.09	19.70	86.19	54.69		
16	1ST-81	35.12	22.52	113.78	142.17	105.44	234.91		17.25	14.25	50.53	78.21	56.49	121.36	
17	2ND	30.75	65.87	99.10	189.47	164.14	211.69		16.36	33.61	49.70	99.70	84.30	112.04	
18	3RD	-56.15	-25.40	-2.88	154.11	65.73	167.48		-22.91	-6.55	7.70	84.39	43.20	94.46	
19	4TH	28.12	-28.03	37.84	167.30	88.88	170.01		11.52	-11.39	22.22	85.90	50.68	92.95	
20	1ST-82	-13.35	14.77	-10.63	174.22	61.93	149.55	224.28	-2.10	9.42	2.87	91.71	40.50	86.36	124.23
21	2ND	-25.94	-39.29	-67.32	43.67	39.63	101.15	144.37	-6.45	-8.55	-19.94	46.88	33.37	68.36	92.10
22	3RD	42.99	17.05	31.82	27.49	120.20	111.86	199.30	15.13	8.68	18.10	39.47	62.08	68.04	112.56
23	4TH	72.76	115.75	76.46	120.72	147.53	212.57	246.47	21.83	36.96	28.41	62.18	66.72	101.32	121.36
24	1ST-83	46.41	119.17	136.22	174.02	148.11	216.72	285.77	16.68	38.51	47.19	67.08	64.31	99.81	133.55
25	2ND	44.81	91.22	206.97	290.64	205.52	256.56	308.12	19.51	36.19	73.15	109.82	86.82	115.28	141.51
26	3RD	3.70	48.51	167.68	367.18	174.10	246.66	279.54	3.29	22.80	61.31	144.01	72.86	110.49	129.35
27	4TH	-.97	2.73	93.95	355.14	142.38	249.33	306.52	.98	4.27	40.46	138.86	57.48	110.79	141.78
28	1ST-84	-16.64	-17.61	30.90	376.82	181.89	270.27	247.62	-6.38	-5.40	17.40	142.01	74.01	117.99	117.21
29	2ND	-30.55	-47.19	-44.46	312.58	123.22	194.29	212.10	-8.96	-15.34	-11.07	117.99	53.53	91.84	104.21
30	3RD	26.19	-4.36	-21.97	192.47	162.76	174.65	224.69	10.42	1.46	-3.94	82.49	66.05	83.17	106.55
31	4TH	19.49	45.68	-1.51	118.98	208.19	206.74	247.82	8.53	18.95	3.61	62.93	81.03	94.70	114.40
32	1ST-85	4.92	24.41	20.05	52.17	170.12	176.54	290.32	3.34	11.87	13.33	38.61	69.24	80.79	131.32
33	2ND	10.25	15.17	60.85	18.83	107.61	156.04	255.14	5.10	8.44	27.39	24.25	52.51	69.53	119.23
34	3RD	-15.02	-4.77	19.64	11.33	46.18	197.17	194.29	-3.76	1.34	13.21	21.32	32.07	88.68	96.38
35	4TH	53.33	38.31	53.48	67.25	54.70	222.38	260.22	18.06	14.30	22.74	41.02	30.62	95.22	117.44
36	1ST-86	67.97	121.30	116.53	235.74	118.97	303.70	293.07	26.98	45.04	46.38	101.40	54.31	124.30	127.17
37	2ND	5.73	73.70	112.01	313.80	125.67	335.37	268.05	4.03	31.01	45.31	130.95	57.36	134.78	114.84
38	3RD	-14.75	-9.02	112.28	259.10	127.56	277.63	309.45	-7.06	-3.03	42.01	108.97	56.68	112.59	130.69
39	4TH	-3.27	-18.02	55.66	216.67	154.84	201.60	278.06	-.76	-7.82	23.19	89.28	64.88	90.00	118.41
40	1ST-87	44.85	41.58	32.56	243.08	173.50	200.04	336.26	19.29	18.53	15.50	99.37	73.75	92.61	139.80
41	2ND	-7.60	37.25	19.23	285.10	146.41	147.63	354.60	-2.56	16.73	8.91	114.76	62.66	70.54	143.69
42	3RD	4.66	-2.94	38.64	243.85	146.15	148.59	316.27	3.23	.67	19.20	101.13	62.55	70.48	131.79
43	4TH	-68.34	-63.68	-26.43	56.87	67.56	81.22	175.17	-36.48	-33.25	-16.52	22.84	20.97	33.02	73.48
44	1ST-88	34.71	-33.63	-36.57	-48.46	117.29	132.57	163.47	15.62	-20.86	-20.19	-29.03	40.35	55.02	72.42
45	2ND	10.48	45.19	-18.49	5.75	74.44	173.60	129.14	6.20	21.82	-11.43	-4.18	28.49	70.18	59.11
46	3RD	-2.12	8.36	-25.27	32.13	4.35	145.29	123.32	.20	6.40	-14.46	10.04	1.71	59.96	56.02
47	4TH	3.08	.96	46.15	-8.49	1.70	128.88	127.37	2.69	2.89	24.71	-5.60	.37	54.12	57.73
48	1ST-89	17.67	20.75	29.11	-24.99	34.12	141.63	161.68	8.62	11.31	17.71	-11.02	16.05	59.40	72.73

diversification. For the 41 24-month periods, only 3 or 7.3 percent were down. When we observe 30-month periods we find no down periods.

Even more supportive of time diversification to my way of thinking are the results of longer time periods. As mentioned above, there were no losing 30-month periods (although there were 39 such periods). Of the 33 4-year periods, the smallest gain was 81.22 percent (which is 16 percent compounded annually)—due to the horrendous losses in the Crash of '87—while in the 29 5-year periods, the smallest gain was 123.32 percent (also including the Crash), which still works out to about 17.5 percent compounded annually.

This limited analysis using TPS Portfolio results is not the same as a rigorous statistical analysis of a random sample of all stocks or of the DJIA 30 stocks. However, it is solid enough evidence, as far as I am concerned, of the apparent reduction of individual stock risk and short-term market risk brought about by time diversification. This "study" shows why stocks tend to be held in TPS Portfolio for over four years on average.

To show a parallel and comparative analysis using the DJIA stocks for the 12 years 4/1/77 through 3/31/89, see Figure 3–2. In this homemade analysis, I added 1 percent per quarter to account for dividend yield (slightly understating the long-term return of dividends). As you might imagine, simply adding back 4 percent a year soon makes an important difference in the positive total return figures. When the dividend returns are added back, the results are such that in only one of the 41 two-year periods was there a total return loss (-.11 percent), whereas if one merely inspects the change in DJIA points without considering dividends (see Figure 3–3), there were six losing two-year periods.

MISLEADING PERFORMANCE NUMBERS

As you may know, when a dividend is paid on a stock, the price of that stock is reduced by an amount equal to the dividend to the next nearest eighth of a point. Thus, five trading days before Chrysler pays its 30-cent quarterly dividend, its stock goes "ex-dividend" and is reduced in market price by 3/8 or 37.5 cents per share. By the end of one year, Chrysler has had its shares reduced $1.50—even though it only paid out

FIGURE 3-2
DJIA Stocks with Dividends (adjusted 1% per quarter)

		QtrEnd	Average	Qtrly%	6-Mos.	12-Mos.	24-Mos.	36-Mos.	48-Mos.	60-Mos.
0		Mar. 31	919.13							
1		June 30	916.30	.69						
2		Sep. 30	847.11	-6.55	-5.84					
3	1977	Dec. 30	831.17	-.88	-7.29					
4		Mar. 31	757.36	-7.88	-8.59	-13.60				
5		June 30	818.95	9.13	.53	-6.62				
6		Sep. 29	865.82	6.72	16.32	6.21				
7	1978	Dec. 29	805.01	-6.02	.30	.85				
8		Mar. 31	862.18	8.10	1.58	17.84	1.80			
9		June 30	841.98	-1.34	6.59	6.81	-.11			
10		Sep. 30	878.67	5.36	3.91	5.48	11.73			
11	1979	Dec. 31	838.74	-3.54	1.62	8.19	8.91			
12		Mar. 31	785.75	-5.32	-8.58	-4.86	11.75	-2.51		
13		June 30	867.92	11.46	5.48	7.08	13.98	6.72		
14		Sep. 30	932.42	8.43	20.67	10.12	15.69	22.07		
15	1980	Dec. 31	963.99	4.39	13.07	18.93	27.75	27.98		
16		Mar. 31	1003.87	5.14	9.66	31.76	24.43	44.55	25.22	
17		June 30	976.88	-1.69	3.34	16.55	24.02	31.28	22.61	
18		Sep. 30	849.98	-11.99	-13.33	-4.84	4.73	10.17	16.34	
19	1981	Dec. 31	875.00	3.94	-8.43	-5.23	12.32	20.69	21.27	
20		Mar. 31	822.77	-4.97	-1.20	-14.04	12.71	7.43	24.64	9.52
21		June 30	811.93	-.32	-5.21	-12.89	1.55	8.43	15.14	8.61
22		Sep. 30	896.25	11.39	10.93	9.44	4.12	14.00	19.51	25.80
23	1982	Dec. 31	1046.54	17.77	30.90	23.60	16.56	36.78	46.00	45.91
24		Mar. 31	1130.03	8.98	28.08	41.34	20.57	55.82	47.07	69.21
25		June 30	1221.96	9.14	18.76	54.50	33.09	52.79	61.13	69.21
26		Sep. 30	1233.13	1.91	11.12	41.59	53.08	44.25	56.34	62.42
27	1983	Dec. 30	1258.94	3.09	5.03	24.30	51.88	42.60	66.10	76.39
28		Mar. 30	1164.89	-6.47	-3.53	7.08	49.58	28.04	64.25	55.11
29		June 29	1132.40	-1.79	-8.05	-3.33	47.47	27.92	46.47	54.49
30		Sep. 28	1206.71	7.56	5.59	1.86	42.64	53.97	45.42	57.33
31	1984	Dec. 31	1211.57	1.40	8.99	.24	23.77	50.47	41.68	64.45
32		Mar. 29	1266.78	5.56	6.98	12.75	20.10	65.97	42.19	81.22
33		June 28	1335.36	6.41	12.22	21.92	17.28	76.47	52.70	73.86
34		Sep. 30	1328.63	.50	6.88	14.10	15.74	60.24	72.31	62.49
35	1985	Dec. 31	1546.67	17.41	17.82	31.66	30.85	59.79	92.76	80.44
36		Mar. 31	1818.61	18.58	38.88	47.56	64.12	72.93	137.04	101.16
37		June 30	1892.72	5.08	24.37	45.74	75.14	66.89	149.11	113.75
38		Sep. 30	1767.58	-5.61	-.81	37.04	54.48	55.34	113.22	127.96
39	1986	Dec. 31	1895.95	8.26	2.17	26.58	64.49	62.60	97.16	136.68
40		Mar. 31	2304.69	22.56	32.39	30.73	89.93	109.85	119.95	200.11
41		June 30	2418.53	5.94	29.56	31.78	89.11	125.58	113.92	217.87
42		Sep. 30	2596.28	8.35	14.65	50.88	103.41	127.15	126.54	209.68
43	1987	Dec. 31	1938.83	-24.32	-17.83	6.26	33.36	72.03	70.09	105.26
44		Mar. 31	1988.06	3.54	-21.43	-9.74	17.32	68.94	86.67	95.93
45		June 30	2141.71	8.73	12.46	-7.45	21.16	72.38	105.13	95.27
46		Sep. 30	2112.91	-.34	8.28	-14.62	27.54	71.03	91.10	91.35
47	1988	Dec. 30	2168.57	3.63	3.25	15.85	22.38	52.21	94.99	92.25
48	1989	Mar. 31	2293.62	6.77	10.55	19.37	7.52	38.12	97.06	116.90

FIGURE 3–3
DJIA Stocks without Dividends

		QtrEnd	Average	Qtrly%	6-Mos.	12-Mos.	24-Mos.	36-Mos.	48-Mos.	60-Mos.
0		Mar. 31	919.13							
1		June 30	916.30	-.31						
2		Sep. 30	847.11	-7.55	-7.84					
3	1977	Dec. 30	831.17	-1.88	-9.29					
4		Mar. 31	757.36	-8.88	-10.59	-17.60				
5		June 30	818.95	8.13	-1.47	-10.62				
6		Sep. 29	865.82	5.72	14.32	2.21				
7	1978	Dec. 29	805.01	-7.02	-1.70	-3.15				
8		Mar. 31	862.18	7.10	-.42	13.84	-6.20			
9		June 30	841.98	-2.34	4.59	2.81	-8.11			
10		Sep. 30	878.67	4.36	1.91	1.48	3.73			
11	1979	Dec. 31	838.74	-4.54	-.38	4.19	.91			
12		Mar. 31	785.75	-6.32	-10.58	-8.86	3.75	-14.51		
13		June 30	867.92	10.46	3.48	3.08	5.98	-5.28		
14		Sep. 30	932.42	7.43	18.67	6.12	7.69	10.07		
15	1980	Dec. 31	963.99	3.39	11.07	14.93	19.75	15.98		
16		Mar. 31	1003.87	4.14	7.66	27.76	16.43	32.55	9.22	
17		June 30	976.88	-2.69	1.34	12.55	16.02	19.28	6.61	
18		Sep. 30	849.98	-12.99	-15.33	-8.84	-3.27	-1.83	.34	
19	1981	Dec. 31	875.00	2.94	-10.43	-9.23	4.32	8.69	5.27	
20		Mar. 31	822.77	-5.97	-3.20	-18.04	4.71	-4.57	8.64	-10.48
21		June 30	811.93	-1.32	-7.21	-16.89	-6.45	-3.57	-.86	-11.39
22		Sep. 30	896.25	10.39	8.93	5.44	-3.88	2.00	3.51	5.80
23	1982	Dec. 31	1046.54	16.77	28.90	19.60	8.56	24.78	30.00	25.91
24		Mar. 31	1130.03	7.98	26.08	37.34	12.57	43.82	31.07	49.21
25		June 30	1221.96	8.14	16.76	50.50	25.09	40.79	45.13	49.21
26		Sep. 30	1233.13	.91	9.12	37.59	45.08	32.25	40.34	42.42
27	1983	Dec. 30	1258.94	2.09	3.03	20.30	43.88	30.60	50.10	56.39
28		Mar. 30	1164.89	-7.47	-5.53	3.08	41.58	16.04	48.25	35.11
29		June 29	1132.40	-2.79	-10.05	-7.33	39.47	15.92	30.47	34.49
30		Sep. 28	1206.71	6.56	3.59	-2.14	34.64	41.97	29.42	37.33
31	1984	Dec. 31	1211.57	.40	6.99	-3.76	15.77	38.47	25.68	44.45
32		Mar. 29	1266.78	4.56	4.98	8.75	12.10	53.97	26.19	61.22
33		June 28	1335.36	5.41	10.22	17.92	9.28	64.47	36.70	53.86
34		Sep. 30	1328.63	-.50	4.88	10.10	7.74	48.24	56.31	42.49
35	1985	Dec. 31	1546.67	16.41	15.82	27.66	22.85	47.79	76.76	60.44
36		Mar. 31	1818.61	17.58	36.88	43.56	56.12	60.93	121.04	81.16
37		June 30	1892.72	4.08	22.37	41.74	67.14	54.89	133.11	93.75
38		Sep. 30	1767.58	-6.61	-2.81	33.04	46.48	43.34	97.22	107.96
39	1986	Dec. 31	1895.95	7.26	.17	22.58	56.49	50.60	81.16	116.68
40		Mar. 31	2304.69	21.56	30.39	26.73	81.93	97.85	103.95	180.11
41		June 30	2418.53	4.94	27.56	27.78	81.11	113.58	97.92	197.87
42		Sep. 30	2596.28	7.35	12.65	46.88	95.41	115.15	110.54	189.68
43	1987	Dec. 31	1938.83	-25.32	-19.83	2.26	25.36	60.03	54.00	85.26
44		Mar. 31	1988.06	2.54	-23.43	-13.74	9.32	56.94	70.67	75.93
45		June 30	2141.71	7.73	10.46	-11.45	13.16	60.38	89.13	75.27
46		Sep. 30	2112.91	-1.34	6.28	-18.62	19.54	59.03	75.10	71.35
47	1988	Dec. 30	2168.57	2.63	1.25	11.85	14.38	40.21	78.99	72.25
48	1989	Mar. 31	2293.62	5.77	8.55	15.37	-.48	26.12	81.06	96.90

$1.20 in dividends—and the dividend returns are not reflected in the stock's price! If Chrysler closed "unchanged" from one year to the next, it would look by merely inspecting its market prices as if nothing were earned on the stock, even though shareholders would have received about a 5 percent total return by including dividends.

When we start using DJIA numbers for examples, we must be careful to stipulate just how we are calculating results for the same reasons referred to above. Taking just the raw numbers, for example, the DJIA closed at 2168.57 on 12/30/88 and at 1938.83 on 12/31/87, for a gain of 229.74 points or 11.85 percent for 1988. Using this return ignores the dividends paid out and their reinvested potential.

We have also not accounted for the actual total-return performance of the 30 stocks in the DJIA without regard to their market capitalization weighting, which involves a series of adjustments to account for stock dividends, split shares, and the replacement over the years of stocks in the average. These adjustments have resulted in the DJIA divisor, which at the current writing (4/89) is .682. That means it only takes a 68.2-cent move in a DJIA stock for the DJIA to advance one point.

Thus, the most-commonly reported DJIA performance of just comparing index values understates its actual total return performance. As common stocks in the S&P 500 have averaged a 10 percent total return gain over the past 63 years, with almost 50 percent of that gain made up of dividends, you can imagine how skewed the figures are without including dividends. *Stock Market Logic* has a fascinating table that shows the accum-ulated differences of accounting for the Dow Jones Industrials (1) by price return alone, (2) by dividend return only, and (3) by a totalreturn, between January 2, 1897, and mid-September, 1975. (See Figure 3–4.)

Norm Fosback, author of the book *Stock Market Logic*, points out that the dividend return, while less risky than the price return, amounts to about half of the total return over long periods. Just accounting for 1988, Lipper Analytical Securities Corporation's "Total Reinvested Percent Change"—assuming quarterly reinvested dividends—arrives at a DJIA figure of 16.21 percent, versus the 11.85 percent simple index calculation, noted above. If we just add the average of each quarter's dividend yield (as reported in *Barron's*) of 3.59 percent, we arrive at a "total return" of 15.44 percent for the year, still understating the *total reinvested return.*

FIGURE 3–4
The Dow Jones Industrial Averages "Returns"

	Price Return	Dividend Return	Total Return
DJIA on Jan. 2, 1897	29.85*	29.85*	29.85*
By mid-September 1975 they had grown to . . .	816.10	1196.59	32684.99
a growth of over . . .	27 fold	40 fold	1095 fold
which is a compounded annual rate of return of	4.29%	4.80%	9.30%

*Adjusted for 12/12/14 change in D.J.I. components.

Source: Adapted from Norman G. Fosback, *Stock Market Logic*, (Fort Lauderdale, Fla.: The Institute for Econometric Research, 1984), p. 276.

SELECTION CRITERIA OR STOCK PICKING

Stock selection criteria and considerations are dealt with in detail in Chapter 2 and Appendix A, which emphasize corporation picking through fundamental analysis. The basic idea is quite simple. We are looking for bargains—undervalued stocks of viable corporations—that have good future prospects.

One of the wonders of the modern world is how a functioning corporation's common shares—which are units of ownership that represent its assets and earnings potentials—can trade for less than 50 percent of its fundamentally assessed current value one year and yet a few years later trade for perhaps 200 percent of its similarly assessed intrinsic value. Scores or hundreds of such undervalued corporations can be discovered each and every year, in good times and bad, waiting for the astute speculator to buy at a discount and, in the fullness of time, sell at a premium.

One could buy the shares of almost any strong and well-run corporation, sooner or later benefitting from its growth, dividends, and increased share prices. If such a corporation's stock were overvalued at the time of initial purchase, the shareholder might have to wait many years to obtain a decent total return. That is, in theory at least, the corporation would have to increase in value beyond its initially overvalued shares' cost. In practice, overvalued stocks often become even more overvalued and invoke the "greater fool theory," which says we can probably sell these expensive shares at an even greater price to a greater fool than ourselves.

The greater fool theory is for some an effective way of playing the market as "trend followers." *High relative strength stocks* are stocks that have advanced faster and further than the market on average and therefore seem likely to continue to do so. Some investors are able with these stocks to capture the overvalued price rises, at least until these stocks' trends do reverse, often falling faster than the market because of their foolish overvaluations. Still, if you can get on the bandwagon while it's surging ahead and jump off before it topples, you can garner some relatively quick and massive gains. However, this is not a strategy for a prudent speculator.

Because there are so few basic ideas needed to do well in the stock market, if they are followed consistently and applied systematically, you will encounter them more than once in more than one chapter of this book. Hopefully their redundancy will not bore you or cause you to gloss over them. To be a successful prudent speculator or investor is to have these ideas as second nature, effective touchstones for motivating strategies of doing something when appropriate as well as doing nothing when that is what is called for. Although this is a book on the stock market and investing in it, the basic focus is on corporations and becoming partners in them through the utter convenience of being able to trade their stocks at our pleasure, when we think it appropriate, in our own good time.

The investor who has not had the privilege of owning a semi-successful business is probably at a disadvantage to the investor who has experienced firsthand how lucrative businesses can be. Businesses are often far more rewarding than they might appear on profit and loss statements or income tax filings. Scandalous stories abound of major corporations paying little or no tax while making huge reported profits and rewarding their top managers with obscene bonuses and perquisites.

How are such high profits and low taxes possible? They are possible through a variety of accounting devices such as tax loss carry forwards, depreciation (including accelerated writedowns and investment tax credits), and reserves for bad loans. Consider also that management benefits and bonuses are a pre-tax cost of doing business, so such "expenses" contribute to reduced taxable profitability.

In my experience of owning two small print shops and an investment advisory business, I have seen my taxable profits reduced by the modest but effective use of depreciation, travel and entertainment expenses, and pension and profit-sharing plans. Each business increased in value as a going concern. My relatively insignificant businesses were tiny examples to me of what is writ large in huge corporations. It is not surprising to me that companies can be sold for two or more times their depreciated and amortized book values, when it would cost much more to replace their physical plants and build their trademarks, patents, and customer bases, even as their earnings do not appear outstanding.

Of course, it is not at all necessary to have been a sole proprietor or a partner in a small business to understand the hidden, "good will" value of corporations. Becoming slightly familiar with the financials of an analyzed corporation, even just the grossest items, can point the way to recognizing undervaluations and potential capital gains in such corporations' stocks in the course of time.

ASSET INVESTING

Becoming "partners," with however small a percentage ownership of undervalued corporations offers at least two main approaches to picking bargain stocks. Let's call the first approach *asset plays* or current valuations. If it's true that Ford Motor Company (F), for example, has a book value around $13.60 per share (all figures are adjusted for stock splits, or "split-adjusted") and is trading at $4 per share—note that it traded between $3.50 and $4.75 in 1981—then astute and brave investors are able to select Ford shares for 29 cents on the dollar more or less. In fact, Ford traded for less than 40 percent of its book value from mid-1980 through the beginning of 1982, and for as low as 26 percent of book value in late '80 and again in late '81.

Considering that Ford's book value had been growing at the rate of 8.5 percent for the previous 10 years (10.0 percent for the previous 5 years), there was a good chance that its underlying fundamental value, as represented by its book value, would become even greater over the next several years, so that a purchase in the early '80s could likely lead to a greater than 100 percent gain as the stock trading a few years down the road tended to reflect its current and increasing assessed valuation.

In fact, Ford's book value did grow substantially over the years so that the $13.60 of 1981 became about $43.87 by the end of 1988. Ford's increase in book value for this time period is 226 percent. More importantly for speculators, Ford's (split-adjusted) share price climbed from a low of $3.50 in '81 to a high of $55.00 in '88, for a gain of 1,471 percent, not counting some substantial dividends along the way.

Many, if not most, investors found it difficult to buy Ford shares in the early '80s. The domestic auto industry was out of favor, to say the least, and Ford had losses for three years running: $2.85 per share for '80, $1.96 per share for '81, and $1.21 per share for '82. Ironically, while Ford was losing money in '82 and did not pay a dividend for that year, its shares advanced from their low of $3.625 at the beginning of the year to over $9 near year-end, for a market price appreciation of 148 percent. In the early '80s, Ford Motor Company was an asset play, *at least*. Of course, Ford was a whole lot more, as time revealed.

We should be constantly aware of the reality that just as stocks trade much of the time at a big discount to their fundamental values, they also trade on many occasions at a significant premium to these valuations, especially when considered as takeover candidates by other corporations. Sometimes, even if a corporation doesn't seem to be reaching its potential—at least its fair return on equity or assets—it nevertheless can provide a handsome capital gain as others recognize its takeover or breakup value.

GROWTH INVESTING

The second major approach to picking bargain corporations is often called *growth investing*. A company may be doing well or poorly, having hit a glitch as the Fishers (Philip and Ken) might say, but with continuing prospects for a rewarding future. Since it is generally accepted opinion that ultimately increasing earnings are the goals of for-profit corporations, a large number of fundamental investors concentrate on finding emerging growth, junior growth, regular growth, and accelerating growth stocks, the prices of which do not reflect their reality or potential.

Happily, we can again turn to Ford Motor Company—of the early '80s and of the present also—for an example of growth investing. Since Ford already has $80 billion or so in sales and $25 billion or so in market capitalization and is a giant corporation, its stock would not be considered junior, emerging, or even a high-growth candidate. Still, in the past 10 years Ford's earnings have grown at 14.0 percent, while its dividend has grown at 33.0 percent per annum for the past 5 years (albeit starting from a low base). At this writing Ford is trading at 4.5 times current earnings, compared to *Value Line's* average annual P/E ratio of 7.0. I believe that Ford should trade at 9-to-10 times earnings when it becomes fully appreciated. Therefore, Ford is a currently recommended stock again in the summer of '89, for its growth potential rather than as an asset play.

We do not live in an Aristotelian world of either/or, and though we often distinguish between growth and asset plays, many undervalued stocks have both characteristics. Ford is not the asset play it was in the early '80s, it haa a book value around $46.56 per share, compared to a price of $50 per share. Thus Ford was trading at 107 percent of book value. Considering Ford traded at 154 percent of its book value before the Crash of '87, it could easily trade at $71.70 (based on Summer 1989 figures without any increase in its book value) in reaching that level again. Furthermore, since Ford's book value has grown at 16 percent per annum in the past five years, its book value could double in the next five years at just under 15 percent per year.

We can also project a conservative example, saying Ford only manages its 10-year book value growth rate of 7.5 percent. In that case, in five years Ford's book value would become $66.84, and if it traded for the aforementioned 154 percent of book value, Ford shares would be priced at $102.94, more than twice their current market price. Hey, it looks as though Ford is still a bit of an asset play after all, at least for the patient speculator.

You can see that even the few basic criteria invoked above can be adequate for finding currently undervalued corporations, believing in their financials and futures, holding them through ugly stock market periods, and finally selling them at enormous capital gains, often receiving substantial dividend income along the way. It's simple in theory, and it works in practice if one's emotions and personality don't interfere.

STOCK DIVERSIFICATION IS A FIRST PRINCIPLE

We may have put the cart before the horse in reviewing time diversification under the topic of patience in the paragraphs above. Generally, *diversification* refers to stock or industry diversification, including sector diversification. There are two distinct schools of portfolio construction and management, which can be summarized by the terms *concentration* and *diversification.*

Those who favor concentration believe in owning relatively few stocks at any one time. Instead of putting many eggs in many baskets, the concentrationists would have us put a few eggs in one basket. In that way, they believe, we would be very careful in the initial choosing of any corporation because if we were wrong in even one stock, the impact on our equity would be significantly detrimental. Some of them also believe that few of us can adequately analyze and understand more than a handful of corporations, let alone keep sufficient tabs on them after we basket them.

Gerald Loeb in his informative, if somewhat dated, book *The Battle for Stock Market Profits* believes in the concentrated approach. He has written

> As to individual stocks, I believe in owning very few. I do not want to buy stock unless I buy enough to show me a worthwhile profit if I am right and potentially hurt me if I am wrong. In practice, if things go my way I would tend to buy more. If things go against me, I would aim to sell out and minimize the damage. I only want to select an individual stock to buy with a unique extra reason that suggests it is the best buy. This is the opposite of building a "portfolio" of "core stocks," that is, a long list of popular leaders in popular groups.[1]

Several personal attitudes are apparent in Mr. Loeb's quotation above. We may contrast Loeb's views with other concentrationists who deviate strongly from one point or another. We may also draw comparisons of his and other concentrationist viewpoints with our own diversification beliefs.

Warren Buffett, a believer in holding core stocks, has said that every investor should be given a book of 20 or so tickets at birth and have one torn out for every stock bought so that, when all tickets are used up, no more stocks can be acquired. That might certainly concentrate one's attention on careful and judicious stock selection, although not necessarily.

In contrast to these estimable and successful gentlemen, I am a firm believer in diversification—the wider the diversification, the better—in order to minimize individual corporate (stock) risk, sometimes called

---

[1]Gerald M. Loeb, *Your Battle for Stock Market Profits* (N.Y.: Simon and Schuster, 1971), p. 90.

unsystematic risk as contrasted with stock market or systematic risk. Even before I learned about risk reduction from studies of diversification, I had an intuitive or commonsense notion that if you had only a small percentage of your estate at risk in any one position, and if that position went against you badly, then you wouldn't be hurt much overall.

My initial sense of stock diversification was that I'd want at least 30 stocks, because 30 was the number that elementary statistics texts claim is a minimum meaningful population or number of events. Figure 3–5, reprinted here through the courtesy of *Stock Market Logic*, illustrates the reduction of unsystematic risk through the increasing number of stocks held in one's portfolio.

I find it interesting that my original naive choice of having at least 30 stocks would turn out statistically to eliminate almost 96 percent of individual stock risk. But there is an important caveat about just the simple number of stocks. These stocks should be scattered among different specific industry groups. If we have five airlines, five paper companies, five gold mines, five banks, five savings and loans, and five oil companies, we would have 30 different stocks, but we would not have the equivalent unsystematic risk reduction implied by that number of positions. The stocks within each of those industry groups would generally tend to act in concert, so the diversification effect would be similar to having only 6 diversified positions rather than 30.

Creating sufficient corporation and industry diversification in a new portfolio poses certain practical problems, especially because of the

FIGURE 3–5
Diversification and Reduction of Risk

Number of Stocks in Portfolio	Percentage of Risk Eliminated
2	46%
4	72
8	81
16	93
32	96
64	98
500	99
All Stocks	100

Source: *Stock Market Logic*, March 1984, p. 254.

amount of cash and the number of undervalued stocks available at any given moment. From time to time we find ourselves "overweighted" in certain industries because that's where the bargains are. Over the years, as portfolios evolve and grow, other undervalued stocks are added to the portfolio or replace some of the overweighted positions, resulting in a more balanced stock diversification.

We certainly can have more than one corporation in the same industry, especially when, for example, two tire companies reflect different niches in the market with their major products, one specializing in the OEM (original equipment manufacturing) market and the other mainly serving the replacement and repair markets. The less our portfolios are represented by a wide spectrum of manufacturing, financial, retail, services, natural resources, and other principal industry groups, the less diversification is at work despite holding a large number of different stocks.

And yet, referring again to Figure 3–5, even if we hold only 15 or 16 diversified industry positions—which might involve 20 to 30 individual stocks—isn't at least a 93% risk-elimination level enough for us? Of course it is. If our selections are halfway decent, and our multi-year market timing (time diversification) protects us against serious but temporary market-wide declines, we will do very nicely, thank you. Still, I want to own as many stocks as I can because of my intuition and experience that casting a wider net increases the possibility of catching more winners. Even if my wide net also catches more losers, I am not terribly concerned, because winners generally win more than losers lose, and by a large measure.

It is simple to observe—but not simpleminded to consider— that a $10 stock can only lose $10 or 100 percent, while it can gain many times $10 over the years. Most of us do not realize how much many stocks have appreciated, because the gains may be hidden in stock splits (and the occasional special large stock or cash dividend that is paid).

As previously mentioned, we must monitor of or research stocks, and question how their current prices came to be when they seem cheap to us. The apparently low price may be the result of a stock split, in which case there is no change in the fundamental value relationship. Or it may be due to a significant decline, in which case the stock may have been driven into undervalued, buy-candidate status.

Other reasons for wide diversification for the small investor or beginning student of speculation—as I was when I began dabbling more than 20 years ago—include our limitations in time, capital, and sophistication. Most of us have neither the time to study each corporation in depth, nor the talent to recognize subtle and esoteric situations. Most of us do not have entree to interview captains of industry or, if we do hear them at annual meetings, cannot discern reality from company cheerleading. Remember, corporate officers are partisans, boosters of their companies, who see and publicize few if any problems that cannot be solved or be regarded as opportunities in disguise. Also, they need not practice candor or be forthcoming, following the Brass Rule, "Thou shalt not knock thy company."

Some individual investors and speculators do have the time and inclination to track companies constantly, recognizing subtle—let alone gross—changes in their fortunes and prospects. Perhaps these talented stock pickers can be concentrationists and keep a careful watch over five or ten positions without regard to diversification. Even the most astute, devoted, and hardworking stock pickers make mistakes as otherwise competent managers and well-run corporations suffer glitches in their operations. Perhaps a promising new product, which has been heavily promoted and inventoried, fails badly in public acceptance and causes a corporation unexpectedly large losses and setbacks. There are many currently good-looking companies that are potential disasters waiting to occur.

Barry Ziskin, one of the best stockpickers and portfolio managers in America, uses a rigid seven-criteria test for stock selection. Though he has managed 30 percent returns on equity for over 10 years, he nevertheless saw two stocks that met his strict requirements, Amfesco Corp. and Commodore International, take a tumble in 1986. Commodore has made something of a comeback, but not all the way.

By the way, the annual reports of Ziskin's Z-Seven Fund are like mini textbooks on conservative investing, explicating his methods for managing his closed-end mutual fund and clients' portfolios. While I appreciate the logic and efficacy of Ziskin's seven criteria, I don't use them systematically myself, finding them too restrictive for my taste and too sophisticated for my accounting. I hold a modest position in the Z-Seven Fund as part of my diversified portfolio and as a bet that Ziskin will continue to outperform the major market averages over the multi-year market cycles.

THE INITIAL 5 PERCENT RULE

Many advisors have suggested that no more than 5 percent of a portfolio be in any one equity. I agree that 5 percent as a criterion is a good limit. If the portfolio has no more than 5 percent in any one position—not counting cash or equivalents such as Treasury Bills held at times—then it can have 20 or more stocks when it is fully formed.

Unfortunately for the small speculator who has only $5,000 or $10,000 available—and does not choose to use margin leverage in order to buy more equities—it is impractical to buy 16–20 stocks. First, there is the penalty of high-commission percentages on small amounts of stock. If you were to buy even 10 positions with $5,000—that is, about $500 each in 10 different stocks—you would have to pay between $250 to $400 in "minimum" commissions. This works out to between 5 percent and 8 percent of your purchase costs, and you would be faced with paying similar-sized sell commissions when you decided to trade those stocks. Perhaps your $5,000 worth of stocks would double in market price (on average) before you sold, so you would "only" pay $250 to $400 on the $10,000 of sales, still 2.5 percent to 4 percent. This means that your stocks would have to appreciate between 7.5 percent and 12 percent just for you to break even—quite a load with which to be burdened, although not insurmountable.

There is another penalty involved for the very small investor, the odd-lot differential, which refers to the tradition of charging you an additinal "eighth" (12.5 cents)—coming and going, buying and selling—for stock lots of less than 100 shares. One hundred shares are called *round lots*. In a few cases for very high-priced stocks, less than 100 share lots may be designated *round*.

With $5,000 and 10 positions, unless you pay $5 or less per share for 100 shares ($500 per round lot), you would be charged an extra 12½ cents per share for the odd lot. For a $6 stock—perhaps you'd buy 77 shares (plus commissions) to approximate your $500 per position limit—you would be paying another 2 percent for the odd lot. Over time, these relatively high commission percentages and differentials combine to seriously lower the net total return performance of a portfolio.

If you do not have the cash (or cash plus margin) to buy over $20,000 worth of stocks, you would probably do well to begin with mutual funds, at least as far as diversification and commission expenses are concerned. Even then I would like to see $10,000 spread among two or three funds, and $20,000 diversified into four or five funds. Although each fund will probably have sufficient stock diversification, ranging from dozens to hundreds of different corporate positions, each fund will have its bias and approach that emphasizes one kind of company over another.

Just as selecting stocks is a serious activity, so too should considerable investigation be done in selecting mutual funds. The selection of mutual funds is beyond the purview of this book, although many of the criteria for stock selection can be applied to mutual fund selection. Mutual funds are able to buy shares at institutional commission rates (from 3 to 7 cents per share) far below normal retail rates, which permits them to trade without the penalty of large commission percentages. But there may be initial or redemption loads (fees), annual 12-b-1 fees (ranging from small fractions of a percent to much more, for promotion purposes). And there certainly are annual management fees (withdrawn daily from the net asset value). All that could combine to cost even more than retail commissions in your own portfolio.

The initial 5 percent limit guideline mentioned above is straightforward enough at the outset but soon requires some interpretation. Suppose you bought 20 stocks in your $50,000 diversified portfolio, which meant you spent on average some $2,500 per position. Sometime later, say after a year, if your portfolio had appreciated 20 percent and thus was priced at $60,000, most likely you would have some stocks that had advanced significantly and others that had declined considerably. Perhaps your best-performing stock position doubled in market price and was valued at $5,000, which then would be 8.3 percent of the portfolio ($5,000/$60,000). Would the 5 percent rule call for your selling $2,000 worth of this most-appreciated stock in order to bring its market value down to 5 percent of the portfolio? No, it would not.

Applying only to *initial* purchases, the 5 percent rule is waived in the case of appreciated stocks that are still significantly undervalued according to their fundamental corporate analysis. I suggest you consider a 10 percent limit of any appreciated position in your portfolio. The idea is to avoid the chance of being badly damaged if a few positions go sour, and if your "best stock" begins to represent more than 10 percent, a sharp (50 percent?) drop in that stock could really set back the portfolio's overall performance. Then too, as a successful corporation's stock appreciates in keeping with your appreciating portfolio, a 10 percent position of the larger portfolio is more than double an original 5 percent position. Besides, you don't have to sell all or even most of the appreciated stock if it is still undervalued, just bring it down to 10 percent or less of the portfolio and reinvest the proceeds in other undervalued stocks, thus increasing your stock diversification.

Suppose that after this pleasant 20 percent appreciation year, you find you have additional funds available for stocks, there are stock-purchase (undervalued) candidates, and the market is not especially threatening. What would be the limit for additional purchases to your $60,000 portfolio? At first glance you might say $3,000, because that is 5 percent of the current market value of the portfolio. Ah, but if you intended to add say $20,000, you are actually considering an $80,000 portfolio, so you are "permitted" to buy up to $4,000 positions.

Of course, you are not required to spend 5 percent per position; that is a rough maximum guideline for portfolios greater than $50,000. In the example above, you might well consider buying six or seven $3,000 positions rather than just five $4,000 positions with your $20,000 additional capital. And, you continue to have the option to buy new—not just more shares in currently owned—positions or to add to current positions (averaging down) that may have declined in market price even as their fundamental values may have been increasing.

As the portfolio increases in value, I would definitely tend to initiate smaller than 5 percent positions. Figure 3–6 represents my personal guideline for initial position percentages and stock diversification. Obviously, small portfolios will need to exceed the 5 percent rule in order to avoid excessive commission expenses and too many odd lots. Remember, position diversification might better be called *industry* diversification rather than *stock* diversification. With 30 stocks, try to be in at least 12 to 15 industry groups.

AVERAGING UP, AND AVERAGING DOWN

Averaging, in the present context, refers to adding to positions already owned, usually at a different price per share than the original cost basis.

FIGURE 3–6
Initial Position Diversification and Percentage
per Portfolio Size

Portfolio Size	No. of Stocks	Dollar Percent
$ 25,000	12–15	6.0–8.5%
50,000	15–20	5.0–7.0
100,000	20–30	3.5–5.0
200,000	25–40	2.5–4.0
500,000	30–50	2.0–3.5
1,000,000	50–100	1.0–2.0

Not unlike the unexamined prejudices against the use of leverage (borrowed funds in margined accounts), is a simply silly slogan, "Never average down!" Anytime you get an "always" or "never" in stock market advice, you're probably getting an overstatement at best and "almost *always*" a bum steer. I disagree that buying more shares of a stock that has declined significantly is for some people "throwing good money after bad." In averaging down, the second purchase may be a wiser move than the first purchase has so far turned out to be.

If you own the stock of a prospering corporation, that prosperity may have been extended to the price of its stock, so that now it trades for appreciably more than you paid, and yet it is still undervalued according to fundamental analysis. With other appropriate conditions, such as the priority of first considering other stocks with greater undervaluations and the percentage limit guideline of this position in the portfolio, it makes perfectly good sense to increase your position in such a stock. As you buy the stock at a higher price, you are averaging up. If the first 100 shares cost $10 per share, and now you buy another 100 shares at $20 per, your average cost will be $15 per share for the 200 shares.

There may be a small psychological letdown after averaging up because your augmented position no longer reflects a doubling of its total cost basis, although you immediately would have a 50 percent gain in the total position in the example above. Such psychological twinges should be of little consequence in a long-term portfolio.

As long as a stock's price continues to represent less than 50 percent of its corporation's fundamental value (or anticipated three-to-five–year market price)—no matter how much it has advanced beyond your cost basis or its original goal price—it is a buy candidate competing for a balanced place in your portfolio. However, if there were an equally or almost equally undervalued stock not in the portfolio, I would tend to want to add that currently unowned stock before increasing current positions, thus adding incrementally to stock diversification and casting the slightly wider net.

If our prospering corporation's stock did well enough, but then began to slow in its appreciation or falter, then perhaps the other added stock would take up the slack. Of course, there is almost always the case where the already-owned, advancing stock continues to advance nicely, even into overvalued territory, while the newly purchased, undervalued stock declines significantly. In such an event we are likely to express one of the famous "Why did I, I shoulda" laments.

"Why did I buy Improving Prospects Unlimited at all—it lost 50 percent of its market price over the past 24 months—when I shoulda bought more shares of Slow and Unsteady Limited, which appreciated 500 percent in the past two years?"

It is certainly okay to hold so-called losers if they are undervalued bargains. Understanding this is the first step to accepting the technique of averaging down for the right reasons. John Templeton has said,

> You will always find in our list some stocks selling below cost but we're not holding them just because they're below cost. We're holding them because we think they are the best bargains, the lowest prices in relation to the long-term earning power of that corporation.
>
> We really try to avoid the question of is it above or below what we paid for it. That has nothing to do with whether it's a good value or not.[2]

Warren Buffett, aside from being arguably the most astute investor of current times, is noted for his wit and down-to-earth themes to make a point. A card player, Buffett enjoys the idioms associated with that activity and has said if you're in a poker game for a half hour and you don't know who's the patsy, you're the patsy. *Webster's New World Dictionary* defines *patsy* as "a person easily imposed upon or victimized." In the present context, Buffett has said,

> If your stock goes down 10 percent and that upsets you—it obviously means you think the market knows more about the company than you do. In that case you're the patsy.
>
> If it goes down 10 percent and you want to buy more because you know the business is worth just as much as when you bought it before, perhaps a little bit more with the passage of time, so you buy more, they're the patsy.[3]

Most investors tend to get emotionally biased when it comes to buying a stock currently or previously owned that has not done well. I've suffered from this syndrome myself, as related in my early trading of Whittaker Corp. (See Chapter 7, page 206.) The Whittaker example showed I was not yet a prudent investor or speculator, as I started by buying an overvalued stock and ended up selling undervalued shares. Since I had been so hurt and

---

[2]*Outstanding Investor Digest*, October 30, 1988, p. 11.
[3]*Outstanding Investor Digest*, June 30, 1988, p. 12.

embarrassed in my losing trades in Whittaker, I was unable to recognize or act upon one of the great buys of late 1974.

Ideas and terms like *averaging up, averaging down, doubling one's position, taking profits,* or *taking losses* should have little influence in decisions of portfolio management. To repeat our song, we buy undervalued stocks to be held for the long term in widely diversified portfolios until they are fully valued or until very severe and threatening overvalued and overbought markets suggest taking defensive measures.

THE BASICS ARE MORE IMPORTANT THAN BEING CLEVER

Our basic investment approach of finding and buying stocks of undervalued corporations can be done quite easily, although not perfectly. To the degree we try to bring in intellectual or academic cleverness, such as outguessing megatrends, the economy, the stock market, inflation, or the next fad, we endanger our strongest suit. All we have to do is our "bottoms up" (individual company) approach, and sooner or later, most of the time, our undervalued corporations will become fairly valued, as reflected in the rising prices of their stocks over a multi-year period.

As I write these lines, inflation is the chief concern of the investment world. There are several kinds of inflation, or at least several components, such as increasing wages, wholesale and retail prices, commodities, interest rates, and service costs. There are simple descriptions of inflation such as too many dollars chasing too few goods. The relationship of productivity increases versus wage increases is important, as the balance of goods to dollars is maintained or lost. You would have to be a very bright and learned economist to keep track of and understand many of the elements that contribute to inflation or deflation, and then you might be able to guess right 50 percent of the time. Meanwhile, you run the strong chance of zigging when you should have zagged, being out of the market when it fools the majority and takes off.

For example, a headline in the *Investor's Daily* (3/16/89) states, "Oil Prices Head Higher, Defying Predictions." Instead of crude oil prices continuing to drop in November 1988 from the $13 per barrel low to below $10 as then predicted, they climbed to over $21 per barrel in April 1989. Thus people who sold—or declined to hold or buy—oil stocks before year-end because of the low crude prices missed handsome gains in most of the major oil companies over that following five-month period, and beyond.

As if trying to outguess crude oil demand, supply, and prices weren't bad enough, some investors presumed that rising oil prices would be negative for airline stocks, since fuel is a major expense for airlines. However, the airlines had a banner first quarter, on average, in both profitability and their stocks' appreciation, powering the Dow Jones Transportation Index to all-time new highs, surpassing pre-Crash of '87 levels. Clever if-this-then-that analysis often doesn't work out in practice, as so many other elements enter into the picture to distort the seemingly simple and apparent if-then relationships.

It will be interesting to see if we are in the much-predicted recession by the time this book is published in the fall of '89—a recession that many economists and market prognosticators were sure would follow the Crash of '87 and each subsequent quarter of '88 and '89. Would it make much difference to the long-term value investor? Not according to Warren Buffett, who was asked whether a recession was imminent at the Berkshire Hathaway annual meeting in May of '88. His answer was, "I don't know . . . But it just doesn't make any difference. If I had spent my time trying to figure out when the next recession would occur, Berkshire's stock would probably be around $15 a share instead of its current $3,675. . . . I wouldn't believe anybody's forecast—especially my own."[4] By the way, Berkshire shares traded for over $8,100 each in September 1989.

Although rising interest rates are generally not supportive of rising stock prices, there have been many periods during which both advanced in tandem, such as the first eight months of 1987, for most of 1988, and during the first quarter of 1989. It seems that the level of interest rates, the strength of their advance, and the perception of future stability or change in direction all contribute to that incalculable balance that tips market fluctuations.

A phenomenon that often confuses stock marketeers is the discounting or anticipating mechanism that the market represents. Markets top out and begin declining during periods of prosperity and enthusiasm, just when it looks as though the good times will go on and on. Markets bottom out and begin advancing during recessions, depressions, and otherwise

---

[4] *Outstanding Investor Digest,* June 30, 1988.

generally gloomy periods when it looks as though the economic viability of America is in dire straits.

There are many cycles, periods, and movements that are neither intuitive nor apparent from daily and weekly stock market activity. There are long stretches (years and decades) when stocks are ''over owned,'' maintaining and keeping up demand and prices until monetary conditions cannot support such excesses. There are times when stocks are under-owned and the need for institutions to invest excess reserves almost demands buying stocks under all but the most adverse conditions.

Currently, as the 1980s come to a close, there is a relative shortage of stocks caused by the massive amounts of shares retired, due to mergers, acquisitions, buyouts, and buybacks, unmatched by relatively few new issues. Over $400 billion in stocks has been ''retired'' from the stock market since January 1984. This five-year reduction in the supply of stocks can only have bullish implications for the longer term, especially as stocks are already underowned by historic averages, and investable funds continue to grow.

TO SELL OR NOT TO SELL, THAT IS THE QUESTION

Most people I've read or listened to agree that knowing when to sell and selling are the most difficult and troublesome aspects of investing. The glib may say that selling is merely the other side of the investment coin—heads I buy, tails I sell—but that really doesn't capture the asymmetrical relationships among buying, holding, and selling. Selling is often analytically and psychologically tough, and almost as important a discipline as buying. I say selling is almost as important as buying because I believe in the idea that a well-bought corporation may almost never need to be sold or will provide many good selling (at a handsome profit) opportunities in the richness of time. Still, there are many guidelines for doing so.

Since so many people have trouble with selling, let's review some of the psychology involved. After deciding to buy stocks but before committing to any trade, we have the luxury of taking our time to review the enormous number of choices available. In Warren Buffett's imagery, we can stand at the plate all day waiting for just the right pitch at which to swing. As individual and independent speculators, no one is forcing us to buy stocks or to hold them only if they show superior quarterly performance, as happens to institutional investors. As long as we are selecting buy candidates, checking them out, and watching their market meanderings, we are safe in the world of the potential position.

Once we buy a stock, subsequent decisions of what to hold begin. Holding one or a group of stocks is an existential exercise for some, a decision each day on whether to continue holding or to sell. It is one thing to peruse a buy list and take one's time in picking and choosing; it is quite another to peruse one's holdings, watching them rise and fall, especially when they decline in price, often for no apparent reason, while the market is advancing on average. This process can be so nerve-wracking for some investors that they take the mechanical way out and place stop loss sell orders. That way, if the stock's price drops a certain amount or percentage, adios and farewell, it's history.

I find it fascinating to hear investors admit in candor that they made a mistake when a stock they picked drops 10 percent (or whatever) in its market price. They believe they are showing how disciplined they are by automatically selling such "mistakes" without additional review or hesitation. Perhaps they have convinced themselves that when the market speaks, they listen. For them, the market's language is price, and the market is always right. I disagree. The market is merely a mechanism for bringing together heterogenous numbers of people, many of whom see the stock market as a game, a way of trying their luck in that big casino in The Big Apple, the Windy City, or other assorted places.

The market is not always right, except in the most sophomoric sense of tortured logic. In reality, the stock market is usually wrong. People assume that a stock's price is the result of an efficient process of informed trading. If that were the case, why would we trade stocks at all? If that were the case, how come some corporations trade today at 5 percent to 50 percent more—or less, for that matter—than they did yesterday? You might say that so-and-so decided to make a bid for the company. Is so-and-so a philanthropist, "giving" away much more than the recent stock price for the benefit of owning the corporation in question? Or was the market "wrong" in pricing that stock yesterday, because it is "correct" today?

Short-term stock price fluctuations often have little to do with long-term corporate conditions or economic conditions. Daily price movements are in effect seemingly random, although daily commentators strive for apparent reasons to explain price fluctuations. Understanding participants take a more sanguine view than professional commentators who are paid to sound knowledgeable, perhaps saying with a twinkle in the eye, "The price dropped today because there were more sellers than buyers" or vice versa.

While much of portfolio management can be mathematical and mechanistic, developing a realistic attitude and exploring one's own mindset are the keys to maintaining long-term perspective and perseverance. Probably the most general mistake, and therefore the weakest link in portfolio management, is in selling too soon. Either because a stock has declined in market price and we are afraid it's going lower, or because a stock has advanced in market price and we are afraid our good fortune cannot continue and the unrealized gains will soon be taken away, many investors lock in small losses and limit themselves to relatively modest gains. This practice is a recipe for not doing well in the stock market. Each loss—plus four commissions buying and selling twice—must be made up before one breaks even, so if the gains aren't generally significantly greater than the losses, one will end with little to show for all the effort, commitment of funds, and risk.

Many conscious or unconscious attitudes we carry into stock speculation sabotage our best efforts. One significant inhibiter of clear thinking is the concept of getting even.

THE GETTING EVEN FALLACY

I have often encountered the *getting even fallacy* from market participants. This attitude takes two distinct forms, each containing fatal errors of reasoning and practice. The first class of investors, after sustaining a price decline, say and think that they are waiting to get even in order to get out of a position or out of the market in general. The other class are those shareholders willing to sell out their "losers" now because, even if their stocks have a likely potential to double in market price, they would only become "even" with their original costs.

Let's start with the terms *realized* and *unrealized gains* and *losses*. A realized gain or loss occurs when a position is sold and the net costs are subtracted from the net proceeds. If the proceeds realized from the sale, after brokerage commissions and transfer taxes or fees, are greater than the purchase costs (which include brokerage commissions), then one has a realized capital gain. Obviously, in the opposite case, where the proceeds are less than the costs, one has a realized capital loss. Realized gains and losses have tax consequences and become part of your income tax return. Realized capital gains and losses are clear and tangible as the outcome of the closed transaction is defined in simple arithmetic.

Unrealized capital gains and losses refer to the differences between the market values of your positions compared to the costs of those positions. Until those positions are sold and the gains or losses realized, there are no tax consequences. What is quite arithmetically clear often becomes emotionally confused, especially when slogans like, "It's not a loss until you sell!" are believed. (The potentially troublesome effects of such a misleading attitude are also touched on in the Chapter 5 on margin.)

People who believe they do not really have capital losses until those lower stock prices are "realized" are often inconsistent as they believe they really do have capital gains before those are realized. In the words of a popular song of some years past, they are accentuating the positive and eliminating the negative, but at the expense of reality. If you can treat these two impostors, unrealized gains and losses (triumphs and despairs) with equanimity, your investment decisions will be more rationally based.

Gains and losses are just that, whether realized or not, and those who do not wish to accept the reality of their unrealized positions are often led into making poor speculative decisions. Most importantly, *current gains and losses have no necessary relationship to the fundamental values of corporations*. Thus, making investment decisions because of unrealized gains or losses in market price is to miss the whole point of long-term value and growth investing.

What is important to the prudent stock speculator, at any given moment, is the fundamental value of the corporation—and therefore the analyzed value of its stock—in which a position is held. For example, I hold Ford Motor Company (F) in my portfolio with a cost basis of $13.01, and it closed 3/31/89 at $48.875. The fact that there was an unrealized gain of over 275 percent had nothing to do with why I continue to hold Ford shares or when I might decide to sell them. The operative factor for holding was that my analysis of Ford at that time showed it likely to trade between $97 and $100 in the next three to five years. Therefore, it was a currently recommended stock and *I might even have bought more shares at near four times my original cost basis*, except that Ford already amounted to one of the largest positions in my portfolio. To buy more Ford would have violated the diversification principle of not buying more than 2–3 percent in any one position in a portfolio the size of mine.

On the other hand, I held General Development (GDV) in my portfolio at a cost basis of $18.88 per share; GDV closed on 7/29/88 at $12.00. Again, I held GDV (and might have bought more shares, thus averaging down) because its estimated 3-to-5–year market price was $34 per share. Logically, *I did not care what GDV cost me in the past*. As long as it was currently trading for half or less of its projected goal price I could buy more shares, and thereafter hold it until its market price meets its analyzed goal price or market conditions dictated selling. By 4/30/89, GDV closed at $14.625, but its goal price had declined to $24 per share, so it was then a strong hold but no longer a buy. In time, GDV's goal price might well advance and make it a buy again, or decline and make it a sell.

In giving examples, I would be remiss not to mention such disappointments as Financial Corporation of American (FIN) and Maxxus Energy (MXS), among many positions that have not worked out well. I held FIN at a cost basis of $8.82; it closed on 7/29/88 at $1.00. I had believed that FIN could be turned around and become a valuable property but finally concluded that long-held expectation unlikely and "realized" my loss. Even though there was little to be received at $1 per share, I would not hold the stock hoping to get even or to make a double from the clearly depressed price. (Several months later, FIN was reorganized by the FSLIC and the common shares became worthless.) Likewise, I had concluded that with all Maxxus Energy's potential, its fundamental analysis led me to want to redeploy the $7.75 per share or so of proceeds—original cost basis $11.63 per share—into a more promising position.

Most overvalued stocks that we sell continue to advance in market price, at least for awhile. We should not be chagrined or disappointed. Only by accident can we catch exact tops and bottoms in stock prices and market movements. You may miss some extra appreciation, but consider what potential appreciation may be gained from new stocks bought with the proceeds, especially over time. We should go with the probabilities that say trim the overvalued stocks—even when they produce a realized loss—in favor of repositioning in undervalued stocks with much greater potential.

So, we do not hold stocks to get even, to show a profit, or to put off realizing a loss. We hold stocks because they are undervalued. We do not sell stocks because their current goal prices are below our cost basis. We sell stocks because they are fully valued or overvalued, no matter what our cost basis, so that we can redeploy the proceeds—with realized gains or losses—into undervalued positions.

It truly grieves me when investors reason that it is correct to liquidate stocks and even portfolios because even if our current projections come true, that would only lead to a portfolio becoming even in two or three years.

Let's say that because of an unusual run of poorly performing selections and the market crash of October 1987, your portfolio declined 50 percent from its cost basis. Let's say that if things went well—of course no guarantees, and future performance may not equal past performance or even be profitable—you might double your post-crash equity in four years (about 18 percent compounded annually), or perhaps in three years (about 24 percent compounded annually). The investor who says, "You mean, even if things go well I will have to wait three or four years, and then only get even?" has missed the point of value and growth speculating and the reality of the situation.

Our unrealized losses are real, as the proceeds from selling out will attest. In this example, our capital is 50 percent gone—it's spilt milk. What matters is what we can do about it from now on. If we can return to making handsome compounded annual gains for the next several years, we will not only "get even" but recover and prevail.

I bought Ambase Corporation (ABC, formerly Home Group) at $18.625 per share, and it is now trading around $13.75 (6/28/89) but has a goal price of $28. I wouldn't consider selling it merely because it would have to appreciate about 50 percent for me to just become even. I would consider buying more, or at least I would hold my current shares because of the probability that I could gain over 100 percent or more from current levels with my ABC shares over the next few years. Conditions may change and I might have to sell Ambase for less than today's price, but as long as it's undervalued and I do not project a crash, I will hold it.

Many stocks happen to trade for 30 percent to 50 percent of their originally recommended or purchased prices only to become huge winners over the years. Consider the early disappointing price history of Puerto Rican Cement (PRN). I bought 500 shares of PRN in 11/83 for $6.75 per share. PRN hit a high of $12.25 in 1984 but fell to a low of $6.00 in 1985. PRN hit a high of $38.50 before the Crash of '87 and thereafter traded at a low of $16.50, thus twice declining more than 50 percent in less than four years. On 3/31/89, PRN closed at $46.50, for an unrealized gain of 589 percent in less than five years. What would my long-term record be if I had sold out when I got even in '86? What would my performance for 1988 have been if I sold out after the crash because I could hope for little more than getting even with the pre-crash unrealized gain?

Successful speculators sometimes make super-sounding statements. George Soros, fabled for his speculative successes, has asserted that he never tries to get even. What's past is over and done. What's important is to get on with the process.

Warren Buffett, as previously cited in Chapter 1, and worth repeating, commented at the 1988 Berkshire Hathaway annual meeting about the probability of a 50 percent decline in one's common stocks. "You ignore that possibility at your own peril. In the history of almost every major company in this country, it has happened. You shouldn't own common stocks if a decrease in their value by 50 percent would cause you to feel stress."[5]

Every market day we are faced with considering our stock positions unless we are truly long-term "partners" in our corporations. If we focus on our corporations rather than the stock market, we may only consider our stock positions weekly, monthly, quarterly, or even annually. Should we sell, hold, or buy more? Most of the time the answer to these questions is the same as yesterday's considered answer. I will hold until I believe the position is fully valued or market conditions become too threatening. From time to time, cash becomes available to invest, and market conditions seem propitious, so I will have to decide whether to buy more undervalued shares of already-owned positions or instead to buy other undervalued stocks. These decisions involve reviews of diversification, limits of concentration, comparative undervaluedness, and perhaps current economic conditions.

Some misguided marketeers say if you wouldn't buy the stocks you own today, then you should sell them—you shouldn't keep holding them. I find this either/or thinking illogical and inefficient. If I find a corporation that fundamental analysis suggests will likely trade at $25 within three-to-five-years, then my discipline permits me to buy that equity up to $12.50 $12.50 per share. Suppose I am able to purchase some of this hypothetical

---

[5]*Outstanding Investor Digest*, June 30, 1988, p. 9.

THE ICEBERG AND THE TITANIC

For those who have intimations of destiny, the story of the iceberg and the Titanic must hold an ironic fascination. As the idea of the great ship took form, the great ice floe that would give birth to that iceberg was moving inexorably toward the ocean. As the Titanic was being provisioned for its gala maiden voyage, the iceberg was breaking off from its glacier and being launched to venture forth on the North Atlantic. In spite of all the planning for the safest ship ever built and a record passage, things went wrong as unexpected disaster followed from these two wondrous objects that had been set in motion, independent of each other.

The story of the Crash of '87 reminds me of the story of the iceberg and the Titanic. Events and conditions were set in motion that had the promise of a record-breaking excursion and the minimized potential for a disastrous collision. The "unseen" colliding conditions for the Crash were the New York Stock Exchange with its programmed trading of stocks for risk arbitrageurs and portfolio insures versus Chicago with its development and rise of derivative instruments such as the S + P 500 futures contracts.

MELTDOWN MONDAY, A.K.A. BLACK MONDAY

This complex story reaches back years as traditional practices and attitudes were modified in the cauldron of greed and under the aegis of barely regulated free markets. It stars the risk arbitrageurs and portfolio insurance hacks who became the darlings of Wall Street because of the control and profits they generated. To get anywhere near the full flavor of the Crash of '87, I strongly recommend a study of the fascinating, informative, and readable book, *Black Monday*, by Tim Metz.[3]

Metz narrates the events and actions of several key players in the years leading up to the debacle he calls *Black Monday*. Much of his information comes from the Brady Commission task force report and the "presumably exhaustive, 874-page Securities and Exchange Commission's study of the crash."[4] Metz paints a clear picture of markets out of control and the efforts to stabilize them, even if existing rules and practices had to be bent or ignored.

---

[3]From *Black Monday* by Tim Metz © 1988 by Tim Metz. Reprinted by permission of William Morrow & Co.

[4]Metz, *Black Monday*, p. 63.

FIGURE 6–2
Daily Data Printout during Crash Period (8/21/87–12/11/87)

ADV	DEC	UpVol	Downvol	1987	NYCI	DJIA	HI	LO	Arms	10-A	10-D	25-A	25-D	A-D	10A-D	25A-D	10NYCI	Z	25NYCI	Z	10 DJIA	Z	25 DJIA	%
803	776	97068	76348	8/21	187.51	2709.50	132	10	.81	.85	.78	.77	.80	27	1019	1255	185.88	.9	180.26	4.0	2679.99	1.1	2589.30	4.6
578	1019	49794	63427	8/24	186.27	2697.07	90	8	.95	.92	.81	.77	.79	-441	-92	1381	186.16	.1	180.71	3.1	2686.11	.4	2597.67	3.8
1023	594	152208	45833	8/25	187.99	2722.42	135	16	.52	.93	.85	.77	.77	429	-140	2406	186.34	.9	181.28	3.7	2690.31	1.2	2607.85	4.4
683	897	76003	109879	8/26	186.94	2701.85	106	19	1.10	.95	.86	.76	.78	-214	-127	2382	186.47	.3	181.82	2.8	2693.56	.3	2617.12	3.2
548	1032	43709	102796	8/27	185.26	2675.06	39	17	1.25	1.02	.93	.79	.79	-484	-877	2217	186.30	-.6	182.31	1.6	2691.92	-.6	2625.24	1.9
395	1231	22406	124225	8/28	182.99	2639.35	29	24	1.78	1.08	.93	.79	.80	-836	-1607	1240	185.93	-1.6	182.68	.2	2687.31	-1.8	2631.40	.3
1007	601	109648	40484	8/31	184.45	2662.95	37	23	.62	1.05	.91	.80	.79	406	-1152	1447	185.70	-.7	183.08	.7	2683.55	-.8	2638.16	.9
428	1197	35047	131497	9/ 1	181.21	2610.97	52	22	1.34	.99	.88	.80	.81	-769	-1022	451	185.40	-2.3	183.32	-1.2	2679.18	-2.5	2641.81	-1.2
443	1216	51266	128281	9/ 2	180.12	2602.04	24	31	.91	.98	.88	.80	.82	-773	-1813	-856	184.98	-2.6	183.45	-1.8	2672.80	-2.6	2644.31	-1.6
625	984	48754	97401	9/ 3	179.34	2599.35	24	37	1.27	1.06	.94	.81	.84	-359	-3014	-1556	184.21	-2.6	183.49	-2.3	2662.06	-2.4	2645.59	-1.7
513	1060	33433	63948	9/ 4	177.58	2561.38	19	43	1.22	1.10	.97	.82	.85	-547	-3588	-2245	183.22	-3.1	183.45	-3.2	2647.24	-3.2	2645.16	-3.2
252	1532	31786	199007	9/ 8	175.59	2545.12	10	74	1.03	1.10	1.01	.82	.85	-1280	-4427	-3139	182.15	-3.6	183.35	-4.2	2632.05	-3.3	2644.68	-3.8
848	763	75490	69427	9/ 9	175.79	2549.27	9	68	1.02	1.15	1.13	.84	.85	85	-4771	-2763	180.93	-2.8	183.28	-4.1	2614.73	-2.5	2644.78	-3.6
1103	494	129079	34950	9/10	177.46	2576.05	22	43	.60	1.10	1.06	.85	.86	609	-3948	-2524	179.98	-1.4	183.24	-3.2	2602.15	-1.0	2645.16	-2.6
1153	449	137554	25133	9/11	180.02	2608.74	44	57	.47	1.03	.98	.86	.86	704	-2760	-2298	179.46	.3	183.23	-1.7	2595.52	.5	2645.74	-1.4
833	752	65870	49078	9/14	180.54	2613.04	43	49	.63	.91	.93	.86	.85	81	-1843	-2370	179.21	.7	183.21	-1.5	2592.89	.8	2646.58	-1.3
430	1159	22959	101326	9/15	177.98	2566.58	31	56	1.64	1.01	.97	.87	.87	-729	-2978	-3769	178.56	-.3	182.99	-2.7	2583.25	-.6	2643.81	-2.9
528	1034	34982	138858	9/16	176.51	2530.19	29	60	2.03	1.08	1.01	.88	.94	-506	-2715	-4752	178.09	-.9	182.61	-3.3	2575.18	-1.7	2637.80	-4.1
691	838	62096	66796	9/17	176.48	2527.90	34	62	.89	1.08	1.01	.90	.95	-147	-2089	-4672	177.73	-.7	182.24	-3.2	2567.76	-1.6	2632.14	-4.0
702	876	80887	88256	9/18	176.30	2524.64	40	49	.87	1.04	.97	.90	.97	-174	-1904	-5112	177.43	-.6	181.81	-3.0	2560.29	-1.4	2625.47	-3.8

489	1069	126957	30289	25	58	1.92	1.11	1.02	.98		-580	-1937	-5386	177.09	-1.6	181.32	-3.9	2553.44	-2.4	2617.77	-4.8
1058	555	167525	24777	31	79	.28	1.04	.86	.92	.94	503	-154	-5034	177.38	.6	180.98	-1.4	2555.73	.5	2612.46	-1.7
1010	605	129685	68503	53	56	.88	1.02	.84	.92	.91	405	166	-3730	177.76	1.0	180.80	-.7	2559.37	1.0	2609.70	-.9
734	828	65755	78193	54	56	1.05	1.07	.88	.93	.91	-94	-537	-3842	177.90	.5	180.58	-1.0	2558.41	.3	2605.73	-1.5
689	789	67820	54095	43	67	.70	1.09	.90	.93	.92	-100	-1341	-4784	177.81	.7	180.26	-.6	2554.55	.6	2600.26	-1.2
1010	593	127045	46771	78	53	.63	1.09	.89	.94	.91	417	-1005	-4394	177.83	1.6	179.99	.4	2553.39	1.9	2595.94	.2
636	940	68232	86266	51	77	.86	1.01	.87	.94	.91	-304	-580	-4257	178.04	1.1	179.74	.2	2555.79	1.4	2591.68	.0
921	674	92730	71689	43	66	1.06	.91	.82	.94	.94	247	173	-4439	178.41	1.0	179.43	.4	2562.40	1.3	2586.64	.4
1029	526	146820	30778	87	35	.41	.87	.77	.93	.90	503	823	-3722	179.06	2.2	179.28	2.1	2573.53	2.6	2584.13	2.1
838	731	94871	58062	92	41	.70	.85	.75	.93	.89	107	1104	-3131	179.77	2.0	179.20	2.4	2585.17	2.2	2582.77	2.3
688	855	82129	59968	83	39	.59	.72	.67	.92	.86	-167	1517	-2462	180.69	1.5	179.22	2.4	2599.90	1.5	2582.80	2.2
338	1332	22570	144432	44	57	1.62	.85	.78	.91	.88	-994	20	-3862	180.74	-1.0	179.00	.0	2597.96	-1.9	2578.23	-1.1
546	1020	57221	105254	13	54	.98	.86	.80	.91	.87	-474	-859	-3567	180.64	-1.2	176.90	-.2	2594.50	-1.7	2575.83	-1.0
404	1193	25764	152152	21	78	2.00	.95	.65	.91	.90	-789	-1554	-3583	180.39	-2.3	178.74	-1.4	2589.52	-2.8	2572.42	-2.2
498	1058	45060	98768	16	89	1.03	.99	.87	.90	.89	-560	-2014	-3784	179.94	-2.9	178.56	-2.2	2580.73	-3.8	2567.73	-3.3
377	1210	29581	95968	8	112	1.01	1.03	.89	.90	.88	-633	-3264	-4070	179.22	-3.2	178.39	-2.7	2567.72	-3.7	2564.14	-3.6
959	629	128399	33037	14	88	.39	.98	.84	.89	.84	330	-2630	-2460	178.81	-1.6	178.41	-1.3	2559.48	-2.0	2562.66	-2.1
287	1406	19695	160980	5	123	1.88	1.06	.88	.88	.86	-1119	-3996	-3664	177.91	-3.7	178.23	-3.9	2541.12	-5.1	2557.19	-5.7
298	1441	29766	218132	6	189	1.52	1.17	1.03	.88	.90	-1143	-5642	-5416	176.36	-5.1	177.83	-5.8	2512.71	-6.3	2548.36	-7.6
111	1749	3616	329776	5	327	5.79	1.68	1.21	.98	.89	-1638	-7387	-7758	173.93	-8.5	176.99	-10.1	2473.29	-9.2	2553.88	-11.3

Figure 6–2—Concluded

ADV	DEC	UpVol/Downval	1987	NYCI	DJIA	HI	LO	Arms	10-A	10-D	25-A	25-D	A-D	10A-D	25A-D	10NYCI	Z	25NYCI	Z	10 DJIA	Z	25 DJIA	Z
52	1973	1129	602781	10/19	128.62	1738.74	10	1068	14.07	3.03	1.61	.92	1.14	-1921	-9141	-9760	168.45	-23.6	174.92	-26.5	2383.14	-27.0	2498.90	-30.4
509	1445	329398	250583	10/20	133.04	1841.01	1	1174	.27	2.89	.95	.92	1.00	-936	-9083	-9967	163.86	-18.8	173.12	-23.2	2312.38	-20.4	2469.88	-25.5
1756	210	424577	19574	10/21	145.02	2027.85	2	108	.39	2.83	.81	.91	.90	1546	-7063	-7915	160.50	-9.6	171.86	-15.6	2260.06	-10.3	2449.79	-17.2
361	1540	35249	346618	10/22	139.45	1950.43	1	172	2.31	2.86	.86	.90	.94	-1179	-7453	-8947	156.82	-11.1	170.38	-18.2	2203.44	-11.5	2426.69	-19.6
670	1048	89414	134593	10/23	139.22	1950.76	1	144	.96	2.86	.86	.90	.95	-378	-7271	-9151	155.27	-9.2	168.89	-17.6	2150.29	-9.3	2403.73	-18.8
134	1791	1862	301434	10/26	127.88	1793.93	0	467	12.11	3.97	.88	.89	.96	-1657	-8095	-10228	148.71	-14.0	167.04	-23.4	2082.54	-13.9	2375.78	-24.5
941	821	173950	64985	10/27	130.51	1846.99	0	341	.43	3.97	.84	.89	.95	120	-8305	-10611	144.16	-9.5	165.12	-21.0	2016.42	-8.4	2346.94	-21.3
591	1153	115873	146651	10/28	130.31	1846.82	0	477	.65	3.85	.83	.89	.93	-562	-7748	-11578	140.06	-7.0	163.15	-20.1	1959.84	-5.8	2317.38	-20.3
1405	366	234773	16212	10/29	136.28	1938.33	2	169	.27	3.72	.85	.89	.90	1039	-5566	-10445	136.95	-.5	161.45	-15.6	1918.16	1.1	2292.26	-15.4
1611	224	249283	30158	10/30	140.80	1993.53	1	39	.87	3.23	.88	.89	.90	1387	-2541	-8958	135.11	4.2	159.92	-12.0	1892.84	5.3	2269.19	-12.1
1093	629	115683	47386	11/ 2	142.74	2014.09	1	34	.71	1.90	.75	.89	.91	464	-156	-8911	136.53	4.6	158.40	-9.9	1920.37	4.9	2245.70	-10.3
493	1211	34524	179220	11/ 3	140.11	1963.55	1	37	2.11	2.08	.88	.89	.93	-718	62	-9325	137.23	2.1	156.80	-10.6	1932.63	1.6	2220.61	-11.6
713	933	81788	102305	11/ 4	139.11	1945.29	2	39	.96	2.14	1.00	.89	.92	-220	-1704	-9792	136.64	1.8	155.15	-10.3	1924.37	1.1	2194.57	-11.4
1281	450	172743	38710	11/ 5	141.81	1985.41	2	45	.64	1.97	.87	.90	.93	831	306	-9464	136.88	3.6	153.51	-7.6	1927.87	3.0	2168.42	-8.4
807	814	56363	97076	11/ 6	140.04	1959.05	0	21	1.71	2.05	.89	.90	.95	-7	677	-9578	136.96	2.2	151.77	-7.7	1928.70	1.6	2141.15	-8.5
412	1285	16210	155030	11/ 9	136.35	1900.20	2	46	2.67	1.10	.81	.91	.96	-873	1461	-10284	137.81	-1.1	149.89	-9.0	1939.32	-2.0	2111.55	-10.0
416	1277	34386	136732	11/10	134.06	1878.15	1	75	1.30	1.19	.88	.91	.96	-861	480	-10151	138.16	-3.0	148.09	-9.5	1942.44	-3.3	2084.73	-9.9
995	587	96818	33268	11/11	135.46	1899.20	2	39	.58	1.18	.89	.92	.97	408	1459	-9289	138.68	-2.3	146.37	-7.5	1947.68	-2.5	2058.65	-7.7
1296	386	176395	18196	11/12	138.88	1960.21	3	20	.35	1.19	.93	.92	.96	910	1321	-7570	138.94	.0	144.87	-4.1	1949.87	.5	2036.39	-3.7
692	912	40970	121569	11/13	137.60	1935.01	3	25	2.25	1.33	1.06	.93	.98	-220	-286	-7230	138.62	-.7	143.39	-4.0	1944.01	-.5	2014.51	-3.9

866	701	78556	51591	11/16	138.16	1949.10	0	29	.81	1.34	1.08	.93	1.00	165	-585	-6232	138.16	.0	141.97	-2.7	1937.52	.6	1993.61	-2.2
399	1204	23101	112255	11/17	136.21	1922.25	1	56	1.61	1.29	1.00	.94	1.00	-805	-672	-7367	137.77	-1.1	140.38	-3.0	1933.39	-.6	1970.18	-2.4
1031	537	97853	40570	11/18	137.58	1939.16	2	56	.79	1.27	.99	.95	1.01	494	42	-5754	137.62	.0	139.03	-1.0	1932.77	.3	1951.23	-.6
366	1287	12612	131884	11/19	134.72	1895.39	3	60	2.97	1.50	1.12	.95	1.00	-921	-1710	-5532	136.91	-1.6	137.72	-2.2	1923.77	-1.5	1932.85	-1.9
714	826	92248	71665	11/20	135.56	1913.63	3	88	.67	1.40	1.02	.94	.96	-112	-1815	-4006	136.46	-.7	136.78	-.9	1919.23	-.3	1919.52	-.3
903	694	86811	41153	11/24	136.13	1923.08	4	68	.62	1.20	.94	.91	.85	209	-733	-1876	136.44	-.2	137.08	-.7	1921.52	.1	1926.90	-.2
1139	502	127240	37630	11/25	137.93	1963.53	5	48	.67	1.13	.87	.91	.91	637	765	-303	136.82	.8	137.28	.5	1930.06	1.7	1931.80	1.6
745	813	54882	67019	11/26	139.90	1946.95	2	49	1.12	1.19	.91	.92	.99	-68	289	-1917	137.27	1.9	137.07	2.1	1934.83	.6	1928.56	1.0
514	957	18812	51753	11/27	135.16	1910.46	6	28	1.48	1.30	1.00	.92	.91	-443	-1064	-1181	136.90	-1.3	136.90	-1.3	1929.86	-1.0	1926.96	-.9
201	1576	7012	255085	11/30	129.69	1833.55	2	211	4.64	1.54	1.09	.93	.95	-1375	-2219	-2178	136.10	-4.7	136.52	-5.0	1919.71	-4.5	1922.27	-4.6
819	771	81236	45675	12/ 1	130.50	1842.34	1	86	.60	1.52	1.06	.94	.89	48	-2336	-473	135.34	-3.6	136.62	-4.5	1909.04	-3.5	1924.21	-4.3
753	755	72921	46266	12/ 2	131.21	1848.97	1	95	.63	1.42	1.00	.94	.92	-2	-1553	-595	134.84	-2.7	136.65	-4.0	1901.71	-2.8	1924.29	-3.9
268	1390	14526	181191	12/ 3	127.01	1776.53	2	169	2.40	1.58	1.10	.95	.95	-1122	-3149	-1155	133.78	-5.1	136.52	-7.0	1885.45	-5.8	1921.48	-7.5
362	1306	45653	120652	12/ 4	125.91	1766.74	0	281	.73	1.36	1.02	.96	1.00	-944	-3172	-3138	132.90	-5.3	136.11	-7.5	1872.58	-5.7	1914.61	-7.7
925	698	96164	33594	12/ 7	126.23	1812.17	2	194	.46	1.34	1.02	.97	1.02	227	-2833	-4298	132.17	-3.0	135.60	-5.4	1862.43	-2.7	1907.36	-5.0
1151	473	131759	63609	12/ 8	131.42	1866.37	1	128	1.17	1.39	1.03	.98	1.03	678	-2364	-4064	131.70	-.2	135.15	-2.8	1856.96	.6	1901.53	-1.7
1119	501	129189	40242	12/ 9	133.56	1902.52	1	74	.70	1.39	1.03	.98	.98	618	-2363	-2748	131.26	1.8	134.89	-1.0	1850.86	2.8	1899.09	.2
512	1065	37765	136963	12/10	131.07	1855.44	3	92	1.70	1.45	1.07	.99	1.00	-573	-2886	-3101	130.38	.5	134.57	-2.6	1841.71	.7	1895.50	-2.1
829	674	91397	40755	12/11	131.79	1867.04	2	70	.55	1.36	1.02	.99	1.02	155	-2290	-3777	130.04	1.3	134.17	-1.8	1837.37	1.6	1890.76	-1.3

The Crash of '87 was a setup. One of the problems of putting historical events into perspective is deciding upon how far back to set the scene. A case could be made that the Black Monday of October 19, 1987, was an offspring of the famous Black Tuesday of October 29, 1929. Actually, we would have to go back at least one more day, as the Black Monday of its time, October 28, 1929, was the greatest one-day plunge in stock exchange history—until 58 years later—resulting in a then-devastating crash of 12.8 percent. The reason Black Tuesday (October 28, 1929) is celebrated as the Crash of '29—the Dow tumbled 11.7 percent that day—is that 16.4 million shares were traded, an all-time record volume, not to be witnessed again for the next 35 years.

Although it would be intrinsically interesting, reviewing the past six decades of stock market history would not necessarily tell us what to expect in the next six decades or even the next six months. One fact is clear: the stock market was a significantly different institution before 1982 than it was after. When we look back to '80 and '81, we see average daily volumes in the 30–50 million share range. A review of the shares traded and their turnover rates for the New York Stock Exchange shows a 50 percent increase in turnover and a fourfold increase in trading between 1981 and 1988 (Figure 6–3).

Crudely observed, the trading volume for 1982 was about 39 percent over 1981, while the turnover percentage increased about 30 percent for '82. However, by 1984, trading volume almost doubled that of 1981, and it redoubled by 1987. Along the way turnover percentage more than

FIGURE 6–3
Trading Volumes and Turnover Percentage, NYSE (in Millions)

Year	Shares Traded	Average Shares Listed	Percent Turnover
1981	11,853.7	36,003.5	33
1982	16,458.0	38,907.0	42
1983	21,589.6	42,316.9	51
1984	23,671.0	47,104.8	49
1985	27,510.7	50,759.4	54
1986	35,680.0	56,023.8	64
1987	47,801.3	65,711.4	73
1988	40,849.5	76,093.0	55

Source: Adapted from Phyllis S. Pierce, *Dow Jones Investors Handbook of 1989* (Homewood, Ill.: Dow Jones-Irwin, 1989), p. 79.

doubled from 33 percent in '81 to 73 percent in '87. Most of this increasing activity is attributable to institutional trading, involving increasing turnover rates due to market-timing techniques augmented by risk arbitrage and portfolio insurance practices, according to Metz.

From 1982 through September 1987 assets in mutual funds grew to more than $827 billion, almost tripling for the period. During the same time, mutual funds invested $233 billion in stocks, more than a 400 percent increase since the end of '82. About 800 U.S. institutions held portfolios of stocks greater than $100 million by the end of '86. According to consultants Amen & Associates (Greenwich, Connecticut), by 1987 almost 40 percent, or more than $500 billion, of assets under management by 786 of the largest institutions were placed in index funds.

In April 1982 the Chicago Mercantile Exchange (CME) introduced the S&P 500 futures contract, a metaphorical iceberg if ever there was one. The next year saw the introduction of other index future contracts and stock index options. There had been option trading before but never anything approaching the scale of these products. Thus the era of derivative instruments began, a tail that would come to wag the dog, the New York Stock Exchange.

In his book, *Black Monday*, Metz points out that,

> Volume of all stock index futures contracts in 1986 would reach 26.5 million contracts, more than quadruple the 1982 level. Index options trading would grow almost tenfold from 1983 through 1986. And, reflecting the relentless advance of institutional trading, the NYSE block trades of 5,000 or more shares accounted for 49.9 percent of the total volume of 1986, up from 41 percent in 1982.[5]

Arbitrage is the noble art of profiting from differences in prices for the same object in different places, or from equivalent items with divergent values over time. It happens that a ''basket'' of S&P 500 stocks and an equal representation of S&P 500 futures have divergences in value because they are traded in different markets with different trading objectives and costs. We do not want to get bogged down in the fine points of program trading, but it is worthwhile understanding the general practice, if only to see how insidious and indifferent to investing values it is.

---

[5]Metz, *Black Monday*, p. 63.

The S&P 500 Index is a weighted index of 500 stocks mostly listed on the NYSE. The S&P 500 futures contracts are bets on where the S&P 500 Index will be during the life of the future's contract. It happens that if the S&P 500 futures price varies a certain amount, say 75 basis points, from "fair value" of the S&P 500 Index, then it can be profitable for an institution to buy $10 to $20 million of one and sell an equivalent amount of the other to lock in the difference. As Metz puts it

> Therefore, if the futures price spikes to, say, 171.75, or a premium of 1.75 points over the index itself, then look for the index arbitrageur to sell futures in Chicago and buy stocks in New York. Or if it drops to 168.25 or less, look for buying in Chicago and program selling on the NYSE. Assuming the full-point fair-value estimate does in fact reflect all the costs of such trades, the index arb's profit is a bit over $44,000 on a $10 million position. That may not seem eye-popping, but what if the arb could do that every day? A $44,000-a-day return over 250 trading days is more than $11 million, or a low-risk return on investment above 110 percent of the $10 million of capital being risked.[6]

Obviously, an institution would not need to program trade every day. Every other day or even once a week would provide a handsome return, as their capital would draw interest while resting between trades. Of course, such action requires sufficient disparity between the futures and the cash price, but this occurs with some frequency.

Consider that the Brady Commission found that U.S. corporations purchased $274.3 billion more in shares than they issued from the end of 1983 through June 1987. As the volume of trading was multiplying, significant net amounts of stock were being withdrawn from trading through mergers, acquisitions, buy outs, and buy backs. This reduction of shares outstanding, which has continued through 1988 and 1989, is considered to be a long-term positive for higher stock prices, based on the classical economics of a reduced supply meeting increasingly available funds for investing in stocks. For some participants, the stock buy-out–buy-back trend was a strong reason for buying or holding stock positions as the market advanced and corporations were being bought out left and right.

In a sense, the decreasing number of shares available for trading was more than compensated for by the increasing number of futures and index option contracts being traded. The near risk-free profits from pro-

---

[6]Metz, *Black Monday*, pp. 73–74.

grammed trading and the sense of security gained from insurance hedging began to increase the stock market's volatility, first seen in the market break of September 11, 1986. On that day the DJIA lost 86.61 points, a record point fall for one day and a percentage decline not seen for decades. There was also record trading volume of 237.6 million shares. The next day the DJIA dropped another 34.17, on another record volume day of 240.5 million shares traded.

The press correctly blamed programmed trading for the dramatic drops on record volume for September 11 and September 12, but neither the SEC nor the markets admitted that or did anything about it. The SEC blamed investor's fears of higher interest rates on the September '86 break, although they conceded that programmed trading may have reduced the time period in which investors adjusted to those fears. In fact, institutions, the stock exchange, and the SEC seemed to support programmed trading and portfolio insurance, both of which grew in size and frequency. Why not? They were money-makers (profit centers) for all concerned.

In August '87, portfolio insurance assets under management grew to more than $60 billion—with some estimates as high as $90 billion—from a 1984 level of a mere $200 million in assets. Contributing to the growth of programmed trading and portfolio insurance was (and is) the New York Stock Exchange's Designated Order Turnaround (DOT) system. The DOT system was begun in 1976 to provide specialists an efficient way to complete small orders, under 200 shares, thus permitting floor traders more time to work on bigger orders. The NYSE began lifting the size limit, first to 599 shares, then 1,099 shares, and by October 1987 to 2,099. By 1984 the exchange made programmed trading easy by modifying the DOT system so that groups of stocks can be traded instead of single stocks.

When more stocks are traded on the exchange, traders, brokers, and specialists all benefit from increased trading commissions. However, this increase in programmed trading and portfolio insurance can exceed stock specialists' liquidity capabilities. As Metz puts it,

> Their buy programs in New York will send the stock market soaring and the portfolio insurers scampering back into the pit to trigger the whole mutually reinforcing cycle again and again. This year alone, the Dow will rise nearly 850 points, or 43.5 percent, to its August 25 peak.[7]

---

[7]Metz, *Black Monday*, p. 86.

Some people have said—without really thinking it through, I believe—that the bull market (or rally) of '85 to '87 was merely driven by derivative instruments that permitted programmed trading and portfolio insurance hedging to drive prices higher. Their argument is that there wasn't much outcry when buy programs were pushing up the DJIA, and therefore one should not be critical when these same programs—only this time sell programs—pushed the DJIA down.

The stock market is a very complex process involving hundreds and thousands of competing forces. From my point of view, programmed and portfolio insurance trading certainly increased the market's volatility (and programmed trading continues to do so), with sharp advances and declines. Still, both the fundamental values of corporations and their earning potentials supported the great advances made during this market cycle. Corporate growth, augmented by the growth of money supply and declining interest rates, essentially fueled the advance. That is why, after the unprecedented crash, the market was able to begin advancing for the next year and one half, regaining all losses on a total return basis that had been generated by the crash.

After all is said and done, programmed trading only intensified the swings and increased the turnover rate. The reason I believe the market could have gone to DJIA 2700 in '87, with or without programmed trading, is because the Dow earnings were estimated at over $200 for '88, and a slightly below long-term average price/earnings multiple of 13.5 would see the DJIA at 2700. With even higher earnings projected for '89—assuming the economic environment, including Federal Reserve policy, were not hostile—the DJIA could easily trade at 18 times earnings, or something well over 3600.

The Titanic and the iceberg comparison to the Crash of '87 echoes the realization that a sequence of events that didn't quite have to happen resulted in a great sinking tragedy. Aside from design flaws in the ship including the insufficiency of lifeboats, there were questions about the radio room being too busy with congratulatory cables to pay enough attention to iceberg warnings, warnings about the speed of the ship in such dangerous waters and about the lookout procedures.

We can see design flaws in the markets—the relationships between Chicago and New York—that permitted vicious cycle waves of panic selling leading almost to the sinking of New York Stock Exchange. We can also witness the seemingly independent events, with the benefit of hindsight, that led to that somewhat inevitable outcome.

In the weeks and days preceding the Crash of '87, an almost unbelievable series of events were unleashed against the normative mode of stock investing. Alan Greenspan, newly appointed Federal Reserve Board (FRB) chairman, led his fellows to raise the discount rate by 1/2 percent to 6 percent just before Labor Day, signalling higher interest rates and increasing the attractiveness of bonds over stocks. About October 9th, rumors begin circulating that the House Ways and Means Committee was crafting a bill to eliminate the tax benefits permitted those doing deals with debt-financed leveraged buy outs. By October 13th, these rumors were confirmed, as takeover candidates (a few of which crashed 45 percent on Meltdown Monday) had fallen 5 percent in the previous days.

The next day—Wednesday, October 14—the U.S. balance of trade deficit was announced as $15.7 billion, more than $1 billion above consensus estimates. The trade deficit shocker led to the 30-year Treasury bond yielding over 10 percent for the first time in 23 months. These events drove the DJIA to a record 95-point loss on not very impressive volume of 207 million shares. According to the Brady Commission study, portfolio insurers sold about $250 million in S&P 500 contracts, while index arbitrageurs used $1.4 billion worth of stocks in program selling, one sixth of the exchange's total trading.

Adding fuel to the fire the next day—Thursday, October 15— Chemical Bank raised its prime rate 1/2 percent to 9 3/4 percent. Already troubled by Secretary of the Treasury Baker's public argument with German financial leaders, stock market participants were further alarmed when the administration announced it had no plans to further reduce the budget deficit. And then, as if adding water to a listing ship, Friday the 16th began with news of an Iranian attack on a U.S. (flagged) protected oil tanker and an emergency meeting of national security officers and President Reagan to determine a probable military response.

Several market analysts had announced that below 2400 was a buying opportunity, and chartist traders thought the 2280–2300 should be as far as the correction would go. Some of these technicians acted on their signals and stepped into the market only to get creamed by programmed selling that in the final 90 minutes drove the DJIA to 2246.74, down a record 108.35 points. The SEC found out later that portfolio insurers sold more than 9,000 S&P 500 contracts worth around $1.3 billion, plus at least another $151 million worth of stock in New York. Keeping up their end of the strategy, index arbitrageurs completed sell programs worth some $1.37 billion.

As chance would have it, I was in Boston on Friday the 16th, and as I dropped into a brokerage office just after the close, I heard several interested onlookers mention in relieved tones that the market had come back on the close. Indeed, in the final 10 minutes the DJIA recovered 22 points, giving hope for a bounce-back rally the following Monday. The SEC findings were that in the final half hour, program traders did 43 percent of the NYSE's total volume.

Metz writes that Friday's massacre should have been far worse, as portfolio insurers should have sold many more contracts during the week than they did, based upon their formulas. He adds, "Among insiders there is no question that the market will plunge on the coming Monday."[8]

SUMMING UP THE CRASH OF '87

Many philosophers have written that we are all fatalists about the past, meaning that once an event has occurred it usually seems obvious that it was bound to happen. From the vantage point of hindsight, the Crash of '87 seems inevitable. From the remembrance of daily events leading up to the crash, its inevitability was not at all clear, and subsequent events have confirmed that the crash was a technical accident rather than a fundamental economic signal. In the two years that have passed since Meltdown Monday, the principal concerns have been a too robust economy threatening an intolerable level of inflation.

In response to the crash, the pessimistic consensus called for a recession beginning in the last quarter of '87—and thereafter each subsequent quarter of '88 and '89—and has given way in the spring of '89 to concerns of too much optimism and therefore the imminent likelihood of economic boom and inflation. Due to the economic slowdown by late June, this consensus flipped again to dire threats of recession and falling profits. Well, sooner or later there will be significant market corrections and economic recessions, but it will be hard to blame them on the Crash of '87.

Nevertheless, the next time the major averages are trading near or above 20 times earnings, yielding 3 percent or less in dividends, and trading above 2.5 times book value, we should certainly be prepared for

---

[8]Metz, *Black Monday,* p. 91.

a significant and probably severe stock market decline. These dangerous fundamental considerations should be examined in terms of the market-wide technical conditions of the time. One lesson learned from the Crash of '87 is that some technical indicators give off buy signals as the market declines and becomes oversold, while others warn of the likelihood of further weakness. Penetration of 150- and 200-day moving averages in both the DJIA and the NYSE Composite Index, as well as new 52-week lows becoming greater than new 52-week highs, augment the storm signals of the major corrective downtrend from too-high fundamental criteria.

To all this we must factor in Federal Reserve Board policy and the general economy. We should avoid knee-jerk reactions such as comparing 1929 to 1987 when their economies were significantly different and trending in opposite directions. With the strength gained in recognizing dangerous waters, avoiding the iceberg of October '87, and recognizing the overdoneness of Meltdown Monday and Turnaround Tuesday, we can then be prepared to react logically to such a market "break" and take advantage of the once-in-a-decade values created by such a panic. We need not have been heroic and bought at the bottom in October, but we could have been logical and bought blue chips after the retest of October 26, and secondary stocks after the bottoming confirmation of December 4.

A BIT OF PERSPECTIVE

I asked earlier, What can we learn from the Crash of '87? Much of the answer to that question has been given in the paragraphs above. With the hindsight of 22 months, we can learn that the crash wasn't the end of the financial world, or even of an economic era. By September 1989 all major indexes have recovered all their crash losses on a total return basis and most have gone on to make new all-time highs. That's not to say that everyone was restored to pre-crash wealth. After all, even if one held all positions and suffered no realized losses, getting back to even, either on the indexes or in dollar amounts after 20 months, is not exactly making money.

As we have pointed out in reviewing the returns of various financial instruments, we should be aware of real—or inflation-adjusted—returns rather than nominal returns. The dollar of summer 1989 probably buys only 90 cents worth of the goods the dollar of summer 1987 bought.

Still, compared to the investors who sold out during or just after the crash, locking in their losses and not participating in the subsequent advances, the long-term shareholders need hardly have been highly disturbed by the traumatic events. And if speculators had the wherewithal and foresight to pick up some more bargains after the crash, they could be holding significant unrealized gains overall, even as the averages show the markets to be slightly above where they were pre-crash.

My portfolio was badly damaged by the Crash of '87. I had the double misfortune of being fully margined with a preponderance of over-the-counter secondary stocks. A large number of my margined stocks were driven below $5 per share, making them unmarginable, which radically reduced the equity supporting the debit balance (margin loan value) and thus created large minimum maintenance calls (see Chapter 5). I had to sell large amounts of stocks at just about their market-cycle lows and so did not have them working in my favor in the subsequent market advance. Even so, the total returns for 12.5 years including the crash have significantly surpassed those of the major market averages.

Some friends suggest I should not write about my setback during the Crash of '87 because too many people seem to focus on that event. Many people equate the use of margin with gambling. I have been called a "river-boat gambler" by one allegedly conservative investment advisor. All I can do is remind readers that my view of the use of leverage is that I am a businessperson employing borrowed funds to enhance my business. If borrowing to open another carefully considered branch store or to take advantage of improving one's inventory at bargain prices is gambling—then so be it. But I believe that what I am following is the same strategy employed when great corporations borrow—raise cash through the sale of bonds or commercial paper—to expand their plants or services.

As is true for anyone who borrows, we must be careful not to borrow more than we can likely repay, and we must guard against changing conditions that would cause us to make forced liquidations during market lows. Having experienced this phenomenon once is no reason to quit being logical and businesslike, even as one becomes more careful and takes greater precautions against becoming overextended. "Once burnt, twice shy" is okay as a guideline, but "If you fall off a horse, get right back on" is a better life and stock market motto for learning from experience and overcoming adversity.

CHAPTER 7

TWELVE YEARS AND COUNTING

As long as I can remember, life has always seemed a little unreal, as if I were taking part in a play which later I could hardly believe had happened. And so it is with my role as an investment advisor and stock speculator. Providence, in the form of a friend, led me, as a relatively penniless, aging grad student, to buy a few shares of stock with a few hundred dollars, surplus funds from my GI Bill and meager part-time earnings.

I was a 38-year-old UCLA grad student studying philosophy of education when I had several practical and serendipitous conversations about the stock market with my fellow teaching assistant, Tom Haldi. All this led to my Ph.D. sponsor, Professor George Kneller, a veteran of three decades in the market, encouraging me to open an account. He sent me to one of his bright young brokers, Peter Palmer, at the old Francis I. duPont office in Beverly Hills. There I opened a pathetically small account with the few hundred dollars which had been burning a hole in my pocket.

I can hardly believe how ignorant I was about the stock market at the age of 38. It did not matter that I had owned two businesses, worked for several major corporations since I turned 18, and had earned two master's degrees. I was quite naive when Mr. Palmer put me into the old Enterprise Fund, saying this fund has doubled in each of the past two years and implying—or did I just imagine he said?—that it would likely double again during the next 12 months. My first purchase was $300 worth of Enterprise Fund (22.239 shares) on December 12, 1968. It turned out that in 1969 the old Enterprise Fund made a "round trip" and instead of doubling, it lost a significant portion of its net asset value.

APPRENTICESHIP

Next, Peter said something like, "Let's buy some Whittaker; it's at 27, down from 37, and we may never see this price again." That sounded good to me, so I bought 30 shares at $25 per share in June 1969 and—Peter was right—I never saw that price again (while I owned it). The stock continued to decline to 1⅛ by December 1984. Now Peter had my full attention.

Thus began the Whittaker Saga and my dogged determination to learn this game. By December, convinced that Whittaker wouldn't go much lower, I bought another 30 shares at $19.75 and another 20 on December 23, 1969 for $15.625. By September 8, 1970, I was able to buy another 100 shares of Whittaker at $7.375. Whittaker was probably around fair value when I bought the next 20 shares at $6.75 on December 22, 1970. WKR must have rallied a bit because I bought another 100 shares on April 2, 1971 at $10.75. Nothing if not persistent, I bought another 100 shares of WKR on June 30, 1972 for $8.75 and still another 100 shares on September 14, 1972 at $7.625. On May 24, 1973 (I cannot remember why) I sold my supply of WKR for $1,007.33, taking a long-term capital loss of $2,683.50.

Selling Whittaker in May of '73 left me with no lasting lesson. Three months later, I could not resist buying 300 shares of WKR at $3 on August 29, 1973 and then another 200 shares at $2.50 on December 4, 1973. One more time, I picked up my final 100 shares of WKR on February 26, 1974 at $2.50. Thus, I had accumulated 800 shares since having sold out my earlier positions. By November of '74, just at the end of the great bear market of '73–'74, I sold out again, first 400 shares for $602.71 on November 19, 1974, creating a long-term capital loss of $1,101.95, and then on November 25, 1974 the final 400 shares for $602.72, creating a long-term capital loss of $547.16.

The irony of this series of Whittaker trades is that I bought overvalued shares at the beginning, was impatient, and sold them when they were undervalued. I then bought undervalued shares, was impatient, and sold them when they were more undervalued, just at the end of a great bear market, which was followed by a great bull market. At that time, I did not know the meaning of the terms *bull* and *bear markets* or for that matter, *market timing*.

By May of '81, Whittaker traded for more than $50 per share. The 800 shares of WKR I sold in November 1974, which had cost $2,854.54, would have been worth $40,000.00, for a long-term capital gain of $37,145.46 or 1,300 percent—not counting dividends or margin leverage—a compounded annual gain of 67 percent per annum for the 6.5–year holding period. Ah, paying those kinds of dues—having taken the repeated losses and missing the great gains—did a lot to develop my patience as a stock speculator.

So, instead of becoming discouraged at what happened to my initial "investments" in '69 through '74, I became intrigued and fascinated. I still felt sheepish and a bit of an imposter entering the august and beautifully appointed offices of Francis I. duPont in Beverly Hills, my old-line prestigious "wire-house" (a.k.a. full-service) brokerage. I would grab all the research reports available in the bins lining the reception area, sheepish that I had only a couple hundred to throw at the market rather than thousands and tens of thousands.

Slowly and unsurely I began to acquire the lingo and read a couple of important books that fortunately made a lot of sense to me, especially Ben Graham's *The Intelligent Investor*. Somehow I managed to escape in these formative years the scourge of chart reading and technical analysis, although in recent years I've become fascinated with technical analysis and wonder if chart reading can be far behind.

And so it went, this vague recollection that, as I studied philosophy, psychology, and history and began writing my dissertation on "The Concept of Consciousness in Higher Education," all the while I had defected intellectually to the seductress stock market. After several years of trying to serve two mistresses, the challenge of stock speculation overwhelmed the challenge of the classroom. Graduate studies (especially many of the courses in philosophy, logic, and ordinary language analysis) and teaching at the university level set the stage for what I've learned and done in speculating and advising.

RECORDED HISTORY

Now the teaching jobs, the two summers spent as an associate professor at Bloomsburg State College, the hundreds of interesting classroom encounters, all seem a lifetime ago. On the other hand, I have for more than 12 years written my newsletter (over 260 issues of *The Prudent Speculator*) and have amassed 20 years worth of trading confirmation slips; yet, in contrast to my perception of my academic years, I have the sense that I have been at this only a few years. Maybe that's what happens when one is having fun.

I'm studying as hard or harder than I ever have, to try to learn more about the mechanics of the stock market and consolidate what I think I know about investing. In fact, one reason for writing this book is to gather together many of the bits and pieces of the past 20 years, focusing them into a recognizable and heuristic tableau, to reinforce my own learning and behavior as well as to help you.

To the end of reviewing actual events in the expectation that what is past is prologue, at least to a meaningful degree, I embark on a sparse review of the 12 + years of publishing *The Prudent Speculator*. I could not imagine 12 years ago that I would be still at it today. Actually, the advisory letter originally was supposed to be a kind of course, which readers would complete in two or three years and thereafter be sufficiently knowledgeable to succeed on their own. I am an advocate of the *Tao Teh King* of Lao Tzu, a tenet of which is, "In teaching, he teaches, not by describing and pointing out differences, but by example." I am a believer in the emphasis on learning as opposed to teaching, eloquently exampled in Carl Roger's *Freedom to Learn*.

By sharing my experiences, learning, and actions—especially because they have turned out to be somewhat successful—I hope to facilitate your learning in terms of the stock market. A distillation of the printed record might better speak for itself, and so we begin with *TPS*, issue 1. As there are over 260 issues of *TPS* I can comment on only a few.

THE FIRST YEAR: 1977

For the first year—actually nine months or 22 issues—of publication, I am going to taste a bit from each issue, showing my thinking at the time and how my advisory letter and stock portfolio developed. This would be too much detail to carry through for the following 11 years, so I will merely summarize the most noteworthy events and recommendations of subsequent years.

I am reminded of short termpapers turned in for college assignments as I look at *TPS 1*, dated March 12, 1977. Typed on a manual typewriter and Xeroxed, only one side of the paper, this "gem" was sent to about 100 friends and acquaintances. A few paragraphs set the stage, which hasn't changed all that much in over 12 years.

Welcome to the *Pinchpenny Speculator* (PS), dedicated to the small speculator. I will express my experience and thinking about "playing" with stocks for fun and profit. My essential commitment is with New York Stock Exchange common stocks. I will take an irreverent view and tone to such goings on, attempting to penetrate mystifications and obfuscations created by jargon and semantics. For example, "playing" is a reasonable term denoting what I and others do when we involve ourselves in buying, selling, and talking about the "market" and stocks. The word investing is frequently used to hide or mask the play of speculating with stocks
 . . . After several years of helter-skelter buying and selling, I learned that successful speculating is more a matter of character than mathematics, analysis, or luck. Obviously the latter are required, but the great gains and losses seem to occur in consequence to individual psychology. This has been my experience; perhaps you recognize it also.
 . . . Essentially, the PS method is to "buy low and sell high." Low refers to "undervalued" (in the market place) stocks, and high refers to fully- or overvalued stocks. These valuations are based upon historical, current, and projected: 1) tangible book value; 2) net working capital; 3) price/earnings ratio; 4) earnings; 5) dividends and dividend policy; 6) price; 7) earned on net-worth percentage; 8) other special considerations unique to the company being analyzed (e.g., management, products, cultural trends); 9) stock market climate; and 10) the individual's needs, capacities, and portfolio. I include items 9) and 10) in the notion of valuation because it is silly to consider any equity independently of them. Thus, any "recommended" stock is in an individual- and market-dependent context.

Pages 3 and 4 of the initial letter review the record of all my sales of common stocks for 1976, Figure 7–1, and my portfolio as of March 11, 1977, displayed in Figure 7–2.
 I thought I was pretty clever back in '77, as I boasted that all sales in '76 resulted in long-term (which was 6 months then) capital gains, having been held from 9 to 19 months. I also pointed out that the gains amounted to 66.43 percent net, since my portfolio was fully margined for the entire period,

> so the gain on invested capital amounted to more than 132 percent. I say *more than* for two reasons: the dividends received were more than the margin interest paid, and some of the stock was bought with surplus in the margin account, that is, leveraged with increases in market values. I must say that 1976 was an "easy" year in which to profit from the terrible declines of '73 and '74, the opportunity of a decade!

FIGURE 7–1
Sales of Common Stocks for 1976

Sold	Shrs Issue	Sale net	Cost net	Gain/Loss	Bought
1/12/76	100 Western Union	$ 1,602.19	$1,092.44	$ 509.75	1/7/75
2/10/76	100 Garfinkle-Brks	1,450.60	1,153.43	297.17	5/28/75
5/ 5/76	100 Avnet Inc.	1,672.74	752.50	920.24	5/28/75
7/27/76	100 Boeing Arcrft	3,976.86	2,056.69	1,920.17	3/ 4/75
9/29/76	100 Western Union	1,980.23	1,257.38	722.85	2/14/75
10/ 7/76	100 Consumers Pwr	2,164.72	1,406.93	757.79	5/9/75
		$12,847.34	$7,719.37	$5,127.97	

Oh man, was I smug. What I did with the proceeds from the "brilliant" trade in Boeing was to buy a brand new Honda 550–4 motorcycle, which at the time cost just about the Boeing profits. What I didn't realize until a while later was that motorcycle cost me about four times what I paid for it as Boeing went on to split twice and reach the equivalent of $120 per share a couple years later. Score another one for long-term holding of undervalued, growing corporations.

On page 4 of the first issue, I began a tradition of displaying my personal, actual ("model" TPS) portfolio. Not only would the triumphs be shown and trumpeted, but the failures would also be highlighted in an effort to learn from sometimes painful trial and error. Figure 7–2 shows

FIGURE 7–2
TPS Portfolio at March 11, 1977

Date BOT	Issue (in 100-Share Lots)	BOT at	3/11/77	+/-
9/28/76	American Medical Int'l	11½	12½	+ 1
10/ 7/76	American Seating	10	11¼	+ 1¼
3/10/74	Chemitron Corp.	30	33⅝	+ 3⅝
9/22/76	Cluett, Peabody & Co.	8¼	9¼	+ 1
9/22/76	Dan River	8⅞	8½	− ⅜
1/17/77	Marathon Mfg.	14	13⅛	− ⅞
9/29/76	McNeill Corp.	12¼	11⅞	− ⅜
9/29/76	Phillips-Van Heusen	10¼	10⅝	+ ⅜
10/ 7/76	Triangle Industries	10⅛	9¼	− ⅞
3/31/75	United Financial of Cal.	7⅜	11¾	+ 4⅜
9/ 8/76	United Financial of Cal.	11⅛	11¾	⅝
9/13/76	Western Pacific Ind's.	11½	18½	+ 7
		$14,525.00	$16,200.00	$1,675.00

at March 11, 1977, how my stock portfolio was listed. The portfolio was fully margined, with equity actually at $8,006. "For the ten weeks in 1977, the portfolio has a 'paper profit' of $575 or 48 cents per share, while the Dow Jones Industrial Average has declined 56.96 points (947.72) and the Average Price per Share of Common has declined $1.91 on the New York Stock Exchange."

To look at the March 11, 1977 portfolio can be shocking if one thinks about the corporations and their stocks that are no longer with us, or so changed as to be for all practical purposes different entities. In just 12 "short years" American Seating, Chemitron, Cluett, Peabody & Company, Dan River, Marathon Manufacturing, McNeill, United Financial of California, Triangle Industries, and Western Pacific Industries no longer exist as independent corporations—9 out of 11 gone! American Medical International and Phillips-Van Heusen are still listed, but they too are under threat of being bought out or "restructured."

TPS 2 (March 26, 1977) features a review on tangible book value (TBV), and quotes the 1971 *NASD Training Guide*, "Because investors place greater importance on the earning power of a corporation, book value and market value per share are usually not related" (p. 19). Of course, some investors focus mainly on book value or asset plays in their stock selection. Phillips-Van Heusen (PVH) and Dan River (DML) were recommended as buys. PVH at 10⅜ was trading for "less than half its TBV and for less than net working capital" with a P/E of 8 and yielding 5.78 percent. DML traded for P/E 5 and 40 percent of TBV. Hard to find those kinds of bargains in the past few years.

Net working capital (NWC)—sometimes called net liquidating value—was the featured topic of *TPS 3* (April 9, 1977). You could find many corporations in those days trading for less per share than the difference between current assets and all liabilities, a fundamental relationship Benjamin Graham sought. Still,

> It is important to note that a company can prosper with a negative NWC, and its stock may be an attractive purchase based upon other criteria. Western Pacific Industries (WPI), with a TBV of some $50.00 per share, and a negative NWC is an example. WPI advanced from 6 to 18⅞ during the recent 15 months.

Who could have known that WPI would go on to be bought out for $163 per share in cash, after paying a $23 return-of-equity "dividend" per share on December 31, 1979?

Hughes & Hatcher (HGH) at 7, and Kroehler Manufacturing (KFM) at 14⅛ were recommended at April 9, 1977. Both traded for less than half their TBVs and about 2/3 their NWCs.

By *TPS 4* (April 23, 1977), the P/E ratio was assayed with a degree of breathless amazement.

> On April 15, 1977, the P/E for Dow Jones Industrials was 9.8, compared to 13.0 on April 15, 1976, and 8.2 on April 15, 1975. These figures show quite a variation over just a 24-month period. Furthermore, the P/Es of DJIA stocks currently range from 4 for Chrysler to 26 for Eastman Kodak.

Reviewing further, I found

> P/E can be a tricky figure. For example, the P/E for Lowenstein & Sons (LST) was 21 at the week ending February 25, 1977. During the next week, LST's P/E became 5, when it reported annual earnings of $2.50 a share for 1976, versus a deficit for the same period 1975. On the other hand, Triangle Industries' P/E of 18 became zero during October, 1976, when its nine-months' *earnings* were published.

The recommended stocks for April 23, 1977 were American Medical International, (AMI) at 13¼, around its book value with a P/E of 8, and United Financial of California (UFL) at 14⅝, at 75 percent of TBV and P/E 5.

TPS 5 (May 7, 1977) dealt with earnings and the unexpected buyout bid for dull-trading Hughes & Hatcher, recommended four weeks earlier, which jumped its price from 7 to 10¾ (54 percent). I quoted my favorite mentor, Benjamin Graham, "Don't take a single year's earnings seriously. . . . If you do pay attention to short-term earnings, look out for booby traps in the per share figure." Marathon Manufacturing (MTM) at 16¼, 60 percent of tangible book value and P/E 5, and McNeil Corp. (MME) at 12⅛ or 50 percent of TBV and P/E 6, were the recommended stocks for May 7, 1977.

"Dividends and Dividend Policy" was the essay for *TPS 6* (May 21, 1977), using non-dividend paying Western Pacific Industries (WPI) as a high appreciation example compared to high-dividend paying Western Union (WU) with a dividend yield of 7.8 percent as a low total return example. In conclusion,

> An important argument is made that a good yield puts a floor under the market price of a stock, however, when all is said and done, The

Pinchpenny Speculator looks principally for stocks he hopes will appreciate significantly, and lets whatever incidental dividends accrue balance the ravages of his margin interest.

By May 21, 1977, Wurlitzer (WUR) at 8¾, 50 percent of TBV and P/E 5, and Triangle Industries. (TRI) at 9½, about 40 percent of TBV and P/E negative, made the recommended page.

TPS 7 (June 4, 1977) celebrated "our first quarter" and espoused the speculation strategy of the margin account, touching on some of the basics revealed in Chapter 5. TPS Portfolio was updated, noting that American Seating (AMZ) was tendered for $15.00 per share net on May 20, 1977. "This year's gain (so far) of 10 percent is modest, but delightful, when compared to the other averages, which show a loss of 8–9 percent . . ."

By June I was aware that recommending two stocks an issue did not nearly represent the population of recommendable stocks I'd been discovering. I was becoming frustrated that some formerly recommendable stocks had already advanced in price too far to be currently recommended. So I listed 71 "closely followed stocks" that "are not all recommended at this time!" Still, I believed "many of them [are] appropriate commitments, depending upon the individual's situation."

TPS 8 (June 18, 1977) was rather upbeat.

> Take Friday the 17th, for example. I was delighted that the market traded almost 22 million shares and though the DJIA was unchanged on Friday the 17th, the average share of common gained five cents. . . . The DJIA continues to mask market appreciation as the broader averages show greater increases, especially among the so-called secondary stocks.

The essay was on price, mostly in relationship to fundamentals. Salant (SLT) at 7⅛ and Faberge at 8⅝ were recommended stocks.

"Serendipity" was the title of a paragraph in *TPS 9* (July 2, 1977).

> I was talking to a wave theorist the other day, a market watcher who claims to follow apparent (chartable or graphable) wave actions based upon price and volume, etc. He suggested that the smaller capitalized and lesser-traded stocks may avoid the consequences or implications of wave theory. I thought to myself, well, these stocks just don't make sufficient waves! But they do often get results nonetheless, and sometimes counter to the apparent trend. And I was pleased to read in the current issue of *Forbes* that people who are too concerned with the 'market' and where it is going, often miss good opportunities present in individual stocks.

The essay for July 2, 1977 was titled "Earned on Net Worth" (ENW) and the two recommended stocks were Spring Mills (SMI) at 12¼, and Gibraltar Financial Corporation of California (GFC) at 10⅜. I suggested readers regard "the pinchpenny angle" when checking out ENW. For instance, SMI for '76 had net income of $15.1 million and net worth of $284.4 million for an ENW of 5.3 percent. "However, SMI's net worth, which was about $32.80 per share, could have been purchased at Friday's close for $14.25." This works out to an earned on the cost of net worth of 12.23 percent. "The astute speculator will look for these relationships which are not immediately apparent in the published ENW percent."

"A funny thing happened to the NYSE on the way to the Bastille Day rally–New York City had an energy knockout which kept the Exchange dark." Thus began *TPS 10* (July 16, 1977), which spent two full pages (out of the four published then) on "some reflections on the individual and the market." The essay called for trying to get our thinking straight about stocks and the market and took a swipe at the system. (This theme is reiterated more forcefully in Chapter 8.)

> I do not like stock brokerage houses nor the role of account executives, because I believe there is an essential conflict of interest in their functions. The account executive generally works on commission and only makes a living if he can have customers who trade stocks, bonds, and options. He cannot say, "The market looks blah; why don't you go to Europe for a year and forget it!" He would be out of business.

Cluett, Peabody & Company (CLU) at 11 and Franklin Mint (FM) at 11⅛ were the recommended stocks on July 16, 1977.

The market tumbled a bit in the fortnight preceding July 30, 1977 when *TPS 11* was published.

> On Wednesday occurred something akin to panic selling, as the DJIA dropped 19.75 points, ending down 33.35 for the week, making a new 18-month low. The heavy, across-the-board declines have been attributed to the tremendous trade deficits (estimated at possibly 25 billion dollars this year); the poor showing of steel companies, with the second largest, Bethlehem Steel, cutting its dividend; a surprising jump in the money supply; and the second monthly decline in leading economic indicators.
>
> Meanwhile, second quarter earnings are generally good, inflation seems under control, unemployment is steady, and stocks are historically cheap. Not to panic, a time to pick up more bargains at even better prices. TPS recommends purchase and accumulation of underpriced, recommended issues.

The essay for July 30, 1977 was entitled "The Individual's Psychology", and began,

> As an investment adviser, I am often disappointed when individuals tell me they are not interested in the stock market because they "took a bath" or "lost my shirt" a few years ago. As a speculator, I am secretly pleased that there are so many such people because they contribute to the recurring opportunities in undervalued stocks.

It's déjà vu, all over again, as Yogi Berra is said to have said. I might write the same sentence in a current edition of *TPS*, except for the scars remaining from the Crash of '87. I cited the example of Consolidated Edison (ED), the NYC utility that traded between $6–$8 per share during the last eight months of '74 after its directors omitted the June dividend. "Today, ED trades at 23⅝ and pays a $2 dividend, a yield of 25 to 33 percent annually, based on the fall and winter of '74 price."

The recommended stocks for July 30, 1977 were Zale (ZAL) at 14¾, and Morse Shoe, (MRS) at 10⅜.

By August 13, 1977 and *TPS 12,* I am still marveling at the average daily volume during the summer decline of less than 19 million shares and how encouraging it is "that there is little apparent rush to sell large amounts of stock at lower prices." I am still exploring "some psychological aspects of speculation, especially the toos, too much procrastination or too little patience." Again, Western Pacific Industries (WPI) is cited as having traded between 6 and 10¾ in '74, between 6 and 8¾ in '75, between 6 and 14 ⅞ in '76, and between 14 and 23⅞ so far this year.

> Clearly one might have stuck with WPI through '74 and '75, at whatever purchase price, and see it more than double or triple in value two or three years later. . . . It is still selling for only four times earnings and looking good otherwise . . . so even though the stock has doubled in price since last September (1976) when it was bought for 11½—it sold for 9½ on October 15! (1976)—it may well double again in the next year or so, and should be held in spite of the 15 percent retrenchment suffered during the recent three weeks.

Western Pacific Industries, (WPI) at 20¾, and Dean Witter Organization (DW) at 12½ were the two stocks recommended in *TPS* as of August 13, 1977. Ironically, we noted that DW is a holding company that has never had an unprofitable year since its founding in 1924. Later, Dean Witter became Dean Witter Reynolds and still later Sears Roebuck acquired that major brokerage at a handsome profit for long-time DW stock owners.

"How come you never ask me about the market?" inquired the speculator to his friend. "How's the market?" "Don't ask!" This was the mood when *TPS 13* (August 27, 1977) was published. The theme for this issue was "Some Thoughts on When to Sell a Stock," and it included such gems as, "In order to determine when to sell a stock, consider the reasons for which it was bought." Of course, that was a takeoff of Gerald M. Loeb's notion of "The Ruling Reason" for buying and owning a stock, the violation of which should lead to the immediate sale of the stock. The ruling reason could be a level or trend of profitability or asset valuation which, if broken or diminished, should lead to getting out of that position.

In *TPS 13* the 20 stocks recommended during the first six months were reviewed. Happily, the overall recommendations appreciated 2.03 percent during a period in which the DJIA declined 7.19 percent and the New York Stock Exchange Composite Index lost 2.45 percent.

TPS 14 (September 10, 1977) mentions watching *Wall $treet Week* and being

> . . . struck again with the wisdom of the venerable and sanguine Philip Carret, who offered as his major single piece of advice to the investor, "Patience." If one has made a good stock selection, he should be unaffected by transitory market conditions or fluctuations in the price of the stock—trading frequently is not the way to consistently make money in the market, although there are no doubt traders who do. Of course, if one discovers an error in his selection, or conditions alter radically, he must be prepared to accept change and act accordingly.

The essay for *TPS 14*, "A Game Plan, or Two," was based on one of those tables I love to construct and review, showing 10 years of compounded annual returns. The recommended stocks were Armstrong Rubber (ARM) at 28, Avco (AV) at 15⅛, and Sterchi Brothers Store (SBI) at 9, each recommended without any fundamental criteria because page 4 was used to review TPS Portfolio. It showed additions of Marathon Manufacturing (MTM), Morse Shoe (MRS), and Zale (ZAL); the tender of American Seating (AMZ); and the sales of Chemitron (CTN), Triangle Industries (TRI), and United Financial (UFL). Alas, I reported

> Chemitron (CTN) was sold the day before the first Crane Co. tender offer was made. . . . CTN closed yesterday at 48½. My impatience cost some

$2,000 on one stock in one month, after owning CTN patiently for some 29 months. I didn't have an inkling of the takeover bid; however, the numbers indicated that CTN was a good stock to own at $30.00 a share on August 1, 1977. I present this information in all candor that readers, clients, and I may learn from my experience. The American Seating was a tender offer by the company itself; it seemed wise to take the 100 percent (margined) profit. I sold Triangle Industries and United Financial (100 shares each) to obtain funds.

The broad market and DJIA stocks were still declining by September 24, 1977 when *TPS 15* opened with

"If you can keep your head when all about you are losing theirs . . ." you may not know what they know. But then, they may not realize what you have either. It is trying to watch the general averages declining all year long and keep shouting that they are only telling half the truth. Look at the new highs (e.g., United Financial, UFL, closed Friday at a new high, 16 ⅝, up 38.5 percent this year) . . .

The first one-page essay for September 24, 1977 was "Lifestyle and Speculating," still another attempt to show that *speculator* was a better term than *investor* and not to be associated with gambling or other pejoratives. The second one-page essay was "The Art Is Learning from Experience" and reviewed my Whittaker Corporation (WKR) experience but extended it to a missed Act II, "missed" because I had quit after Act I.

WKR worked its way to $1.125 per share by December, '74. Did I know that WKR had a book value about $5.00 per share, paid no dividend, sold for over 16 times earnings, and had a negative net working capital? I do not remember even being aware of those kinds of facts when I started buying the stock. All I knew is that WKR had sold for higher prices, was a "bargain," and was recommended by a man who was recommended to me by a man who made a lot of money in the market during the '60s.

Nor was I aware that by December '74, WKR was selling for three times earnings and only 20 percent of book value, making it a good speculation near the bottom of a great and exhausted bear market. As hindsight shows, WKR tripled in market value between December 1974 and May 1975, about five months, to $4.625 per share. I was only "aware" in December 1974 that I had bought and sold WKR at ever-decreasing prices (e.g., 3.50 on May 24, 1973; 1.625 on November 25, 1974), and would not go near the stock again because I had been "burnt" so much already. So I was emotionally blocked from having perspective about profiting, no matter what the numbers suggested. I see a lot of that kind of thinking and acting still going on, as people who took big losses in the early '70s and missed out on the big gains since then are still unable to recognize fundamental values in the market.

The three recommendations mentioned in the previous issue were detailed as recommendations on September 24, 1977: Armstrong Rubber (ARM) at 26⅛, Avco (AV) at 15, and Sterchie Brothers Stores, (SBI) at 9. It was startling to see that ARM traded with a P/E of 3.46 and for less than 50% of tangible book value, while AV's P/E was 2.62 and traded for less than TBV, and SBI with a P/E of 6.56 traded for less than net working capital. Those were the days.

"The Market versus the Stock" was the theme for *TPS 16* (October 8, 1977), expanding on the maxim, "This is a market of stocks, and not a stock market." I noted that while the DJIA hit 21-month lows, 79 stocks made new 52-week highs during the week ended September 30, 1977.

> The reasons I cannot predict what The Market will do are the same reasons that are given every day by market commentators (post hoc) as to why the market advanced, was unchanged, or declined. Example: Friday morning (October 7, 1977) the pre-opening news was: 1) major banks raised their prime rate to 7½ percent, bearish; 2) unemployment figures showed a decline from 7.1 percent to 6.9 percent, bullish; 3) wholesale prices rose 0.5 percent for the reported month, bearish; and 4) the money supply M1 decreased 1.2 billion, bullish. Meanwhile, the Fed is "tightening up," short-term interest rates are rising—bearish. However, construction and consumer credit is up—bullish. Thus, the economy is a) doing well, b) merely getting by, c) pretty shaky. Take your pick. The market opened nicely up, then settled back. It closed off 1 cent, APSC [Average Price per Share Common], virtually unchanged for the day, although many stocks took gains and losses. Who knows what it will do next week?

Rockower Brothers (ROC) at 11½ with a P/E of 5.18 and Pier 1 Imports, (PIR) at 6⅛ with a P/E of 4.94 were the recommended stocks for October 8, 1977.

Another tough fortnight was the message in *TPS 17* (October 22, 1977), with Citibank raising its prime rate to 7¾ percent and *The Wall Street Journal* headline "Consumer Confidence Found at 15-Month Low". The essay pointed out the glories of the "earnings-to-price ratio," or how much in earnings you would get per dollar's cost of stock. The recommended stocks were Allis-Chalmers (AH) at 23 ⅝ with a P/E of 4.75, trading for about 50 percent of TBV, and Cooper Tire & Rubber (CTB) at 12⅜ with a P/E of 2.64, trading for about half of TBV and ⅔ of NWC!

By November 5, 1977, *TPS 18*, the question was, Had the market bottomed on November 2 at DJIA 800.85? The essay, "A Technique within an Approach within a Game within the System," attempted to describe the desirability of focusing on one kind of stock selection augmented by using margin as a form of being in business. The recommended stocks were Oxford Industries (OXM) at 9⅝ with a P/E of 2.38, trading at less than 50 percent of TBV and ⅔ of NWC, and Zayre (ZY) at 6¾ with a P/E of 3.48, trading at less than NWC and less than 30 percent of TBV. Prophetically, I wrote, "The ruling reason for speculating with ZY is that it could be selling for four to six times its current price if it continues to improve as a business and the market climate turns bullish." Zayre's stock appreciated over 2,400 percent between November 15, 1977 (adjusted cost basis $.959 per share) and April 1988, when we closed out the original recommendation at $24.00 per share.

"Finally, the summer rally, and just in time!" was the lead sentence in *TPS 19* (November 19, 1977).

> True, it seems to have lasted only six trading days (Nov. 4–11), but what a week the penultimate one was, including two days of 30-plus-million share days. For those six days, the DJIA gained 43.22 . . . far and away the largest advance of the year.

I'm not sure how many (if any) readers were amused at a summer rally in November, but a quick 5 percent market gain is almost always satisfying. The little essays were "The Market as an Animal" (bull, bear or pig), "The Market as a Condition" (under valued, valued, or overvalued), and "Important to Keep Invested in Under-Valued Markets" (because "For TPS, the week of Nov. 7–11 alone added one-third again as much appreciation earned during the previous 44 weeks of this calendar year").

The recommended stocks for November 19, 1977 were Budd (BF) at 23⅝ with a P/E of 3.87, and International Harvester (HR) at 29⅛ with a P/E of 4.85. The former International Harvester—now renamed Navistar International (NAV)—has yet to work out.

The following fortnight saw the DJIA lose 1.41 percent while TPS Portfolio gained 5.71 percent, although the first week was a winner with the second a loser. The essay in *TPS 20* (December 3, 1977), "Buy 'at Market'," pointed out the pennywise but pound-foolishness of trying to save a few dimes on the cost basis while missing a position that advances several dollars. The recommended stocks were Magic Chef (MGC) at 9⅝ with a P/E of 5.12, and Eastern Air Lines (EAL) at 6¼ with a P/E of 5.10. For the first time I began listing goal prices: $18–$25 for MGC and $18–$27 for EAL. It's interesting to see that MGC did well enough—advancing to $73.00 (658 percent) on May 23, 1986, before being bought out by Maytag (MYG) on June 2, 1986 for 1.671 shares of MYG—as if to compensate for how poorly EAL has performed overall.

TPS 21 (December 17, 1977) reported on a negative market during the first two weeks of December. The theme article was "The Stock Market Waltz Is Rarely in Three-Quarter Time," based on the Spanish proverb, "With patience, everything is possible." The recommended stocks were Cummins Engine (CUM) at 38⅜ with a P/E 4.21 and a goal of $86 + , and Elixir Industries (EXR) at 4⅞ with a P/E of 4.78 and a goal of $11–$14.

The final issue for the year, *TPS 22* was dated December 31, 1977 and reported on a small Santa Claus rally. For the year TPS Portfolio gained 38.71 percent in appreciation with an estimated margined gain of over 77 percent, while the DJIA declined 17.27 percent and the NYSE Composite Index dropped 9.3 percent. There is a small disparity with the audited figures for TPS Portfolio (see Figure I–2) because they date from March 11, 1977 and not for the whole year. "The Recent Year" was reviewed in a few paragraphs pointing out the strong advances for the American Stock Exchange and NASDAQ Composite.

For "The Upcoming Year" my advice was "BUY! The rally so many of us expected for January '77, which did not occur, and the many who do not believe a rally will happen in January '78, combine to make a metaphysical irony too great to resist." TPS Portfolio—fully margined all year—was displayed and reviewed. Based on an equity value of $7,158.61 on December 31, 1976 and a $5,125 appreciation, the gain was 71.59 percent; however, during the year $2,816.16 was withdrawn for living expenses. The 35 stocks that had been recommended during 1977 were reviewed, showing a market appreciation of 7.38 percent, not annualized for time held.

All in all a very good year for TPS Portfolio, especially in comparison with the DJIA and NYSE Composite Index. I didn't save subscription records, but I doubt that there were over 30 paid subscribers and perhaps another 45 copies sent to other newsletter writers or other very important people. Still, I was getting into the swing of things and looking forward to another good year.

THE BEGINNINGS OF A TRACK RECORD: 1978

Some investment books are entertaining, with delightful anecdotes and colorful stories of smart moves that do not actually give much help to the reader in making other future smart moves. Other financial manuals are academic treatises, replete with charts, tables, and statistical analysis, which tend to overwhelm all but the highly trained and mathematically addicted buffs. I am trying to tread a middle ground, with real examples and learning experiences that are recognizable and useful to the not-highly trained financial or stock market student.

Still, investing and speculating in stocks is very much an activity of bookkeeping and number crunching. Plowing through a certain number of tables and technical events in order to gain perspective and insight is a chore well worth undertaking. In Appendix C is a list of all stocks recommended in *The Prudent Speculator* (*TPS*) for the 12.5 years from 1977 through the first six months of 1989 that were still "holds" or currently recommended at the publication deadline for this book. In Appendix D is a list of all stocks recommended in *TPS* since 1977 that have been closed out, through recommended sale, buyout, or merger.

I have not gone into extended analysis of the total return of all *TPS* recommended stocks, dividends included, per period of recommendation, because I feel this would be relatively meaningless and require a large number of caveats that could become very confusing. For instance, almost all of the stocks were recommended more than once at both higher and lower prices than their original recommendation. A large number of the stocks were bought out, mostly for cash, but many with choices of accepting their acquirer's stock completely or partially, or other instruments such as preferred stocks and bonds.

What I believe does have learning value is a list for each year of the stocks being recommended at the beginning of that year, usually obtained from the final issue of *TPS* for the previous year. We can, if interested, compare these annual recommendations with subsequent recommendations and the final disposition of the stocks in question. We can also see how, year after year, certain patterns tend to recur, that generally lead to better-than-market returns over multi-year holding periods. Numbers after names represent stock splits (e.g., 3:2 equals 3-for-2 shares).

For Figure 7–3, which lists stock recommendations for 1977, I've used the original TPS Portfolio at the time of the first issue of *TPS*.

FIGURE 7–3
Stock "Recommendations" for 1977 (Original Price, Split-Adjusted Year-End Values)

Symbol	Corporation	3/11/77	12/31/77	% Change
AMI	American Medical Int'l	12.500	19.500	56.00
AMZ	American Seating	11.250	13.750	22.22
CTN	Chemitron (Al'y Lud'm)	33.625	47.500	41.26
CLU	Cluett, Peabody	9.250	10.625	14.86
DML	Dan River	8.500	11.625	36.76
MTM	Marathon Mfg. 3:2	13.125	25.125	91.43
MME	McNeill Corp.	11.875	12.125	2.11
PVH	Phillips-Van Heusen	10.625	9.250	−12.94
TRI	Triangle Industries	9.250	7.250	−21.62
UFL	United Fin'l of Cal.	11.750	16.500	40.43
WPI	Western Pacific Ind's	18.500	24.750	33.78
	Average	13.695	18.00	27.66

Notice that the 11 positions are all in so-called secondary stocks, with no large capitalization, blue chip stocks owned. Inadvertently, though I would love to claim it was by design, I had chosen that segment of the market to be in during 1977. We have noted elsewhere that the "total reinvested percent change" for the DJIA for 1977 (full year) was −12.84 percent according to Lipper Analytical Securities Corporation. The equivalent return for the S&P 500 was −7.2 percent, while for small company stocks it was +25.4 percent, according to Ibbotson Associates' *Stocks, Bonds, Bills, and Inflation: 1989 Yearbook (SBBI)*. All subsequent quotes for common stocks (S&P 500) and small company stocks (representing small capitalization stocks) are taken from *SBBI*.

Obviously, with the 27.66 percent market appreciation for TPS Portfolio for some nine months of '77 my portfolio outperformed the major averages and, with the leverage of margin, the actual audited rate of return was +70.28 percent. If you review much of the stock market commentary for 1977 you will find that the year was considered a difficult period, but, of course, that was true only of the large capitalization portion of the stock market. The old cliche, "A market of stocks, not a stock market" can be seen as important and meaningful in '77.

1978 WAS ANOTHER TOUGH MARKET YEAR

The tremendous gains of '75 and '76—following '73–'74, the worst market period since the '30s—were still being corrected in '78. We note that the DJIA made a total return of only +2.81 percent, while the S&P 500 did a bit better with +6.6 percent, both well below their 50-year average returns. Simultaneously, very small capitalization stocks continued to prosper, with a total return of +23.5 percent. The market was jarred in October with the first of its "October Massacres," a sharp and swift selloff that was repaired over the succeeding months.

There were 30 stocks being recommended in *TPS* as '77 drew to a close—these form the recommendations for '78—including 3 in TPS Portfolio. This batch (see Figure 7–4) was to garner a market appreciation of only 12.96 percent (not including dividends or reinvestment), performing far better than the big cap stocks but only a bit over half as well as the small company stocks. The 3 stocks still recommended from 1977's list (Figure 7–3) all showed gains, the early evidence of an important pattern now known as time diversification (see Chapter 3).

Also worthy of note are the losses registered in several stocks that went on to become big winners over the years. Cooper Tire and Rubber, Dean Witter Reynolds, and Elixir Industries are examples of stocks that fit this pattern. Of course, some winners in '78 turned sour in succeeding years, such as Gibraltar Financial, while many other stocks that showed little appreciation in their first year of recommendation provided handsome total returns in the months and years to come.

1979 WAS A SOLID STOCK MARKET YEAR

In these summaries of years, I am not going into great detail of the concerns that plagued the stock market or the conditions that supported stock prices. We observed some of these "news" items in detailing 1977, hopefully showing how unpredictive and misleading they could be. These 13 year-by-year pictures support the idea that the stock market is only a vehicle to allow anxious people to sell undervalued corporations to astute speculators, and in turn to allow fully valued stocks to be given back to greedy investors.

The 34 beginning-of-the-year recommendations for 1979 (Figure 7–5) begin to show some cumulative effects of long-term investing

FIGURE 7–4
Stocks Recommended for 1978 (Original Price, Split-Adjusted Year-End Values)

Symbol	Corporation	12/31/77	12/31/78	% Change
AH	Allis Chalmers	24.750	29.000	17.17
ARM	Armstrong Rubber	23.375	24.500	4.81
CCF	Cook United 6% stk	2.875	3.710	29.04
CLU	Cluett, Peabody	10.625	10.875	2.35
CP	Canadian Pacific	15.625	21.500	37.60
CTB	Cooper Tire & Rubber	13.625	10.125	−25.69
CUM	Cummins Engine	38.125	33.250	−12.79
DWR	Dean Witter Reynolds	12.000	10.500	−12.50
EAL	Eastern Air	6.125	8.500	38.78
EXR	Elixir Industries	4.875	4.250	−12.82
GFC	Gibraltar Fin'l 3:2	11.000	15.375	39.77
GR	B.F. Goodrich	21.000	17.375	−17.26
HR	Int'l Harvester	30.250	36.250	19.83
HSM	Hart,Schaffner,& Marx	11.875	11.250	−5.26
HZ	Hazeltine Corp.	10.375	12.250	18.07
ICA	Imperial Corp. America	15.875	16.125	1.57
JOL	Jonathan Logan	12.625	11.875	−5.94
MG	Monogram Industries	14.875	24.750	66.39
MGC	Magic Chef	9.375	10.125	8.00
MRX	Memorex Corp.	31.750	29.375	−7.48
OXM	Oxford Industries	10.500	9.375	−10.71
PIR	Pier 1 Imports	5.250	8.000	52.38
RAY	Raybestos-Man. 10% div	31.125	32.175	3.37
SLT	Salant Corp.	6.750	5.750	−14.81
SMC	Smith (A.O.) Corp.	13.875	18.250	31.53
UFL	United Fin'l of Cal.	16.500	19.500	18.18
WPI	Western Pacific Ind's	24.750	34.375	38.89
YES	Yates Industries	11.000	18.125	64.77
ZAL	Zale Corp.	15.625	16.000	2.40
ZY	Zayre Corp.	8.500	10.125	19.12
	Average	15.496	17.088	12.96

in widely diversified portfolios. With 14 stocks carried over from 1978's list and United Financial of California (UFL) recommended for the third year, one begins to get a glimmer of what *long-term* means in operational terms. In these days of negativism toward savings and loan companies—which parallels similar appraisals during the high interest-rate periods of the early '70s—we see how some S&Ls overcame difficult periods and

FIGURE 7–5
Stocks Recommended for 1979 (Original Price, Split-Adjusted Year-End Values)

Symbol	Corporation	12/31/78	12/31/79	% Change
ARM	Armstrong Rubber	24.500	18.250	−25.51
AV	Avco Corp.	22.875	27.750	21.31
CAL	Continental Air	8.750	10.000	14.29
CNV	City Investing	13.625	18.000	32.11
CPS	Columbia Pictures	22.375	34.125	52.51
CRO	Chromalloy American	15.500	23.000	48.39
CTB	Cooper Tire & Rubber	10.125	11.875	17.28
CUM	Cummins Engine	33.250	31.000	−6.77
DWR	Dean Witter Reynolds	10.500	11.000	4.76
EAL	Eastern Air	8.500	7.750	−8.82
EXR	Elixir Industries	4.250	4.875	14.71
FBG	Faberge Inc.	8.250	11.250	36.36
FLX	Flexi-Van Corp.	14.625	14.125	−3.42
FWF	Far West Financial	11.875	12.625	6.32
GDV	General Development	7.000	11.500	64.29
GFC	Gibraltar Financial	10.250	11.250	9.76
GDW	Golden West Financial	11.750	16.000	36.17
GR	B.F. Goodrich	17.375	19.625	12.95
GW	Gulf + Western	14.125	18.500	30.97
HSM	Hart,Schaffner,& Marx	11.250	11.875	5.56
ICA	Imperial Corp. America	16.125	25.500	58.14
IU	IU International	10.250	11.125	8.54
NPH	N.American Phillips	25.375	26.750	5.42
OXM	Oxford Industries	9.375	10.750	14.67
SHA	Shapell Industries	22.750	40.625	78.57
SHP	Stop & Shop Companies	16.250	15.625	−3.85
SMC	Smith (A.O.) Corp.	18.250	17.000	−6.85
SMI	Spring Mills	14.750	18.750	27.12
UFL	Un. Fin'l of Cal 5:4	19.500	41.563	113.14
WIX	Wickes Corp.	10.500	16.750	59.52
WNT	Washington Nat'l	23.250	25.500	9.68
Z	F.W. Woolworth	19.375	25.125	29.68
ZAL	Zale Corp.	16.000	20.250	26.56
ZY	Zayre Corp.	10.125	10.875	7.41
	Average	15.077	18.546	23.26

provided handsome market price gains. UFL appreciated a handsome 40.43 percent in '77, a satisfying 18.18 percent (split-adjusted) in '78, and then a terrific 113.14 percent (split-adjusted) in '79, being bought out for cash by National Steel.

Western Pacific Industries (WPI) was trading above its recommendable level by December 31, 1978, but another interesting position, Stop & Shop Industries (SHP), saw its stock lose 3.85 percent during a strong market year. Meanwhile, Zayre (ZY), a repeat from '78 during which it gained 19.2 percent, was up only 7.41 percent for '79. You might notice a stock that interested you during this period, perhaps Gulf + Western (GW, now Paramount Communications, PCI), which managed a 30.97 percent appreciation—a stock I still hold ten years later. More about GW in due course.

For '79 the DJIA registered a total return of + 10.68 percent, while the S&P 500 was considerably better at 18.4 percent. Small company stocks scored an amazing 43.5 percent total return. Our list managed a satisfying 23.26 percent (not including dividends or cash reinvested).

1980 WAS A GOOD YEAR FOR STOCKS

With the DJIA showing a total reinvested return of + 22.13 percent, the S&P 500 registering 32.4 percent, and the small company total return at + 39.9 percent, I could almost be embarrassed by the 22.02 percent market appreciation (not including dividends or reinvested proceeds) indicated for 1980's recommended list (see Figure 7–6). Actually, my margined portfolio (see Figure I–2) managed only a 15.69 percent total return, which could be of concern, given that a fully margined "unmanaged" portfolio of the stocks listed below should have produced about a 35 percent return. There was another October Massacre in '80, so aggressive portfolios buying stocks heavily just before the big correction showed sharply decreased annual performance.

By the end of 1979, there were many stocks that met our criteria as buy candidates—51 in the list below. About this time a couple of subscribers were beginning to complain that they didn't know where to begin selecting a stock or 2 or 10 from such extensive recommendations. I was quite sympathetic to their plight in that I couldn't afford to buy nearly all the recommendable stocks. Of course, 14 of the recommendations were holds or repeats from 1979's list; and another 8 were holds,

FIGURE 7–6
Stocks Recommended for 1980 (Original Price Split-Adjusted
Year-End Values)

Symbol	Corporation	12/31/79	12/31/80	%Change
AR	Asarco Inc.	37.375	43.250	15.72
AV	Avco Corp.	27.750	29.000	4.50
BG	Brown Group	25.500	31.000	21.57
CP	Canadian Pacific	33.875	36.375	7.38
CHD	Chelsea Inds.	10.625	7.500	−29.41
CNV	City Investing	18.000	21.500	19.44
CLU	Cluett, Peabody	9.750	9.500	−2.56
ETN	Eaton Corp.	25.625	28.500	11.22
FMC	FMC Corp.	26.000	30.500	17.31
FCA	Fabri-Centers Amer.	5.125	8.375	63.41
FLX	Flexi-Van Corp.	14.125	20.250	43.36
FM	Franklin Mint	9.625	25.000	159.74
FQA	Fuqua Industries	18.500	14.500	−21.62
GDV	General Development	11.500	13.875	20.65
GR	B.F. Goodrich	19.625	24.875	26.75
GOR	Gordon Jewelry	23.375	19.125	−18.18
GW	Gulf + Western 5:4	18.500	19.844	7.26
HSM	Hart, Schaffner, & Marx	11.875	14.250	20.00
HR	Int'l Harvester	39.125	25.625	−34.50
KCC	Kaiser Cement	26.625	25.000	−6.10
KOE	Koehring Co.	20.000	37.000	85.00
LES	Leslie Fay	6.625	8.875	33.96
MGC	Magic Chef	8.375	8.000	−4.48
MHT	Manhattan Inds. 4% stk	6.875	7.410	7.78
MRX	Memorex Corp.	17.875	12.750	−28.67
MG	Monogram Industries	39.000	40.000	2.56
MRS	Morse Shoe	13.500	22.250	64.81
NPH	North Amer. Phillips	26.750	38.125	42.52
OXM	Oxford Industries	10.750	12.125	12.79
PN	Pan Am Corp.	6.000	4.250	−29.17
PHL	Phillips Industries	5.500	7.125	29.55
PVH	Phillips-Van Heusen	14.125	10.875	−23.01
RAY	Raybestos-Manhattan	22.375	29.375	31.28
SVN	Sav-On-Drugs (Jewel)	9.875	19.000	92.41
SCI	Sea. Cst. Ln. (Chessie)	29.375	52.375	78.30
SHC	Shaklee Corp.	15.125	29.000	−91.74
SMC	Smith (A.O.) Corp.	17.000	13.750	19.12
SMI	Spring Mills	18.750	17.375	−7.33
SHP	Stop & Shop Companies	15.625	15.250	−2.40
SMB	Sunbeam Corp.	17.625	16.750	−4.96

FIGURE 7–6
Stocks Recommended for 1980—Continued

Symbol	Corporation	12/31/79	12/31/80	%Change
TRI	Triangle Industries	8.125	11.750	44.62
USG	U.S. Gypsum	31.500	33.000	4.76
USL	U.S. Leasing	14.875	27.000	81.51
WRC	Warnaco Industries	11.625	15.625	34.41
WNT	Washington National	25.500	38.000	49.02
WH	White Motor	5.875	3.500	−40.43
WIX	Wickes Corp.	16.750	13.500	−19.40
WWW	Wolverine World Wide	13.250	21.000	58.49
Z	F.W. Woolworth	25.125	24.750	−1.49
ZAL	Zale Corp.	20.250	27.625	36.42
ZY	Zayre Corp.	10.875	21.250	95.40
	Average	17.988	21.304	22.02

having been recommended for '77 or '78. Actually, 52 stocks would not be too many to own in a portfolio of $200,000 or more, which means that each position would represent about $4,000 or 2 percent of the portfolio.

I've noticed that some investors with a couple hundred thousand dollars or more would consider it beneath their dignity to buy fewer than 100 shares of any stock, lest they be thought of as odd lotters or amateurs. There is nothing wrong with buying 35 or 50 shares of a high-priced undervalued stock if that amount approximates the average dollar position in the portfolio. I have long held over 100 positions in my portfolio, happy to have less than 1 percent to 2 percent in any given stock. When the bad ones bomb, only a percent or fraction thereof is given up, while a good position gaining several-fold its cost has a significant cumulative effect on one's total return, especially if the portfolio is heavily leveraged (margined).

Apparently the big winner for 1980 was Franklin Mint (FM), up 159.74 percent, although several other recommended stocks advanced handsomely. We see that Zayre (ZY), after gaining only 7.41 percent in '79, was able to almost double (95.40 percent) in its third recommended year. Alas, Zayre advanced beyond recommendation—while remaining a strong hold—and was able to appreciate 2,400 percent before it was closed out in April 1988. Although ZY's originally recommended price was $8.50 in late '77, due to several splits, its cost adjusted price became

96 cents (.959) per share by the time it was closed out at $24.00 per share. One must be very careful when comparing historical prices to remember to check for splits, stock dividends, and returns of capital over the years.

It would not be fruitful for me to try to analyze each of the hundreds of recommended stocks for the past 12 years or to comment on their particular performances. As you can imagine, each company has its own unique story as well as what happened to its stock in a fickle, irrational, and rarely efficient market. As I gaze at the recommendations for 1980, I see little gems such as Magic Chef (MGC), which lost 4.48 percent in market price that year and then advanced nicely over the years (as mentioned above), and which I still hold in the form of shares in Maytag (MYG), the appliance manufacturer that acquired Magic Chef.

1981—THE PAUSE BEFORE THE NEXT LEG UP

After the strong 1980, 1981 was a bit of a downer according to the major averages, with the DJIA declining 3.65 percent and the S&P 500 managing a total return of − 4.9 percent. Meanwhile, the small company stocks' total return registered a much better 13.9 percent gain. When we review TPS recommended stocks at year-end '81 (Figure 7–7), we see that they appreciated 13.48 percent without dividends included or reinvested, just a tad better than the small company stocks' performance.

Even in a down year, at least according to the DJIA and S&P 500, it is quite possible to obtain a positive return through decent stock selection and a well-balanced portfolio. TPS Portfolio actually lost .74 percent in its margined condition in '81, although a hypothetically unmargined TPS Portfolio would have gained 17.28 percent. The apparent disparities among these figures is easily understandable. TPS Portfolio in 1981 represented mostly undervalued stocks that had been held for several years with many appreciating strongly, such as Cluett, Peabody (CLU), Fuqua Industries (FQA), and Stop & Shop (SHP), to name a few. The margined loss developed through the purchase of additional undervalued stocks that generally remained out of favor during 1981 and dragged down the overall performance.

Meanwhile, we see that, of the 36 recommendations for 1981, 13 were also recommended for 1980, and 9 had been recommended in previous years. One third of the recommendations declined in 1981,

FIGURE 7–7
Stocks Recommended for 1981 (Original Price, Split-Adjusted Year-End Values)

Symbol	Corporation	12/31/80	12/31/81	% Change
AFL	American Family	7.500	7.625	1.67
AR	Asarco	43.250	25.750	−40.46
BG	Brown Group 3:2	31.000	42.563	37.30
CP	Canadian Pacific	36.375	35.125	−3.44
CPH	Capital Holding	17.750	22.250	25.35
CEC	Ceco Corp.	16.875	19.250	14.07
CNV	City Investing	21.500	22.750	5.81
CLU	Cluett, Peabody	9.500	15.000	57.89
CPG	Colonial Penn	16.250	15.000	−7.69
CNK	Crompton & Knowles 3:2	19.500	25.500	30.77
FLX	Dan River	14.750	13.375	−9.32
DSO	DeSoto Inc.	12.500	17.000	36.00
FQA	Fuqua Industries	14.500	21.250	46.55
GOR	Gordon Jewelry 3:2	19.125	25.500	33.33
GW	Gulf + Western	15.875	15.875	.00
HML	Hammermill Paper	27.000	27.750	2.78
INB	Industrial National	19.750	26.875	36.08
INA	INA Corp.	40.500	44.125	8.95
IU	IU International	17.500	13.750	−21.43
KT	Katy Industries	14.875	10.750	−27.73
LES	Leslie Fay	8.875	13.875	56.34
LEV	Levitz Furniture	24.500	34.500	40.82
NAC	National Can	22.500	21.250	−5.56
OI	Owens-Illinois	25.500	29.625	16.18
PCF	PennCorp Financial	7.125	5.625	−21.05
PVH	Phillips-Van Heusen	10.875	15.750	44.83
PII	Pueblo International	3.625	3.625	.00
RVB	Revere Copper	16.250	14.750	−9.23
SLF	Scot Lad Foods	5.125	4.000	−21.95
SHP	Stop & Shop Companies	15.250	22.000	44.26
SMB	Sunbeam (All. Int'l)	16.750	27.750	65.67
TA	Transamerica	18.750	23.375	24.67
UK	Union Carbide	50.250	51.375	2.24
WRC	Warnaco Industries	15.625	27.000	72.80
Z	F.W. Woolworth	24.750	18.000	−27.27
ZAL	Zale Corp.	27.625	21.000	−23.98
	Average	19.701	21.682	13.48

although over longer periods of time our experience is that about 20 percent of all recommended stocks fail to advance. As the majority tend to advance over time, and winning stocks win more than losing stocks lose, the average multi-year gains accumulate nicely, in spite of October Massacres and Meltdowns.

LATE IN 1982 THE GREAT BULL MARKET BEGINS A BIG LEAP FORWARD

Many market historians count the great bull market of '82 to '87 as beginning on August 12, 1982, with the DJIA closing at 776.92 (easily remembered as "777"), a two-year low. Just seven years later, it hardly seems possible that conditions felt so bad in the Summer of '82, yet the market advanced so forcefully over the next five years—almost 2,000 points on the DJIA!

In *TPS* 137, dated August 5, 1982, under "Current Approaches" I wrote, "BOLD SPECULATORS can hold 150 percent (margined) positions, given the currently oversold market conditions and the extreme undervaluations of select common stocks." Under "Recent Stock Market Activity and Outlook" I wrote,

> Suicide is not the answer, patience is. I am taking my lumps this year for a variety of reasons, many of which have little to do with speculating in the stock market, such as using capital funds for personal reasons. When one considers how well the stock market is bound to do over the next few years, this period of adjustment (bottoming) in this current market cycle will seem relatively trivial.

From the December 31, 1981 DJIA close of 875.00 to the August 12, 1982 DJIA close of 776.92, the Dow Jones Industrial Average declined 11.2 percent. Thereafter, the DJIA advanced to close on December 31, 1982 at 1046.54, a gain of 34.7 percent for the four and one half months, resulting in 19.6 percent gain for the year! Nineteen eighty-two is a strong argument against market suicide during a cycle low.

By the end of 1981 there were 41 recommended stocks for 1982, with 7 holdovers from '81 and 8 rerecommended from prior years (see Figure 7–8). The overall list managed a market price appreciation of 28.65 percent not including dividends or reinvestment. This compares very favorably with the S&P 500's total return of 21.4 percent, and favorably with the DJIA's reinvested return of 27.20 percent and the

FIGURE 7–8
Recommended Stocks for 1982 (Original Price, Split-Adjusted
Year-End Values)

Symbol	Corporation	12/31/81	12/31/82	% Change
ARE	Amerace Corp.	17.000	18.250	7.35
AMZ	American Seating	13.375	29.125	117.76
ASR	Amstar Corp.	25.875	25.125	−2.90
ARM	Armstrong Rub. 2:1	32.750	61.000	86.26
BNK	Bangor Punta	18.875	18.500	−1.99
CIL	Cont'l Illinois	33.125	20.375	−38.49
CTB	Cooper Tire & Rubber	14.500	36.750	153.45
CNK	Crompton & Knowles	17.000	19.375	13.97
DSO	DeSoto Inc.	12.250	24.250	97.96
DYN	Dynalectron Corp.	9.000	10.875	20.83
FWB	First Wisconsin	30.375	30.250	−.41
GOR	Gordon Jewelry	17.000	18.375	8.09
GW	Gulf + Western	15.875	16.750	5.51
INB	Industrial National	26.875	28.375	5.58
KT	Katy Industries	10.750	12.125	12.79
LTV	LTV Corp.	16.375	11.375	−30.53
MGC	Magic Chef	9.000	20.750	130.56
MHT	Manhattan Ind's 4%	12.125	14.040	15.79
MGU	Michigan Sugar	15.000	19.000	26.67
MOB	Mobil Corp.	24.125	25.125	4.15
MWK	Mohawk Rubber	15.375	24.125	56.91
NOM	Natomas Co.	24.000	16.250	−32.29
OXY	Occidental Pete.	23.000	19.750	−14.13
OM	Outboard Marine	20.000	28.875	44.38
OSG	Overseas Shipping	16.250	15.250	−6.15
OI	Owens-Illinois	29.625	28.250	−4.64
PII	Pueblo International	3.625	8.500	134.48
PRN	Puerto Rican Cement	3.375	3.500	3.70
RCI	Reichold Chemical	11.375	19.000	67.03
RS	Republic Steel	24.500	15.625	−36.22
RD	Royal Dutch Pete	34.875	34.625	−.72
SLF	Scot Lad Foods	4.000	4.625	15.63
SCN	Sea Containers	21.000	23.500	11.90
VO	Seagram Co. Ltd.	57.625	73.750	27.98
SHW	Sherwin Williams	22.000	44.000	100.00
SMI	Spring Mills	23.500	38.625	64.36
TK	Technicolor Inc.	14.625	22.625	54.70
TX	Texaco Inc.	33.000	31.125	−5.68
TYC	Tyco Labs	12.375	17.500	41.41
X	U.S. Steel	29.875	21.000	−29.71
WWW	Wolverine World Wide	14.000	20.875	49.11
	Average	19.738	23.687	28.65

small company stocks' total return of 28.0 percent. Of course, if these stocks had been margined, they would have gained twice as much or more, depending upon what stocks were bought during the year, with increasing buying power based on increasing equity.

During the turbulent 1982 year, we see 13 of the recommended stocks declining in market price (just under one third of the total number recommended) losing from 0.41 percent to 38.49 percent, while the remaining 28 advanced from 3.7 percent to 153.45 percent, not counting dividends in either case. Again, there are so many sagas associated with these stocks ranging from the continuous three-year recommendation of Cooper Tire (CTB, up +153.45 percent) to the emergence of lowly Puerto Rican Cement (PRN), which, at this writing, is up over 1,200 percent less than seven years later.

If you are really curious about any of the stock sagas, you can refer to the lists of all formerly recommended stocks still open in Appendix C, and all formerly recommended stocks closed out in Appendix D, to see their dispositions as of June 30, 1989.

1983, OR ONE GOOD YEAR DESERVES ANOTHER

The explosive year-end rally of 1982 carried through 1983, with the DJIA registering a 26.06 percent reinvested return, about 1 percent less than for 1982. The S&P 500 showed a total return of 21.4 percent, and the small company stocks gained a fantastic 39.7 percent. It was a great time to be fully invested and leveraged (margined), though undoubtedly some investors probably lost money in '83 by being in the wrong stocks and trying to trade the market counter to its trend. My TPS Portfolio showed a margined return of +117.74, or a hypothetical cash account (unmargined) return of 45.44 percent.

After 1982's fall and winter rally there were fewer undervalued stocks to recommend, so the list in Figure 7–9 shows only 21 stocks.

Of the 21 recommended stocks for 1983, 8 are carryovers from 1982's list. The 31.84 percent market price appreciation compares very favorably with the major averages mentioned above but looks anemic compared to TPS Portfolio's margined return, or even with the hypothetical TPS cash return. These differences, I submit, are due to the long-held and maturing nature of TPS Portfolio's undervalued stock positions, which tend to do better after a year or two than when they are so out of favor (and consequently severely underpriced) when first selected.

FIGURE 7–9
Stocks Recommended for 1983   (Original Price, Split-Adjusted Year-End Values)

Symbol	Corporation	12/31/82	12/31/83	% Change
BK	Bank of New York 2:1	49.750	65.500	31.66
CIL	Continental Illinois	20.375	21.875	7.36
DYN	Dynalectron Corp.	10.875	12.500	14.94
FHR	Fisher Foods	8.125	10.000	23.08
FLT	Fleet Fin'l Group	34.500	47.750	38.41
GBS	General Bancshares	20.000	37.750	88.75
GLM	Global Marine	9.250	7.875	−14.86
KAB	Kaneb Services	15.000	14.375	−4.17
KT	Katy Industries	12.125	30.125	148.45
KEN	Kenai Corp.	5.375	4.000	−25.58
MHT	Manhattan Inds. 4%	13.500	24.875	84.26
MM	Marine Midland	18.750	24.750	32.00
MCN	MidCon Corp.	25.750	35.000	35.92
NBD	NBD Bancorp	30.250	45.875	51.65
NOM	Natomas (Dia. Sham.)	16.250	25.593	57.50
PSA	PSA Inc.	30.625	21.750	−28.98
PRN	Puerto Rican Cement	3.500	8.750	150.00
RD	Royal Dutch Pete	34.625	45.000	29.96
SCN	SeaCo Inc.	23.500	26.250	11.70
TOS	Tosco Corp.	11.125	5.000	−55.06
UER	United Energy Res.	27.125	24.875	−8.29
	Average	20.018	25.689	31.84

The greatest gainer for 1983, Puerto Rican Cement (PRN), up 150 percent, did not make the 1984 recommended list because it had risen to more than 50 percent of its then goal price. PRN attained the status of a long-term hold but, as we know now, did continue to advance another 400 percent from its 1983 closing price. PRN is still a hold, as its goal price has continued to rise during the years (see goal prices in Appendix C). Tosco (TOS), which I had the misfortune to recommend on *Wall $treet Week* in September 1983 at about $10 per share, has yet to recover from its tumble but is begining show signs of improving in market value in 1989.

1984 WAS A HANGOVER YEAR

The tremendous gains of late '82 and '83 actually petered out on November 29, 1983 when the DJIA made a closing high of 1287.20.

With the DJIA opening at 1252.74 for 1984, its high for the year was made January 6th at 1286.64, with the yearly low at 1086.57 on July 24th, and a close of 1211.57, off 3.74 percent for the year. The "total reinvested percent change" for '84, according to Lipper Analytical Securities Corporation, was +1.35 percent, gained by accounting for reinvested dividends. For 1984, *SBBI* shows the S&P 500 total return plus 6.3 percent, while their small company total return registered a minus 6.7 percent, reversing the multi-year trend of smaller capitalization stocks outperforming larger cap stocks.

TPS Portfolio came up with a loss of 12.71 percent in its actual margined account, but as a hypothetical cash account would have earned +2.14 percent. Because of the magnificent advances during 1982–83, there were only 10 stocks to recommend at year-end for 1984 (see Figure 7–10). These managed to appreciate 4.13 percent in market value, not counting dividends, keeping up with the S&P 500's results and avoiding the small cap's underperformance. Of course, this list contains several large cap stocks including Chrysler, Ford, and Royal Dutch Petroleum.

1985 MADE UP FOR 1984'S PAUSE

When the DJIA closed at 1211.57 on December 31, 1984 it sported a P/E ratio of 10.7. This ratio was based on the DJIA stocks having earned

FIGURE 7–10
Stocks Recommended for 1984 (Original Price, Split-Adjusted Year-End Values)

Symbol	Corporation	12/31/83	12/31/84	% Change
C	Chrysler Corp.	27.625	32.000	15.84
F	Ford Motor	42.375	45.625	7.67
FWB	First Wisconsin	20.375	24.750	21.47
GFC	Gibraltar Financial	10.375	9.500	−8.43
MM	Marine Midland	24.750	28.500	15.15
PGT	Pacific Gas Trns"A"	16.625	20.000	20.30
RD	Royal Dutch Pete	45.000	49.375	9.72
SMP	Standard Motor Prod.	18.375	13.250	−27.89
TSO	Tesoro Petroleum	14.000	10.000	−24.53
WKT	Wayne-Gossard	13.375	9.625	−28.04
	Average	23.288	24.263	.13

$113.58 for 1984, actually a handsome increase over 1983's earnings of $72.45. Ironically, in 1985 the DJIA stocks earned only $96.11, a 15.4 percent drop from 1984, but the DJIA closed at 1546.67—335 points higher for the year—resulting in a P/E ratio of 16.1! Next time someone tells you stocks cannot advance during a declining profits year, point to 1985.

If nothing else, the DJIA relationship between 1984 and 1985 shows that you can't count on lower earnings alone keeping the market from rising. If general or specific conditions are perceived to be improving so that the following year's earnings, interest rates, inflation, the dollar, or what have you, look to be better, then the anticipating market will make its own adjustments.

Because of the droopy market action of '84, and the increasing fundamental stock values, we found 37 stocks to recommend at year-end (Figure 7–11). Of this group, only three were holdovers from '84 although another five had been recommended in prior years. To show how strong a year '85 was, only eight on this recommended list failed to show a price gain—22 percent "first-year losers" versus our "average" 33 percent to 40 percent. The average gain of the recommended list for '85 was 30.99 percent, not including dividends or reinvestment. This gain compares with the DJIA total invested percent change of 33.62 percent (actual nominal point gain of 27.66 percent). The S&P 500's total return was 32.2 percent, while the small company stocks' total return was "only" 24.7 percent, continuing the trend of small cap stocks underperforming large cap stocks.

While the hypothetical unmargined TPS Portfolio managed only a 23.41 percent gain for '85, the actual margined account recorded a 50.72 percent total return. A nice performance goal is 15 percent, per year, compounded, so any time portfolio performance or the major averages exceed that 15 percent you would have to say you were having a good year. Fortunately and unfortunately, many of the years between '82 and '87 far exceeded 15 percent, thus unduly raising expectations for systematic stock market profits. Perhaps the rich years of this secular bull market—from December '74 through August '87 (if indeed the Crash of '87 was no more than just a "normal" 50 percent correction)—have led individual investors to expect too much, become disappointed too easily, and try too hard to find high returns in highly speculative options and futures contracts.

At any rate, 1985 was undoubtedly another leg—in a manner of speaking—of the great bull market that began from very undervalued

FIGURE 7–11

Stocks Recommended for 1985 (Original Price, Split-Adjusted Year-End Values)

Symbol	Corporation	12/31/84	12/31/85	% Change
ANT	Anthony Industries 5%	12.750	15.356	20.44
ABZ	Arkansas Best	15.875	29.125	83.46
CAL	CalFed Inc.	16.000	27.375	71.09
C	Chrysler Corp.	32.000	46.625	45.70
CBU	Commodore Int'l	16.375	10.625	−35.11
CUB	Cubic Corp	15.625	22.375	43.20
CUM	Cummins Engine	77.625	72.000	−7.25
DBRSY	DeBeers Consolidated	4.125	4.719	14.40
DUCK	Duckwall-Alco (LBO)	13.500	17.750	31.48
EFG	Equitec Fin'l Group	10.375	9.625	−7.23
FRA	Farah Mfg. Co.	19.375	21.125	9.03
FBT	First City Banc Tex	14.625	12.875	−11.97
FFHC	First Fin'l Wisc. 2:1	18.000	35.000	94.44
F	Ford Motor	45.625	58.000	27.12
GRX	Gen'l Refractories	8.250	11.375	37.88
GLEN	Glendale Federal	8.875	17.500	97.18
GDW	Golden West Fin'l 3:2	23.750	46.500	95.79
GRR	G.R.I. Corp.	4.500	4.125	−8.33
HR	Int'l Harvester	8.125	8.500	4.62
ITT	ITT Corp.	29.375	38.000	29.36
KZ	Kysor Industrial	16.625	22.125	33.08
MGC	Magic Chef	35.375	52.875	49.47
MXM	MAXXAM Group	12.750	11.000	−13.73
MSL	Mercury S&L 6% stk	6.125	11.395	86.04
MODI	Modine Mfg. 5:2	35.750	58.125	62.59
PN	Pan Am Corp.	4.625	7.750	67.57
PRN	Puerto Rican Cement	6.875	8.125	18.18
RADC	Radice Corp. "A"	8.750	14.625	67.14
RBSN	Robeson Ind's 10%	6.000	5.775	−3.75
ROP	Roper Corp.	14.625	15.875	8.55
RD	Royal Dutch Pete	49.375	63.000	27.59
SCR	Sea Container Ltd.	29.500	30.500	3.39
SC	Shell Transport	30.500	38.750	27.05
SM	Southmark Corp. 10%	6.750	10.725	58.89
TCL	Transcon Inc.	8.250	7.875	−4.55
U	US Air Group	33.250	34.375	3.38
YNK	Yankee Oil	5.500	6.625	20.45
	Average	19.064	24.543	30.99

and sold-out levels in December 1974 and that was renewed in August 1982. Some of the stocks on the '85 recommended list, such as First City Banc of Texas, Roper, and Arkansas Best, are gone because of bankruptcy or buyouts. Others have yet to retrieve their originally recommended price, while some have made a comeback, such as Commodore International (CBU), which reversed its '85 loss to sell at a small profit.

1986 KEPT 1985'S MOMENTUM GOING

With 1986, we are getting into "current history" concerning the stock market, especially as '86 set up the great advance that carried through the first three quarters of '87. After advancing so strongly in '85, there were only 26 stocks to recommend at year-end '86. Old stalwarts such as Chrysler, Ford, Sea Containers, and Shell Transport (40 percent of the Royal Dutch Petroleum complex) continued to be recommended. Savings and loans began to reflect a larger portion of the list.

The 26 stocks (displayed in Figure 7–12) show a market price gain of 23.60 percent, not counting dividends or reinvestment. This handsome return about equals the DJIA total dividend reinvested return of 27.25 percent. The S&P 500 total return for '86 is reported at 18.5 percent, while the small company stocks' total return is a measly 6.9 percent.

Thus continued the trend of large cap stocks outperforming small cap stocks, but even more so, the DJIA became the premiere performing average due to programmed trading and the emphasis on such derivative instruments as those based on the Major Market Index (MMI, an index of 20 stocks designed to emulate the DJIA), the S&P 500, and S&P 100 index futures and options contracts.

1987 KEPT 1986'S MOMENTUM GOING, FOR A WHILE AT LEAST

In Chapter 6, "The Crash of '87," 1987 is dealt with in some detail, but it's still part of the recommended stocks series and each year's performance, so we continue with the end-of-1987 recommendations listed in Figure 7–13.

While 1987 was a traumatic experience for many market participants, especially those of us who were fully invested and on margin,

FIGURE 7–12
Stocks Recommended for 1986 (Original Price, Split-Adjusted Year-End Values)

Symbol	Corporation	12/31/85	12/31/86	% Change
ACF	AirCal	7.500	14.500	93.33
AINC	American Income Life	10.625	14.500	36.47
AFS	Amfesco	1.375	2.000	45.45
AZP	AZP Group	27.250	28.375	4.13
CAL	CalFed Inc.	27.375	33.500	22.37
CARG	Carriage Industries	7.750	7.500	−3.23
C	Chrysler Corp. 3:2	31.083	37.000	19.04
DBRSY	DeBeers Consolidated	4.750	7.500	57.89
FWF	Far West Fin'l 3:1	16.583	13.875	−16.33
FFOM	First Fed'l S&L Mich.	16.125	22.875	41.86
F	Ford Motor 3:2	38.667	56.250	45.47
GDF	General Defense	12.875	15.865	23.22
GDV	General Development	15.500	17.500	12.90
GFC	Gibraltar Financial	10.625	10.750	1.18
GDW	Golden West Financial	31.000	34.875	12.50
HERE	Heritage Entertainment	2.625	7.375	180.95
HFD	Home Federal S&L SD	26.500	26.375	−.47
MXM	MAXXAM Group	11.000	8.750	−20.45
PLM	PLM Financial	5.250	6.500	23.81
SCR	Sea Containers	30.500	13.625	−55.33
SC	Shell Transport	38.750	58.500	50.97
SHG	Sheller Globe (LBO)	30.500	46.650	52.95
SM	Southmark Corp. 15%	8.478	8.375	−1.21
TKA	Tonka Corp. 3:2	18.333	19.875	8.41
TUR	Turner Corp.	25.750	20.625	−19.90
WLC	Wellco Enterprises 2:1	7.938	13.750	73.22
	Average	17.873	21.049	23.60

conservative investors who emphasized owning the DJIA or equivalent stocks did not have that bad a time of it. Common stocks, as represented by the S&P 500, actually had a 5.2 percent total return, slightly outdone by the DJIA's total reinvested change of 5.55 percent. Not so for small company stocks, as they lost 9.3 percent on a total return basis, continuing their out-of-favor trend.

Obviously, our recommendations fared very badly in 1987, significantly underperforming the major market averages. It was a difficult year for secondary stocks in general and especially bad for

FIGURE 7–13

Stocks Recommended for 1987 (Original Price, Split-Adjusted Year-End Values)

Symbol	Corporation	12/31/86	12/31/87	% Change
ARAI	Allied Research	5.375	3.500	−34.88
AFC.A	American Fructose "A"	12.750	6.250	−50.98
ANT	Anthony Industries	10.875	11.875	9.20
CAL	CalFed Inc.	33.500	21.750	−35.07
C	Chrysler Corp. 3:2	24.667	22.125	−10.31
DBRSY	DeBeers Consolidated	7.500	9.375	25.00
ELCN	Elco Industries	16.750	24.250	44.78
FWF	Far West Financial	13.875	9.875	−28.83
FIN	Financial Corp. Amer.	7.500	1.125	−85.00
FFOM	First Fed'l S&L Mich.	22.875	9.000	−60.66
FFHC	First Financial Wisc.	17.250	12.750	−26.09
F	Ford Motor	56.250	75.375	34.00
GEMH	Gemcraft, Inc.	7.000	.875	−87.50
GDV	General Development	17.500	10.875	−37.86
GFC	Gibraltar Financial	10.750	3.500	−67.44
GDW	Golden West Financial	34.875	25.000	−28.32
GTA	Great American 1st	17.500	12.625	−27.86
HHH	Heritage Entertainment	7.375	3.125	−57.36
HFD	Home Federal S&L SD	26.375	20.750	−21.33
HUM	Humana Corp.	19.125	19.250	.65
ICA	Imperial Corp. America	13.221	7.500	−43.27
JII	Johnston Industries	13.875	18.500	33.33
LK	Lockheed Corp.	50.125	34.375	−31.42
MSL	Mercury Savings	10.625	5.875	−44.71
NTK	Nortek Corp.	13.000	7.000	−46.15
PFIN.A	P&F Industries	4.000	2.250	−43.75
RI	Radice Corp.	9.250	.938	−89.86
RIHL	Richton Int'l	4.125	3.250	−21.21
SM	Southmark Corp.	8.375	4.625	−44.78
TKA	Tonka Corporation	19.875	8.875	−55.35
TCL	Transcon Inc.	8.125	2.750	−66.15
TUR	Turner Corp.	20.625	16.125	−21.82
WLC	Wellco Enterprises	13.750	12.125	−11.82
WILF	Wilson Foods	9.000	7.625	−15.28
	Average	16.695	12.796	−30.83

out-of-favor undervalued stocks, which underperformed for most of the year before the crash and then were doubly trounced during the October and November period, not bottoming out until the first week in December.

1988, A YEAR OF RECOVERY

Many people threw in the towel, the sink, and all their stocks after the Crash of '87. This was particularly ironic as history shows time and again that after a terrible selloff, the market usually recovers perhaps 50 percent, as it did in early 1930, following the 1929 crash.

Many of the gurus who had anticipated a selloff—and many who didn't but quickly joined the bearish camp—were convinced that the worst was yet to come. They predicted recessions, depressions, much lower market prices, and perhaps a breakdown of the world economic system. They certainly urged readers and listeners to stay out of the market, especially with the availability of handsome "risk-free" returns on U.S. government bills, notes, and bonds. They also missed the significant rebound in 1988 as the risk-free investments turned out to have a considerable negative "opportunity risk," risk in not participating in the historically and potentially greater gains from common stock appreciation.

For 1988, S&P 500 common stocks earned a total return of 16.8 percent, just a bit better than the DJIA's total reinvested change of 16.21 percent. Finally, after several years in the doldrums, small company stocks accelerated to a total return gain of 22.9 percent, or 36.3 percent more than their larger cap cousins.

The list of recommended stocks in *TPS* was the largest in its history at the end of 1987, numbering 99 (See Figure 7–14), but gaining 18.55 percent for the year not counting dividends or reinvestments—comparable to the small company stocks' performance. Several stocks were bought out such as Stop & Shop (SHP), Roper (ROP), Mohasco (MOH), USG (USG), Triangle Industries (TRI), and Arkansas Best (ABZ), so there is no telling how much greater gain from stocks recommended for 1988 may have been achieved by reinvesting these proceeds into other or additional undervalued recommended stocks.

FIGURE 7–14
Stocks Recommended for 1988   (Original Price, Split-Adjusted
Year-End Values)

Symbol	Corporation	12/31/87	12/31/88	% Change
AEPI	AEP Industries	8.250	12.750	54.55
AFC.A	American Fructose "A"	6.250	9.500	52.00
AIIC	American Integrity	2.875	1.188	−58.70
AINC	American Income Life	9.750	17.625	80.77
ARAI	Allied Research	3.500	2.500	−28.57
APK	Apple Bank	25.250	30.750	21.78
ARV	Arvin Industries	19.250	19.375	.65
ARX	ARX Inc.	6.875	6.375	−7.27
C	Chrysler Corp.	22.125	25.750	16.38
CAL	Calfed Inc.	21.750	22.000	1.15
CCI	Citicorp	18.625	25.875	38.93
CCTC	CCT Corp.	6.500	2.500	−61.54
CFG	Copelco Financial	5.000	8.750	75.00
CGE	Carriage Industries	4.375	5.250	20.00
CHCR	Chancellor Corp.	7.500	6.000	−20.00
CI	CIGNA Corp.	43.875	47.125	7.41
CIS	Concord Fabric	3.813	3.125	−18.03
COFD	Collective Federal S&L	8.750	7.375	−15.71
CSA	Coast S&L	16.000	14.750	−7.81
DHTK	DH Technologies	4.750	5.625	18.42
DPT	Datapoint	4.625	4.500	−2.70
DSL	Downey S&L	11.500	15.375	33.70
EFG	Equitec Fin'l Group	5.750	3.000	−47.83
ELK	Elcor Corp.	6.000	8.750	45.83
ENVR	Envirodyne	16.500	31.250	89.39
ESCA	Escalade Corp.	8.250	9.000	9.09
EXC	Excel Industries	5.909	12.000	103.08
F	Ford Motor	37.688	50.500	33.99
FBC	First Boston	24.875	52.625	111.56
FED	First Federal Financial	11.800	13.875	17.58
FFHC	First Financial Wisc.	12.750	14.000	9.80
FG	USF&G Corp.	28.375	28.500	.44
FNB	First Chicago	18.875	29.625	56.95
FWES	First West Financial	6.125	6.250	2.04
FWF	Far West Financial	9.875	7.875	−20.25
GD	General Dynamics	48.750	50.750	4.10
GDV	General Development	10.875	12.625	16.09
GDW	Golden West Financial	25.000	31.375	25.50
GDYN	Geo Dynamics	8.000	9.750	21.88
GLN	GlenFed Inc.	22.000	19.625	−10.80
GNT	Greentree Acceptance	15.125	10.375	−31.40

FIGURE 7–14—*Continued*

Symbol	Corporation	12/31/87	12/31/88	% Change
GRR	GRI Corp.	4.875	9.625	97.44
GTA	Great American 1st	12.625	11.250	−10.89
GXY	Galaxy Carpets	11.500	14.375	25.00
HEI	Heico Corp	16.375	18.250	11.45
HELE	Helen Of Troy	6.875	15.625	127.27
HFD	Home Federal S&L SD	20.750	24.875	19.88
HME	Home Group Inc.	12.000	11.000	−8.33
HOF	Hoffman Inds.	2.750	5.625	104.55
HTHR	Hawthorne S&L	16.750	22.000	31.34
HYDE	Hyde Athletic	7.000	8.875	26.79
ICH	ICH Corp.	7.750	4.750	−38.71
IRE	Integrated Resources	16.500	13.875	−15.91
ITT	ITT Corp.	44.500	50.375	13.20
JII	Johnston Industries	18.500	16.375	−11.49
KB	Kaufman & Broad	14.500	13.500	−6.90
KLM	KLM Royal Dutch	15.750	21.000	33.33
LADF	LADD Furniture	14.000	13.750	−1.79
LEN	Lennar Corp.	16.625	17.625	6.02
LK	Lockheed Corp.	34.375	41.250	20.00
LNDL	Lindal Cedar Homes	5.165	8.750	69.40
MRI.A	McRae Industries	6.000	5.500	−8.33
NTK	Nortek Corp..	7.000	9.125	30.36
NUVI	NuVision Inc.	6.250	8.125	30.00
PFINA	P&F Industries	2.250	2.000	−11.11
PGI	Ply Gem Industries	11.000	11.875	7.95
PLM.B	PLM Financial "B"	5.125	5.875	14.63
PMSI	Prime Medical Services	1.875	.875	−53.33
PNRE	Pan Atl Insurance	7.000	6.250	−10.71
RAY	Raytech Corp.	7.125	2.875	−59.65
RBSN	Robeson Industries	1.063	1.500	41.18
RGB	R.G. Barry	6.250	5.500	−12.00
RIHL	Richton International	3.250	2.500	−23.08
RLI	RLI Corp.	9.625	7.625	−20.78
ROP	Roper Corp.	15.500	54.000	248.39
RTN	Raytheon	66.625	67.000	.56
S	Sears, Roebuck	33.500	40.875	22.01
SBIG	Seibels Bruce	11.250	11.375	1.11
SBOS	Boston Bancorp	17.750	15.375	−13.38
SCR	Sea Containers	17.500	30.125	72.14
SIA	Signal Apparel	6.000	4.750	−20.83
SM	Southmark Corp.	4.625	1.625	−64.86
SMC.A	Smith A.O. "A"	13.875	16.500	18.92
SP	Spelling Productions	4.625	6.375	37.84

FIGURE 7–14—*Concluded*

Symbol	Corporation	12/31/87	12/31/88	% Change
SPF	Standard Pacific	8.000	12.000	50.00
SUPD	Supradur Companies	6.250	12.500	100.00
TGR	Tiger International	11.000	19.750	79.55
THMP	Thermal Industries	6.250	4.750	−24.00
TMK	Torchmark	24.500	30.500	24.49
TRI	Triangle Industries	26.750	32.625	21.96
TSOF	TSO Financial	3.125	4.375	40.00
TT	TransTechnology	17.750	17.750	.00
TUR	Turner Corp.	16.125	16.750	3.88
USH	USLIFE Corp.	28.500	34.875	22.37
VFC	VF Corp.	24.500	28.750	17.35
WDC	Western Digital	16.250	14.750	−9.23
WLC	Wellco Enterprises	12.125	15.250	25.77
WLD	Weldotron	4.625	7.250	56.76
ZY	Zayre	14.000	24.000	71.43
	Average	13.815	16.485	18.55

1989, ANOTHER STRONG FIRST EIGHT MONTHS

I am including the recommended stocks at the year-end 1988, so you can see how they did for the year as time unfolds. Post deadline time (September 1, 1989) they were a little behind the major averages. For the first eight months of 1989, the DJIA gained 26.91 percent, not counting dividends, compared to the recommended list's 23.60 percent, not counting dividends.

By September 1, 1989, only 16 stocks were recommendable—compared to the 46 below at year-end '88—which indicates that the market was getting close to a top, at least in terms of fundamental valuations. Of course, there are hundreds of stocks that range from somewhat to almost 50 percent undervalued and are strong holds or buys in other systems that do not require a 50 percent-of-goal-price bargain level. And, with every correction of any magnitude many stocks drop into the buy level through lower prices, just as other stocks become candidates by reporting higher earnings and improved fundamentals as their prices remain fairly stable.

On June 30, 1989, the DJIA closed at 2440.06—dropping a sharp 91.81 points for the week ending June 30—up 12.52 percent for the six months, not counting reinvested dividends. By September 1, the DJIA advanced to 2752.09, up 26.91 percent for the year to date.

FIGURE 7–15
Stocks Recommended for 1989   (Original Price Split Adjusted)

Symbol	Corporation	12/30/88	9/1/89	% Change
AFC.A	American Fructose "A"	9.500	20.000	110.53
ALWC	Williams (AL)	14.500	21.375	47.41
BAC	BankAmerica Corp.	17.625	32.875	86.52
BS	Bethlehem Steel	23.250	22.500	−3.23
BVFS	Bay View Federal	17.875	24.750	38.46
C	Chrysler Corp.	25.750	27.000	4.85
CAL	CalFed Inc.	22.000	26.750	21.59
CCI	Citicorp	25.875	32.750	26.57
CCTC	CCT Corp.	2.500	2.250	−10.00
COFD	Collective Bancorp	7.375	11.000	49.15
CSA	Coast S&L	14.750	19.500	32.20
DAL	Delta Airlines	50.125	80.000	59.60
F	Ford Motor	50.500	54.250	7.43
FBO	Federal Paper Board	20.250	28.500	40.74
FED	First Federal Financial	13.875	21.875	57.66
FFA	FirstFed America	15.500	27.000	74.19
FNB	First Chicago	29.625	48.250	62.87
FWES	First Western Financial	6.250	8.500	36.00
FWF	Far West Financial	7.875	13.000	65.08
GD	General Dynamics	50.750	58.250	14.78
GDV	General Development	12.625	14.375	13.86
GLN	GlenFed Inc.	19.625	24.375	24.20
GTA	Great American 1st	11.250	13.000	15.56
HME	Home Group (Ambase)	11.000	15.750	43.18
HOC	Holly Corp.	12.500	28.375	127.00
HTHR	Hawthorne Financial	22.000	34.250	55.68
ICA	Imperial Corp. America	9.125	4.375	−52.05
INDB	Independent Bank Corp.	10.750	11.250	4.65
IRE	Integrated Resources	13.875	2.250	−83.78
JII	Johnston Industries 3:2	10.917	12.375	13.36
LEN	Lennar Corp.	17.625	22.125	25.53
LK	Lockheed Corp.	41.250	51.500	24.85
LMS	Lamson & Sessions	12.875	11.250	−12.62
LNDL	Lindal Cedar Homes 10%	7.955	6.750	−15.15
MRI.A	McRae Industries Cl A	5.500	5.250	−4.55
PGI	Ply-Gem Industries	11.875	14.000	17.89
RBSN	Robeson Industries	1.500	2.125	41.67
RLI	RLI Corp.	7.625	8.875	16.39
SBOS	Boston Bancorp	15.375	17.625	14.63
SPF	Standard Pacific	12.000	18.500	54.17
STO	Stone Container	32.000	32.000	.00

FIGURE 7–15—*Concluded*

Symbol	Corporation	12/30/88	6/30/89	% Change
SUPD	Supradur Companies	12.500	11.750	−6.00
UAC	Unicorp American	5.750	3.625	−36.96
UK	Union Carbide	25.625	30.875	20.49
WDC	Western Digital	14.750	9.250	−37.29
WLC	Wellco Enterprises	15.250	15.000	−1.64
	Averages	17.367	21.766	23.60

SUMMARY, OR TO BE CONTINUED

This chapter does not need a summary so much as a *to be continued*. Overnight, market psychology flipped—on June 27 with the release of the leading economic indicators down 1.2 percent—from belief in a "soft landing" with reduced but sustainable growth to fears of a "hard landing" recession. From a scenario that would permit decreasing interest and inflation rates with continued slow economic growth, the script was rewritten to include a recession in progress or just around the corner with corporate earnings about to tank. Time will tell, but we know that markets advance smartly after recessions begin, in anticipation of the next up cycle.

The process continues year after year, each year having its crisis or two, and yet over decade-length periods the market or well-selected portfolios rise on average. After so many years, it seems silly to get concerned over daily, weekly, or even monthly fluctuations in the market. Just become "partners" with a large diversified number of corporations—especially when conditions look pretty bad—and benefit over the years by their long-term growth (on average) until euphoria whistles in your ear to take profits and a long vacation.

CHAPTER 8

POTPOURRI—A STOCK MARKETEER'S STEW

This is a small, catchall chapter, but it is not just afterthoughts or minor miscellaneous subjects. Included are important ideas that are not chapters in themselves yet have been helpful to me and are worthy of your consideration. Some ideas are taken from the better essays of 12 years' worth of *The Prudent Speculator* newsletter. Some are partially reviewed elsewhere but deserve repeated or specific emphasis, such as the following topic.

THE STOCKBROKER IS NOT YOUR FRIEND

In my 20 years of speculating and my dozen years as a money manager, I have known a few good registered representatives—also known as *account executives, vice presidents, financial consultants, first vice presidents, senior vice presidents, investment representatives*—but generally called *stockbrokers* or *my broker* by the investing public. For the most part, I have been disillusioned and disappointed with brokers and brokerage houses.

In Chapter 5, I reviewed some of the questionable practices brokers use in relation to margin accounts and their maintenance levels. For anyone using a margined account, it is vital to be clear on what could happen to you in a crunch. For years you might have a wonderful, conflict-free relationship with your broker, only to be abused during a period of chaos in a sharp market selloff. I wrote about the subject of brokers for the March 28, 1984, edition of *The Prudent Speculator*, and nothing much has changed from my additional experience since then. In fact, during the Crash of '87, some brokers and brokerage houses behaved worse than I ever thought likely.

At the risk of offending "the brokerage industry," but in the service of my most needful readers, let me state that the small investor ought not to think of his or her broker (account executive) as a friend, fiduciary, or investment counsel. With a few notable exceptions, the typical account executive has not the time, talent, nor expertise to pick stocks, time markets, or manage portfolios.

Essentially, the typical account executive is a telephone-order taker and "product" salesperson. The broker generally works strictly for commission income, the percentage of which increases as gross commissions are generated (except in most discount brokerages); thus, no trades mean no new shoes for the kids or no new toys for the parents. A registered representative may be on the phone 50 to 100 or more times during a long working day—perhaps from 6:30 a.m. to 6:30 p.m. on the West Coast—often prospecting by making cold calls in a frantic effort to build up a "book" of customers, otherwise canvassing active and inactive clients in an effort to induce trades or sell brokerage-sponsored products, such as CDs or limited partnerships.

The account executive is given canned research, which may be out-of-date and inappropriate for a given client's portfolio. He or she rarely has the time, skill, or documentation to analyze the brokerage's recommendations. The account executive is often told to sell new issues and secondary distributions, with the infamous prevarication, "And there's no commission when you buy this stock." An egregious dissembling is the "no commission" ploy, as the "commission" is factored into the net price of the stock or product, usually at a much higher amount paid to the broker than a normal trading commission would amount to. With apologies to those wonderful brokers I know of, you readers might better think of your account executive as your adversary than your ally.

The realities of the system work against the benefit of the small investor. It takes no more time to write a ticket order for 500 shares of a $50 stock than for 100 shares of a $9 stock. On the latter, the brokerage house makes its minimum commission, often crying all the way to the bank that it costs more to service that transaction than it makes. And the account executive gets his 25 percent to 40 percent, a paltry $10-$20, perhaps, for the small placement, while for the larger item—the $25,000 ticket—several hundred dollars may be charged in commissions, even though the percentage rate is much smaller than for the $900 trade.

In whom is the account executive and his or her boss, the branch manager, going to be interested, given their druthers, the $900 investor or the $25,000 trader? An extreme example perhaps, but I have seen the principle applied to myself—in both directions over the years—and to many others. The big, active investor gets attention and service, the small fry gets tolerance, perhaps. But don't blame the broker for this. Think of your own business or activity. Do you want to deal with and spend much time on people who usually do not know the score and clearly cannot contribute much to your well-being? There is a lot of lip service about goodwill, and developing the little investor into the big client over the years, but time and reality intrude and take their toll.

Nor are discount brokerages always a relief from the "better service for the VIP" syndrome. They are sometimes manned with burnt out or beginning registered reps who cannot or will not compete in the full-service brokerage business jungle. For your discount, you may get long waits on the telephone, no advice (probably a blessing), and the runaround when something goes wrong. And many things can go wrong with all brokers. If Las Vegas or Atlantic City operated like most brokerage houses, they would be out of business within one year. As recent history shows, many brokerage houses have not survived deregulation, slack markets, or the Crash of '87 and have either closed their doors or saved their faces with timely (shotgun) mergers.

Perhaps I paint too strong a picture. If I overstate, it is in the hope that a few readers will be saved from placing unwarranted trust in the brokerage industry. Many brokerages are shameless. Many will issue checks on out-of-state banks—in spite of the scandals associated with such float strategies—often causing the small investor, who needs the money, delays in getting the check cleared. This scheme gives the brokerage house a float of two or three days to earn interest on your funds. You must be prepared to defend yourself against your broker and be willing to ferret out the few who can and will give you the kind of service you need and deserve.

Few novices know about *negotiated commissions,* a phrase many account executives abhor. Investors with accounts of $100,000 or more regularly obtain 25 percent to 50 percent commission reductions from full-service brokerages, based sometimes upon trading frequency. Even small investors may be able to obtain a discount from a full-service brokerage if the brokerage is pressed to give one. Most everything in the financial community is negotiable, and there is still considerable competition, although the industry has closed ranks on certain subjects such as arbitration versus court trials. You should be aware of all these considerations—and those detailed in Chapter 5—in selecting a broker-age house and an account executive. And you might consider one more truism—one usually only gets what one pays for, if that much. Free advice is usually worth what it costs, while expensive investment advice is generally overpriced.

IS IT ONLY MONEY?

One of the small comforts of investing in stocks and not doing well (which is to say, losing) is the cheerful little rationalization, "It's only money."

Of course, we should not speculate with money we cannot afford to lose, especially for the short term. I knew a person who was planning to buy a house in the fall of '87 with money accumulated by the Spring of '87 but decided to get on the booming stock market bandwagon for just six months in order to enhance his down payment. After October, his funds were insufficient for a minimum down payment and, to add insult to injury, he also had to forfeit a substantial option deposit on the house of his choice.

For about four months of my life I studied gaming in Las Vegas, especially the craps and 21 tables. The sagest thing I ever heard in Vegas was, "There are two kind of players, those who make money bets and those who make mental bets. If you bet money, that's all you can lose, but if you make mental bets you can lose your minds."

We should not make investing in the stock market a test of our worth as human beings, win or lose. If we have a good day in the market, that doesn't make us any brighter, wiser, or even kinder, necessarily, although it's easier for most people to be kinder after a good day than a bad one. If we have a good year in the market, we may not be more interesting, warm, intelligent, or loving than before, although a good year may be interesting in a limited way, and we may feel more generous and loving than we would after a bad year.

It is this reinforcement of high self-esteem that "winning" may give and the opposite reinforcement of low self-esteem that "losing" may engender that makes speculating in stocks such a dangerous and personality-distorting enterprise. If it were only money at stake, that would be bad enough, but for some it may be a question of mental health. And I'm not even talking about compulsive gamblers or other neurotics who have a need to "keep up with the Joneses" or who are punishing themselves by losing in that sophisticated casino (for them) called the stock market.

There is a considerable danger that success in speculation could turn you into a tunnel-visioned, self-deluded, and insular person as more and more time is spent on studying corporations, the market, the economy, newsletters, and government regulators, and finding satisfaction only in conversations about the market, especially those in which your smartness is displayed. It is very easy, especially for those who have met with the winning ways of a bull market, to become stock market junkies, paying dearly for their initial good fortune over and over again in bear markets, as well as in diminished sociability. Early or big success leads to unrealistic expectations and frustration with historically reasonable, somewhat better-than-average returns.

PAPER TRADING IS NOT ACTUAL TRADING

People who trade so well in their imaginations or on paper usually do less well when real dollars are involved in real time. One can easily forget a bad trade one would have made while recalling another trade that would have turned out great. One can remember a low entry price, perhaps lower than it actually was at the time the stock was considered. What about the mental effect of seeing a price higher than one would have been likely to realize, and be trapped in the optimism (or greed) of a roaring blowoff that quickly collapsed?

When "paper trading," one can easily ignore trading commission expenses—after all they amount to "only" 1 percent or 2 percent of the transaction. Ah, but every position involves at least two trades, buying and selling, so that turning over the portfolio two or three times a year involves perhaps 8 percent to 12 percent in commissions. Considering that the long term common stock total returns range from 10 percent to 12 percent— depending upon what kinds of stocks are dealt with—it would be very easy to spin one's wheels by paying as much for the privilege of trading as one might expect as an average annual return. And the total return includes dividends, many that would not be received in a heavily traded portfolio.

Sometimes when people are practicing, clocking, back checking, or trying other forms of paper trading, there is a tendency to fix on the closing or average price of a stock for that day's "trade." In reality, one often pays a bit more, due to buying at the asking price, or receives a bit less, due to selling at the bid price, than the closing or average price for a day. These eighths or quarters (or more) of additional costs or reduced proceeds can add up to a significant penalty.

Say you bought a stock intraday for $10.25 that closed at $10.00 and sold another stock intraday for $9.75 that closed at $10 per share. The effect of these two trades—not unlike buying and selling the same stock— cost you 2.5 percent each way compared to the closing prices. If this occurs often, or if the differences turn out to be even greater, say 3/8 or 1/2 of a point, real-time results would vary from the paper trading results by several percent, depending upon the number of trades and varying executions. It should not be surprising that many an investor cannot seem to match real performance to simulated or paper performance. Bob Prechter, editor of *The Elliott Wave Theorist* (P.O. Box 1618, Gainesville, GA 30503), has for a decade in speaches at investment conferences pointed out that paper trading is not actual trading, especially in obtaining executed orders.

THE PERFECT IS THE ENEMY OF THE GOOD

Whoever said, "The perfect is the enemy of the good" could have been talking about the stock market. So many investors who have done rather well in the market still tend to be dissatisfied because they read of those few who have done spectacularly well—often for only a short period of time. This syndrome of, "The returns are always greener in another system," leads some investors into discontent and impatience, often producing worse results from shifting to last year's hot strategy than sticking with one's own long-time "adequate" strategy.

The appearance of short-term, erratic returns versus the reality of long-term, relatively consistent gains has often been the subject of editorial comment in *The Hulbert Financial Digest* (316 Commerce Street, Alexandria, Va. 22314). Not only does the *HFD* report on the performance of a large number of newsletter portfolios, it also reviews investing strategies and historical comparisons worthy of consideration. Perhaps the greatest service the *HFD* performs is to explode false and outrageous performance claims, while bringing reasonable and realistic expectations to its readers' attention.

There are any number of reasonable goals to strive for in terms of invested returns. John Templeton's expressed goal is 15 percent compounded annually over a multi-year period. My goal is 18 percent compounded annually over a multi-year period in a cash account, but 27 percent compounded over a five-to-ten-year period in a heavily margined account. Barry Ziskin's goal is to obtain a 30 percent annual gain, defined as, during a market cycle from peak to peak or trough to trough. Ziskin bases his goal on the premise that the corporations he selects tend to grow at 30 percent or more per year.

We know that 10 percent is the 63-year average for S&P 500 stocks, and 12.3 percent is the 63-year average for very small capitalization stocks, so those might be minimums. Given that one *should* do a bit better than average following a systematic strategy such as this book presents, a return of 15 percent to 18 percent could be considered reasonable, handsome, and likely attainable over a multi-year period.

During various economic cycles, one might set a total return goal in terms of after-inflation returns, or after-inflation and after-tax returns. Again, we can turn to the long-term historical statistics for comparison (Figures 8–1 and 8–2). Remember, the effect of inflation reduces the purchasing power of the original capital investment as well as after-tax gains.

FIGURE 8–1
After-Inflation, After-Tax Returns, Assuming 40% Total Tax Liability

Inflation	Returns					
	10.00%	12.50%	15.00%	17.50%	20.00%	22.50%
3%	2.82	4.28	5.73	7.19	8.64	10.10
4	1.76	3.20	4.64	6.08	7.52	8.96
5	.70	2.13	3.55	4.98	6.40	7.83
6	-.36	1.05	2.46	3.87	5.28	6.69
7	-1.42	-.03	1.37	2.77	4.16	5.56
8	-2.48	-1.10	.28	1.66	3.04	4.42
9	-3.54	-2.18	-.81	.56	1.92	3.29
10	-4.60	-3.25	-1.90	-.55	.80	2.15

From an after-tax, after-inflation return point of view, we might consider a net 3 percent return fair or adequate. Currently, if you are in the top tax bracket and in a high-tax state, you might well be paying at a 40 percent or greater income tax rate on capital gains and investment income. If so, Figure 8–1 shows that with a 3 percent inflation, a 10 percent total return would result in a 2.82 percent after-tax, after-inflation

FIGURE 8–2
After-Inflation, After-Tax Returns, Assuming 30% Total Tax Liability

	Returns					
Inflation	10.00%	12.50%	15.00%	17.50%	20.00%	22.50%
3%	3.79	5.49	7.19	8.88	10.58	12.28
4	2.72	4.40	6.08	7.76	9.44	11.12
5	1.65	3.31	4.98	6.64	8.30	9.96
6	.58	2.23	3.87	5.52	7.16	8.81
7	-.49	1.14	2.77	4.39	6.02	7.65
8	-1.56	.05	1.66	3.27	4.88	6.49
9	-2.63	-1.04	.56	2.15	3.74	5.33
10%	-3.70	-2.13	-.55	1.03	2.60	4.18

gain. Indeed, in the inflation environment during the summer of '89—
with inflation running about 5 percent to 6 percent—you would want to
obtain a 15 percent to 16 percent total return in order to keep up your
living standard and add incrementally to your growing capital.

Perhaps a 30 percent tax bracket is more appropriate for many small
investors than the 40 percent assumption. If so, Figure 8–2 shows that with
a 5 percent inflation rate a 12.5 percent gross return would provide a
relatively "fair" after-tax, after-inflation return. One reason the subject of
after-tax, after-inflation returns is rarely reviewed is the great variation in
tax liabilities individual investors may face. To cover everybody's case we
would have to display tables not unlike those in the Internal Revenue
Service 1040 instruction manuals, and still there would be variations.
Nevertheless, we can appreciate that in a 6 percent inflation, with a 40
percent tax bite, we lose purchasing power if our total return is only 10
percent, as we would with a 10 percent total return and a 7 percent inflation
with a 30 percent tax liability.

BEING A CONTRARIAN IS CORRECT
BUT COMPLICATED

Although I think of myself as a contrarian thinker and speculator, willing
to go against the crowd, discover and commit funds to the out-of-favor
stock—assuming it is sufficiently fundamentally undervalued—I still
have trouble with a contrarian rallying cry, "The majority is always

wrong.'' For starters, *always* is usually inaccurate, and beyond that, it is often difficult to determine which group is the majority or what is their strongly held attitude, let alone how much of a cohesive majority is needed in how extreme a condition before they are wrong.

We contrarians believe that usually at market extremes ''the majority'' is wrong. This is the principle of sentiment measures, when what seems an oxymoron, ''Too much bullishness is bearish,'' becomes both reasonable and somewhat predictive. That is, when the overwhelming majority is enthusiastically bullish and the market is making historic highs as registered in its major averages, most of the likely participants are in the market, with most of their capital invested; thus there is little capital left to drive the market higher. What does not go up—at least in stock market physics—sooner or later comes down. But, ''the majority'' can be bullish for quite a while as the market continues advancing into overbought territory.

And, the reverse is true at sold-out market bottoms, where most (a large majority?) of the stock market participants who wanted to sell or had to sell have already sold, so thereafter the line of least resistance is a market rise, in spite of the pessimistic majority. These are rationales for and descriptions of overbought and oversold markets, which we've reviewed before.

Still, it seems to me that many times the majority is right, and for long periods of time. As with any trend-following system, following the majority is right until the trend reverses (the market reverses) and one gets caught as part of the wrong majority. Often, the majority is a better indicator of market lows than of market highs. As the market was plunging in November 1988, it looked as though the worst fears of the bearish gurus were about to be realized—the other shoe was dropping— and soon the market would revisit and exceed the October '87 crash lows. Bearishness was rampant, and bullishness was in small supply.

Investors Intelligence, edited by Michael Burke (Chartcraft Inc., New Rochelle, N.Y. 10801), a publication that tracks investment newsletter (advisory) opinion as well as presents its own technical and charting information, reported in its December 9, 1988 issue that only 21.1 percent of the advisory services it monitors were bullish, while 55.3 percent were bearish. The publication pointed out that, ''You have to go all the way back to June 1982 to find as few bulls or as many bears as we saw 2 weeks ago and this indicator is very bullish.'' In the December 8, 1988 issue of *The Prudent Speculator* we noted this condition, summarizing: ''On this sentiment indicator basis, we have a screaming contrarian buy signal.''

It is good to be aware of market majorities, if they can be identified, and to consider such sentiment indicators along with other technical indicators and fundamental criteria of value. It is also good not to try to outguess an alleged majority, thus altering one's basic approach, hoping to catch a trend reversal based on intuitive expectations.

Over the years I have written about the BB syndrome—the bullish-but or bearish-but psychology of individual, institutional, or stock advisory participants. The BB syndrome occurs when people report, "I'm bullish (or bearish) *but* I'm waiting to see how the market develops." Often that means they are not buying or selling, so their bullishness or bearishness is not really affecting the market's trend. This is one of the reasons why it is so difficult to get a clear picture of what is a majority and what it is doing.

By the way, a "newsletter" that has been a source of inspiration and comfort and that I have enjoyed for many years is *The Contrary Investor*, written by James L. Fraser, C.F.A. (309 South Willard St., Burlington, Vt. 05401). This low-key, two-page, green-tinted, biweekly generally quotes and comments upon the Contrarian's coping with the Crowd. In keeping with his New England, away-from-Wall-Street location, Fraser takes and reviews "the road less travelled." For instance, in the June 28, 1989 issue, as part of an essay on "What Do You Think of the Market?", Fraser writes,

> The normal person does best with a dollar averaging program that keeps emotions in the background. To be sure, the true Contrarian can do better but that means concentrating hard on your own feelings and being able to associate them with the Wall Street community. You buy when you feel bad and you sell when you feel good. That is a lot to ask from the healthy and normal thinking person. Reverence for the latest investment fashion or whoever is doing well at the moment should be set aside. The most sacred of investment duties is to be disciplined without losing your power of imagination.

SHUN SLOGANS, MINIMIZE MAXIMS

Stock market slogans and cliches generally fall into a category of half-truths or contingent truths. That is, the kinds of slogans and maxims mentioned in previous chapters and reviewed below have elements of truth to them but are often misleading and sometimes false. If you find yourself parroting some stock market slogan because it makes you comfortable or rationalizes current conditions, beware that you have not been seduced by platitude, euphemism, or delusion. Bob Prechter has also long been critical of conflicting cliches such as, "You can never go broke taking a profit" versus "Cut your losses short and let profits run."

"Nobody ever went broke taking a profit" or "You can never go broke taking a profit" are examples of rationalizations rather than rationales. These slogans are at best misleading and at worst false. If the profits you take are less than the after-tax, after-inflation penalties, you might not go broke, but your purchasing power and standard of living will probably decrease if you are dependent upon stock market gains. However, there likely are people who did go broke taking profits, especially consistently taking small profits that were more than wiped out by realized or unrealized large losses. If your average realized profit is 10 percent to 15 percent, and your average loss is 20 percent to 25 percent—and you manage about as many winners as losers, not an unheard of balance—you could go broke over time.

You must have profits that more than compensate for your losses. Many successful investors have claimed that if you are right only 3 or 4 times out of 10, you can make a fortune in the stock market. They are assuming (based on experience) that when you are right your profits will be in the 100 percent to 1,000 percent or more range, while when you are wrong your losses will tend to be less than 100 percent and perhaps only 25 percent or less, on average.

In fact, to counteract the "No one ever went broke taking a profit" rationalization, we have the more widely quoted slogan, "Cut short your losses and let your profits run on." How you take profits while letting them run on is a trick I have not mastered. One strategy to reconcile these paradoxical maxims is to sell half your position after a 100 percent gain. In theory that would mean that you couldn't lose, since you had recovered your costs, and you continue playing with "house money." This "Swiss technique" violates the principle that a position is a buy, hold, or sell. Either the whole position should be sold because it is fairly valued (and the profits locked in), or the whole position should be held because it is undervalued (letting the profits run on).

Although letting profits run on is a good idea and cutting short losses is a good-sounding idea, the reality is that often a short-term loss turns into a long-term gain. If you are quick to dump a stock that has a small decline, you have not only cut short your (temporary) loss in that stock, you have also cut short your potential for profit in that stock. You have "locked in your loss." As mentioned frequently in this book, many early losses or sharp declines thereafter are merely part of the pattern of market price fluctuations along the way to great gains. True, some stocks continue to lose and never recover, but the best policy is to base sells on fundamental values, accepting the occasional disaster.

BEWARE ILLOGICAL EXAMPLES

"I never buy at the bottom or sell at the top; I'm content with the 60 percent in between." This self-serving slogan is a real come-on used by snake-oil-type salespersons. First, any statement that has the words *always* or *never* in it is suspect if not outright false. Second, who does buy at the bottom or sell at the top? Such events are generally accidents and certainly not predictable. As for the being content with only taking a large chunk out of the middle, this come-on is so illogical that it is worth explicating how ridiculous it is.

In Chapter 1 I wrote about some of the problems and tricks associated with performance statistics, specifically the confusion of averaged annual gains with compounded annual gains (see Figure 1–2). There are endless examples of weak or illogical analogies or arguments.

One terrific-sounding and great-looking but absurd proposition is made when investment advisors or portfolio managers claim that they are not greedy because they never try to buy at the bottom or sell at the top: they merely capture the great gains in between. Immediately, we should be alert to the reality that no one can know the bottom or top until after the fact, and therefore no one could possibly decide in advance to trade at slightly above or below those points. Otherwise, if you could determine bottoms and tops, why wouldn't you trade at those points exactly in order to maximize your gains and minimize your losses?

Some people who would normally see the fallacy of charlatans who claim concurrent or advance knowledge of market tops and bottoms may become mesmerized by the attractive use of graphics, specifically a picture of a bell-shaped curve such as the left curve in Figure 8–3. The con artist shows that if one waits for a 20 percent rise off the low, participates in the next 60 percent of the up cycle, and then gets out about 20 percent before the top, great returns will be gleaned by capturing 60 percent of the move. Ah, but how do you know where 20 percent off the low is, since you have no foreknowledge of how far the apparent trend will continue? Likewise, how do you know that you are 20 percent away from the top before the top has been made and the trend reverses?

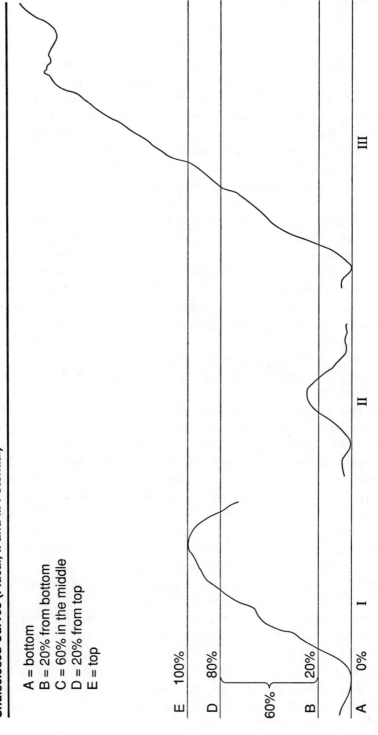

FIGURE 8-3
Undisclosed Curves (I Ideal, II and III Potential)

A = bottom
B = 20% from bottom
C = 60% in the middle
D = 20% from top
E = top

Actually, few trends are as smooth and none is as predictable as Figure 8–3's leftmost curve would indicate, but the smooth-talking salesperson may be able to convince many a naive but otherwise reasonable, investor that this "ungreedy" timing method is a winning strategy. And there is much that is appealing about using an "ungreedy" method. Meanwhile, Figure 8–3's middle or right curves may be as probable as its left one, as examples of a stock's price moving from point A to point B and what might happen thereafter.

Over the years I have criticized and explored the consequences of admonitions to "Never meet a maintenance call," "Never average down," and "It's not a loss until you sell." One challenge, "Never confuse brains with a bull market," might well be an absolute guide, even though it uses the word *never*. A true bull market is a wonderful thing to behold and participate in. Month after month, even year after year, the majority of stocks advance in price as on a stairway to the stars. You can make many mistakes in a bull market, and the market will bail you out. Sooner or later almost all groups participate, and while there will always be the stocks that fail, they are so overcome by the stocks that advance it becomes easy to imagine that you have a special insight into the secrets of the market.

Sooner or later the day of reckoning arrives for many, and what was a brilliant participation in the strong uptrend becomes a terrible overcommitment to the tricky decline. The long-expected correction, which was supposed to be a minor pause to refresh, turns into a deeper selloff than expected. After the briefest of technical bounces up, the expected resumption of the major advance turns into a mockery as prices fall slowly or sharply. Profits are erased and it seems too late to sell, if not too early to buy, "into weakness." Losses begin to mount up and one quickly realizes what a good move it would have been to have sold during the first of the setbacks or into the "bear market rally."

Braggadocio turns to lament, gurus become ex-gurus, and oaths with the words *never again* in them are sworn. After the down cycle, few people identify their brains with the market at all. Who ever heard of someone saying, "Don't confuse brains with a bear market"? And yet, in the deepest despair of a stock market bottom, the next bull market is being born, the darkest investment night gives rise to the brightest investment day. At least our brains should remember the nature of markets, not unlike the nature of existence.

Vanity of vanities, saith the Preacher, vanity of
    vanities; all is vanity.
What profit hath a man of all his labor which he
    taketh under the sun?
One generation passeth away, and another generation
    cometh: but the earth abideth for ever.
The sun also ariseth.

Ecclesiastes 1:2–5

One generation of investors drops out, and another generation comes along, but the market goes on.

Clearly, many investment slogans are true some of the time or under certain conditions, but often they block clear thinking. The next time you find yourself mouthing a slogan, perhaps in stentorian tones with your audience nodding in affirmative assent, try running it up the flagpole—your critical analytical flagpole—and see how it fits in with the current winds and conditions. Speculating by slogan is a great way to miss what's going on.

A SMALL CONFESSION ABOUT A LARGE GAIN

Since the dust settled on the Crash of '87 during the first week of December '87, I have bought only one stock (200 shares of the Z-Seven Fund) and sold only seven or eight stocks, mostly because they were sell candidates in *The Prudent Speculator*. I tried to hold onto as many shares as I could after the crash and continue to let them "mature." Thus, The Prudent Speculator Portfolio, which has generated the performance displayed in Figure 8–4, has remained as an almost passive investment for over 22 months. Of course, several stocks were taken away in buyouts and mergers, which provided additional cash when needed.

I would like to have bought more stocks with the cash received from buyouts, sales and with the loan value developed through portfolio appreciation. Obviously my total gains would be considerably greater if I had leveraged and pyramided the buying power generated over the past 22 months. I chose rather to reduce exposure during periods when the market looked vulnerable, although the portfolio remained fully margined, and to pay some debts.

I confess to this passive speculative approach in another attempt to convince readers that long-term holding (time diversification), when combined with wide stock diversification of selected undervalued equities, can really pay off. True, there were some stocks that went bad, such as Financial Corporation of America (FIN), or did poorly, such as Equitec Financial Group (EFG), Southmark (SM) and Integrated Resources (IRE). But, as usual, the stocks that did well more than compensated for the ones that failed or have yet to approach their intrinsic values.

Displaying the performance of TPS Portfolio since December 4, 1987 also gives us a chance to review what is probably the best way of accounting for investment performance, using net asset value (NAV) (the way open-end mutual funds must account for their net assets each day). Notice in the Figure 8–4 that TPS Portfolio (TPSP) has a beginning equity value of $258,883. (We round up to dollars in terms of market value, debit balance, and equity.) We arbitrarily assign 258,883 "shares" to TPS Portfolio (TPSP) with a NAV of $1 as of December 4, 1987. Thereafter, whenever cash is added, it will "buy" that amount of TPSP shares at their then current value, just as you would buy shares in an open-end fund at that day's NAV. And whenever cash is withdrawn, TPSP shares will be "sold" at their current value, just as you would liquidate your mutual fund shares at that day's NAV.

Although these computations are the simplest approach and the most accurate representation, they may seem a bit confusing until you realize what is going on. It should be obvious that we must account for cash added to a portfolio so that the portfolio's increases in value and calculated performance gains are not confused with the cash additions that increased the portfolio's values but were not gains from market appreciation. Likewise, we must account for withdrawals of cash, otherwise it would look as though the portfolio had lost in market depreciation because of the lower market value and equity amounts actually caused by cash withdrawn.

For greater accuracy, it would be best if NAV were calculated daily, as is done for mutual funds. However, mutual funds must do that in order to account for the shares that are being purchased and redeemed daily, as well as their daily withdrawal of management fees and other costs. In a personal portfolio, where only periodic additions or withdrawals are made, monthly or even quarterly calculations could be reasonably sufficient, although provision should be made for large changes on the day they occur. We keep such figures for TPS Portfolio on a weekly basis.

Observe in Figure 8–4 that after the first week (December 11, 1987), the net equity value increased $15,675 or 6.05 percent. As there

FIGURE 8–4
Net Asset Value Analysis, TPS Portfolio 12/4/87–6/30/89

Date	Value	Debit	Equity	Add/Del	Shares	NAV
12/4/87	689205	430322	258883		258883.000	1.0000
12/11/87	704241	429683	274558		258883.000	1.0605
12/18/87	747508	439044	308464		258883.000	1.1915
12/24/87	761103	428979	332124	−5000	254686.676	1.3040
12/31/87	751794	437899	313895		254686.676	1.2325
1/8/88	768489	437208	331281		254686.676	1.3007
1/15/88	781263	436550	344713		254686.676	1.3535
1/22/88	782230	436500	345730		254686.676	1.3575
1/29/88	808779	439101	369678		254686.676	1.4515
2/5/88	802100	444257	357843		254686.676	1.4050
2/12/88	805437	440036	365401		254686.676	1.4347
2/19/88	815100	439469	375631		254686.676	1.4749
2/26/88	828787	442546	386241		254686.676	1.5165
3/4/88	865413	444522	420891		254686.676	1.6526
3/11/88	871928	443815	428113		254686.676	1.6809
3/18/88	883081	443192	439889		254686.676	1.7272
3/25/88	868731	443157	425574		254686.676	1.6710
3/31/88	866367	445928	420439		254686.676	1.6508
4/8/88	886592	445413	441179		254686.676	1.7322
4/15/88	829313	412466	416847		254686.676	1.6367
4/22/88	835299	412466	422833		254686.676	1.6602
4/29/88	847242	415398	431844		254686.676	1.6956
5/6/88	837060	407472	429588		254686.676	1.6867
5/13/88	832811	409792	423019		254686.676	1.6609
5/20/88	822250	409168	413082		254686.676	1.6219
5/27/88	828653	408186	420467		254686.676	1.6509
6/3/88	855554	442806	412748	−33000	234697.805	1.7586
6/10/88	870447	440688	429759		234697.805	1.8311
6/17/88	860594	431653	428941		234697.805	1.8276
6/24/88	858699	426895	431804		234697.805	1.8398
7/1/88	862587	429167	433420		234697.805	1.8467
7/8/88	838212	409958	428254		234697.805	1.8247
7/15/88	822128	389252	432876		234697.805	1.8444
7/22/88	811971	415007	396964	−31800	217456.401	1.8255
7/29/88	815081	407675	407406		217456.401	1.8735
8/5/88	811350	421541	389809	−14300	209823.655	1.8578
8/12/88	792287	421489	370798		209823.655	1.7672
8/19/88	790010	420805	369205		209823.655	1.7596
8/26/88	779812	420435	359377		209823.655	1.7128
9/2/88	771576	411441	360135		209823.655	1.7164
9/9/88	774682	410845	363837		209823.655	1.7340
9/16/88	783586	420716	362870	−10600	203710.668	1.7813

FIGURE 8-4 —Continued

Date	Value	Debit	Equity	Add/Del	Shares	NAV
9/23/88	787088	420800	366288		203710.668	1.7981
9/30/88	791230	424082	367148		203710.668	1.8023
10/7/88	807777	423246	384531		203710.668	1.8876
10/14/88	806898	423434	383464		203710.668	1.8824
10/21/88	823712	422395	401317		203710.668	1.9700
10/28/88	812818	422283	390535		203710.668	1.9171
11/4/88	805874	428496	377378		203710.668	1.8525
11/11/88	791196	428304	362892		203710.668	1.7814
11/18/88	769189	425878	343311		203710.668	1.6853
11/25/88	774993	424595	350398		203710.668	1.7201
12/2/88	787939	426838	361101		203710.668	1.7726
12/9/88	798432	431555	366877	−5500	200607.911	1.8288
12/16/88	802075	430413	371662		200607.911	1.8527
12/23/88	804955	430320	374635		200607.911	1.8675
12/30/88	807386	434336	373050		200607.911	1.8596
1/6/89	824328	433415	390913		200607.911	1.9486
1/13/89	831182	428615	402567		200607.911	2.0067
1/20/89	834882	427966	406916		200607.911	2.0284
1/27/89	843217	427347	415870		200607.911	2.0730
2/3/89	835816	414189	421627		200607.911	2.1017
2/10/89	817403	396075	421328	−5000	198228.937	2.1255
2/17/89	827706	398871	428835		198228.937	2.1633
2/24/89	813229	398397	414832		198228.937	2.0927
3/3/89	828468	420370	408098	−20000	188671.867	2.1630
3/10/89	839030	419661	419369		188671.867	2.2227
3/17/89	834490	435122	399368	−16000	181473.552	2.2007
3/23/89	827148	433122	394026		181473.552	2.1713
3/31/89	834710	437103	397607		181473.552	2.1910
4/7/89	843283	436310	406973		181473.552	2.2426
4/14/89	849301	436310	412991		181473.552	2.2758
4/21/89	857066	432882	424184		181473.552	2.3374
4/28/89	861986	441197	420789		181473.552	2.3187
5/5/89	855175	433208	421967		181473.552	2.3252
5/12/89	865596	433082	432514		181473.552	2.3833
5/19/89	884961	432610	452351		181473.552	2.4927
5/26/89	892821	431162	461659		181473.552	2.5439
6/2/89	905621	440942	464679	−6800	178800.540	2.5989
6/9/89	913364	440539	472825		178800.540	2.6444
6/16/89	901935	439484	462451		178800.540	2.5864
6/23/89	919074	456580	462494	−17900	171879.743	2.6908
6/30/89	892792	462494	430298		171879.743	2.5035
7/7/89	907586	456307	451279		171879.743	2.6256
7/14/89	918446	456018	462428		171879.743	2.6904
7/21/89	917539	455392	462147		171879.743	2.6888

FIGURE 8–4 —*Concluded*

Date	Value	Debit	Equity	Add/Del	Shares	NAV
7/28/89	922489	449234	473255		171879.743	2.7534
8/4/89	925531	452502	473029		171879.743	2.7521
8/11/89	946203	452362	493841		171879.743	2.8732
8/18/89	938212	451752	486460		171879.743	2.8302
8/25/89	935595	451184	484411		171879.743	2.8183
9/1/89	941839	462309	479530	−8000	169041.166	2.8368
Total Cash Out				−173900		

was no cash added or withdrawn, there were no changes in TPSP shares. Thus, the NAV per TPSP share increased to $1.0605, a figure obtained by dividing the number of TPSP shares into the net equity value.

After the second week (December 18, 1987)—which was a very big week in TPS Portfolio, with its equity value jumping up $33,906 (a gain of 12.35 percent)—I withdrew $5,000 in cash, which is to say I borrowed $5,000. In doing so, I "sold" (liquidated) $5,000 worth of TPSP shares. By December 18, TPSP shares were worth approximately $1.1915 each, so $5,000 required "selling" only 4,196.324 shares, thus reducing the TPSP shares to 254,686.676, a number that remains unchanged until the next time cash was withdrawn. Between December 4, 1987 and September 1, 1989, no cash was added, so all the computations are to account for withdrawals and market fluctuations.

The bottom lines are that TPS Portfolio appreciated 183.68 percent in NAV between December 4, 1987 and September 1, 1989, and that $173,900 in cash was withdrawn during that period. I find it particularly satisfying that the cash withdrawals over the past 21 months amount to 67 percent of the net equity on December 4, 1987, and yet, even after these withdrawals, the net equity value was $479,503 on September 1, 1989, or 85 percent greater than that of December 4, 1987. Of course, we must not confuse brains with a bull market as mentioned above, especially as bull markets tend to overcome a large number of poor choices and strategic mistakes. For the curious, TPS Portfolio as of June 30, 1989 is displayed in Appendix B.

A superficial scan of the table above, with its handsome gain over the 21 months, might lead some to believe that it was an uninterrupted advance, just week after week of gains with nary a setback along the way. A closer inspection reveals that up to March 11, 1988, the NAV had gained 68.09 percent—a tremendous 4-month appreciation—but by

November 8, 1988, the NAV was again at 68.53 percent, thus indicating no meaningful gain in value for that period of eight months and one week. Even more troubling at the time, the NAV had gained 97.00 percent by October 21, 1988, only to lose $58,006, or 14.45 percent in the following four weeks, wiping out all the gains since March 11, 1988. But these kinds of fluctuations are par for the course. As a matter of fact, the October 21, 1988 to November 18, 1988 correction was relatively mild and not very damaging in the scheme of things.

HEDGING WITH OEX PUT OPTIONS

For over three years, I have been studying the efficacy of hedging stock portfolios with OEX stock index put options. The OEX is based on the S&P 100 Index, with contracts traded on the Chicago Board Options Exchange (CBOE). A put is where the option writer (seller) agrees to buy the contract at a specified price during the life of the contract. As such, the put buyer benefits if the option falls below its cost (or premium) and strike price (or index level). In short, a put option is a bet that the index (market) will decline and that the buyer will gain the difference between his costs and the value of the option at or before its expiration. Hedging with options is a complicated subject and a difficult enterprise, and it's too involved to explain in adequate detail in this book. All brokerages have free booklets on the basics of OEX stock index options.

I have not written about hedging with OEX put options because I'm still learning about the strategy. I believe that it can be done effectively, and I am close to finding the complex keys. For now, I like to buy OEX puts 3 percent to 5 percent out-of-the money (below their current OEX/S&P 100 Index level) with three to four weeks before expiration, paying between $1 and $2 a put ($100 to $200 a contract of 100 puts). For example, if I believe the stock market is ready for a sharp selloff in the next few days or weeks, and the OEX is trading at 325.00, I would probably buy the OEX 310s. Because the OEX at 325.00 represents $32,500 worth of stock, I would buy one contract for each multiple of that amount. For a $100,000 stock portfolio, I would buy three contracts, or maybe four if my sell indicators were very strong.

The market would not have to decline 5 percent before the OEX puts significantly increase in value due to other buyers wanting to take positions and willing to pay higher premiums as the puts approached at-the-money or in-the-money levels. This is the tricky part. If the sharp selloff sends the market into a short-term oversold condition, we might want to liquidate the puts, fearing that a bounce-back rally might render them worthless. On the other hand, if the market is likely to continue down, then we'd want to keep the insurance hedge for even greater protection.

In the past when I have made good buys, I have held onto them for too long as "insurance." Because market timing is generally counterproductive for most investors, perhaps we should just forget about hedging, expecially with portfolios that are not margined. I continue to work on the subject as a potentially effective technique. So, the learning process goes on, even after 20 years of market study.

THE NIFTY 1990s

I am bullish on the stock market for the 1990s. Here are my reasons:

1. Stocks are a positive sum investment and the long-term trend is up.
2. Stocks are severely underowned by historical standards.
3. Productivity increases are likely in the future.
4. Book values are generally understated.
5. There is a potential shortage of common stocks.
6. The rapid movement toward world peace is positive for stocks.

While stocks have done well over the past several years, they are currently not overvalued according to price/earnings criteria and should be able to maintain at least their long-term averages. On the other hand, several astute students of the market point out that the Dow Jones Industrial Average will probably grow at 7 percent or more for the next five years. With the Dow 30 currently earning about $230, and a 7 percent traditional growth rate, in five years it would be earning about $323. At a price/earnings multiple of 16 (compared to the 22 in 1987), the DJIA would be at 5328.

According to the Sindlinger Household Money Supply Report, as quoted in *The Contrary Investor*, "A recent report estimated that only 24.1 percent of all households own stock in a public company, private company or mutual fund. This is an all time low for the more than 30 years that Sindlinger has tracked the stock market."[1] The July 1988 newsletter from

---

[1]"Sindlinger Household Money Supply Report," *The Contrary Investor*, August 1988, pp. 1.

Ladenburg, Thalmann & Co. shows that all major participants in the stock market have significantly reduced stocks as a percentage of their financial assets over the past 20 years. Private pension funds held 63.4 percent of their assets in stocks in 1968, but only 49.6 percent in 1987. Stocks represented 89.9 percent of mutual fund assets in 1968, but only 38.7 percent in 1987. Foreigners reduced their stock exposure from 33.6 percent of U.S. financial assets in 1968 to only 15.8 percent in 1987.

From the same August issue of *The Contrary Investor*, James Fraser displays a table from Peter L. Bernstein's August 1 report on productivity. Fraser summarizes "that the best time spans for an increase in output per hour, that is, productivity growth, 'were periods when the labor force lagged the growth of the total population.' " This condition is nicely in the works with the "labor force growth declining up to the year 2000."[2]

Although the takeover and leveraged buyout mania has probably been excessive, one of its causes has been the undervaluation of corporations, especially their assets and cash flows, which have stimulated sharp financial types to benefit from this condition. With secondary stocks, even more undervalued that blue chip stocks, there are plenty of opportunities for the small investor to benefit from these stocks.

It is now old news that well over $400 billion worth of stocks has been removed from the stock market through buyouts, buybacks, and mergers. This is a "net" figure including the addition of new issues. While stock can be created by corporations deciding to expand their shares outstanding or by more initial public offerings (IPOs), this has not been the case, and such a trend would probably take some time to make a difference in significantly increasing the supply of stocks. Meanwhile, money accumulates on the sidelines as pension funds and individuals find themselves with additional cash to invest.

Finally, although I would not know how to quantify it, I believe that the weakening or abandoning of the cold war, coupled with the relative democratization and capitalization of communist and socialist countries, can only be a long term plus in the global economic picture, with America getting its share of the increased world trade pie. Without being Pollyannish and forgetting any of the economic and political problems facing the United States, the next decade may indeed be a new era of peace and prosperity.

---

[2]J. Fraser, *The Contrary Investor*, August 1988, pp. 2.

APPENDIX A

EXTENDED FUNDAMENTAL ANALYSIS

This is not a textbook on security analysis, yet it does involve some basic accounting. I want to get across the idea that one needn't be an accountant to develop financial statement awareness and the character or willingness to systematically review corporate conditions and stock selection criteria. I said it was simple, but I didn't say it was easy.

If you are willing to take the big picture approach you can find undervalued stocks using two, three, or seven criteria, as reviewed in Chapter 2. If you are a bit more concerned and less cavalier, you can make "almost final" selections from those basic criteria sets and go on to analyze other criteria that may be confirming, insignificant, or disconfirming.

Professionals or chartered financial analysts go far beyond the basics reviewed in this book. They check corporate 10-K (annual) and 10-Q (quarterly) reports for items sometimes not included in the reports sent to shareholders or for items that are buried in the footnotes. For example, they look to see if a corporation has underfunded pension liability, which is not reflected on the balance sheet and which will impact its earnings and equity in the future.

Neither stock selection nor portfolio management are sciences; they are crafts; they might better be likened to an art in the sense of working with techniques and materials. Stock selection considers corporations and their valuations in the stock market. Portfolio management, on the other hand, considers other conditions such as the practice of patience, stock diversification, time diversification, and risk management—which include the states of the market, economy, Federal Reserve, and the administration's (government's) policy. Actual individual stock selection may be only a small part of the process. If so, it is nonetheless crucial, as there are few things more frustrating than to see the market advancing while your selected stocks are declining. Conversely, there are few things more satisfying than to see the market decline while your portfolio advances.

In *The Money Masters* by John Train, the author quotes Philip Fisher, "If the job has been correctly done when a common stock is purchased, the time to sell it is—almost never."[1] This is a wise observation. Other people have pointed out similar advice that the well-bought stock will take care of itself on the sell side. Note that of the 11 positions in TPS Portfolio in March, 1977, 9 were bought out at handsome profits and the remaining 2 are considered buyout or takeover candidates currently (see Chapter 7).

While statistical evidence strongly supports selecting stocks from the lowest 5 percent of the price/earnings pool and from the lowest 5 percent of market capitalization issues, even among this population one might want to guard against over-indebted corporations or those showing declining trends in earnings, sales, and book value. In keeping with our responsibilities as editor and publisher of a stock advisory newsletter and as investment advisors, we at *TPS* update our fundamental analysis *daily*, incorporating price changes and newly released financial information. This computerized updating leads to a daily buy-and-sell candidates' list.

Once a week we print out the total population of closely watched stocks in the form of Figure A-1. This "stock analysis" began with hand calculations, progressed through early personal computers (the Osborne, using SuperCalc), was converted to mainframe IBM 360s and 370s (using COBOL at a public, time-share computer center), was returned to personal computers, and is now run on AT clones in-house using RBase V. The results of our analyses leads to a list of currently recommended stocks published in our newsletter every three weeks.

Our stock analysis still could be done by hand, but working with a personal computer (PC) using any of the popular spread-sheet programs or database management programs saves time and permits greater coverage. With a relatively inexpensive PC you can also employ such programs and data bases as StockPak II, the Standard & Poor's monthly data on diskette system that permits reviewing and screening over 4,000 stocks on the New York and American exchanges and the over-the-counter market. Still, just monitoring *The Value Line Investment Survey* or corporate financial reports can be enough research. If you go to a decent public or college library, this basic public information is free, and to obtain corporate reports requires only a request to the corporation's shareholder relations department.

STOCK ANALYSIS PRINTOUT

I am reproducing "page 7" of April 14, 1989 (Figure A-1) as a typical example of our stock analysis printout and because we can refer to the

---

[1]John Train, *The Money Masters* (N.Y.: Penguin Books, 1981), p. 78.

FIGURE A-1
Page 7 of Stock   Analysis Printout—Input Data—April 14, 1989

	BTU	BVFS	C	CA	CAL	CANX	CAO	CARL	CAW	CB	CBAM	CBK
1 SYMBOL	BTU	BVFS	C	CA	CAL	CANX	CAO	CARL	CAW	CB	CBAM	CBK
2 COMPANY	PyroEnrgy	BayViewFd	Chrysler	CompAssoc	CalFed	CannonExp	CarolnaFt	Carlkorch	CaesarsWld	ChubbCorp	Cambrex	ContlBank
3 EXCHANGE	NYSE	OTC	NYSE	NYSE	NYSE	OTC	NYSE	OTC	NYSE	NYSE	OTC	NYSE
4 PRICE	8.37	19.12	24.50	35.75	22.00	7.00	23.12	26.50	33.62	68.62	14.75	21.25
5 DIVIDEND	.00	.60	1.20	.00	1.60	.00	.60	.16	.00	2.32	.00	.80
6 12 MO EARN	.64	3.00	5.08	1.79	4.97	.89	1.67	1.93	2.54	8.37	1.25	5.19
7 3 YR EARN	.49	2.91	5.76	.82	5.68	.42	1.72	1.19	2.03	7.20	1.23	-5.96
8 PROJ EARN	.90	3.15	5.50	2.25	4.50	1.00	2.60	2.30	3.25	8.80	1.40	4.50
9 5YR ER Growth	17.5	20.0		48.5	7.5	15.0	10.5	-2.0	31.0			6.5
10 P/E NORM	13.0 +	11.0 +	10.0 +	19.0 v	8.0 *	13.0 +	14.0 +	15.0 +	15.0 +	10.0 +	13.0 +	8.0 *
11 TANG BV	6.05	26.18	21.00	7.59	32.25	3.59	20.19	6.41	6.54	53.84	13.04	18.68
12 BOOK VALUE	6.05	27.15+	32.53+	7.59v	55.43*	3.59	20.19	6.41v	8.33v	55.49	15.23+	18.68
13 5YR BV Growth	32.0	13.0		63.0	7.0	15.0	21.0	14.0	10.5			
14 BV NORM	2.0	1.2	2.0	3.5	1.0	2.0	2.0	2.0	3.0	1.2	2.0	1.5
15 CASH FLOW	2.00		9.45	2.65		1.65	6.70	4.25	4.45		2.35	
16 5YR CF Growth	13.0			53.0		20.0	11.0	6.5	13.5			
17 P/CF NORM	6.0		4.0	13.0		6.0	6.0	8.0	7.0		8.0	
18 REVENUES	168.00		35472.00	925.00		14.90	653.00	446.00	856.00		120.00	
19 5YR RV Growth	6.0		5.5	38.0		18.0	8.5	8.0	2.0			
20 SHARES COMM	13.16	6.02	233.10	79.60	24.98	1.69	6.53	11.70	24.82	40.60	5.50	40.68
21 CUR ASSETS	37.0	586.00	33916.0	507.0		5.2	114.0	90.0	274.0		61.0	
22 CUR LIABS	34.0		19650.0	286.0		2.4	94.0	140.0	146.0		16.4	
23 L/T DEBT	68.00		16600.00	177.00	2920.00	6.80	85.00	79.00	428.00	363.00	6.00	942.00
24 TOT ASSETS	188	2707	48567	1156	27478	16	347	276	848	9741	112	32391
25 PREF STOCK			.30				2.21					665.00
26 YR END CST	6.50	17.87	25.75	27.37	22.00	7.12	24.62	22.62	31.00	58.00	14.75	20.75
27 YEAR HIGH	6.62	19.37	27.75	38.00	29.00	8.25	30.62	26.00	32.40	63.40	19.25	23.50
28 YEAR LOW	3.62	13.12	19.62	23.87	19.50	4.25	17.25	11.25	18.40	51.30	11.00	9.00
29 15 YR HIGH	17.00	18.75	35.63	38.00	30.00	8.25	42.50	44.75	35.80	78.10	24.00	
30 15 YR LOW	1.00	11.62	1.37	1.43	11.38	3.87	2.06	7.13	.90	8.00	11.00	
31 VL / S&P	2.6		3.5	2.4	4.0		3.2	1.4	3.5	3.4		

FIGURE A-1—*Concluded*
Page 7 of Stock Analysis Printout—Calculations from Input Data—April 14, 1989

Metric	1	2	3	4	5	6	7	8	9	10	11	12
32 PROJ. ROE	13.84+	11.08	15.85+	25.81*	7.91v	24.44*	12.26+	30.74*	32.64*	14.98+	8.78v	21.91*
33 CUR P/E	13.08v	6.37+	4.82*	19.97v	4.42+	7.86+	13.84+	13.73+	13.23v	8.19+	11.80+	4.09+
34 DIV YIELD ✗	.00	3.13	4.89	.00	7.27*	.00	2.59	.60	.00	3.38	.00	3.76
35 PR/TangBV	1.38	.73	1.16	4.71	.68	1.94	1.14	4.13	5.14	1.27	1.13	1.13
36 PRICE/BV	1.38+	.70*	.75*	4.71v	.39*	1.94+	1.14+	4.13v	4.03v	1.23+	.96*	1.13+
37 CUR RATIO	1.08v	v	1.72v	1.77v	v	2.16*	1.21v	.64v	1.87v	v	3.71v	v
38 RET SALES	5.01*	v	3.33*	15.40*	v	10.09*	1.67v	5.06*	7.36*	v	5.72*	v
39 RET ASSETS	4.48	.66	2.43	12.32	.45	9.11	3.14	8.18	7.43	3.48	6.13	.65
40 RET EQUITY	10.00	12.00	15.00+	23.00*	10.00	25.00*	9.00v	32.00*	33.00*	16.00+	8.50v	16.00+
41 IntGrowthRt	10.00	9.71	11.72	23.00	6.44	25.00	6.92	29.77	33.00	11.78	8.50	13.15
42 PR/NET WKCP		.40	12.87		4.22	7.55	-6.20	6.52			1.81	
43 PRJ EN/PR	10.74	16.47	22.44	6.29	20.45	14.28	11.24	8.67	9.66	12.82	9.49	21.17
44 PRICE/REV	.65+		.16*			.79*	.23*	.69+	.97*		.67+	
45 PRICE/CF	4.18		2.59*	13.49v		4.24+	6.23	6.23	7.55		6.27*	
46 MV CHANGE ✗	28.84	6.99	-4.85	30.59	.00	-1.75	-6.09	17.12	8.46	18.31	.00	2.40
47 MKT VALUE	110.21*	115.28*	5710.95	2845.70	549.56	11.83v	151.00*	310.05	834.57	2786.17	81.12*	864.45
48 P/CF Goal	12.00		37.80	34.45		9.90	40.20	34.00	31.15		18.80	
49 P/E Goal	8.32v	33.00	50.80*	34.01v	39.76	11.57	23.38	28.95	38.10	83.70	16.25	41.52
50 ProjE Goal	11.70	34.65	55.00*	42.75	36.00	13.00	36.40	34.50	48.75	88.00	18.20	36.00
51 BV Goal	12.10	33.93	65.06*	26.56v	55.43*	7.18	40.38	12.82v	24.99v	69.36	30.46	28.02
52 2 x PRICE	16.75	38.25	49.00	71.50	44.00	14.00	46.25	53.00	67.25	137.25	29.50	42.50
53 RECOMMENDS	2A,3C	2A,3D	1A,2C,3D	2A	3C	2A,3C	2B,3D	2A	2A	2A	2A,3C,	2B.
54 Goal Price	11.03	33.86	52.16	34.44	43.73	10.41	35.09	27.56v	35.75	80.35	20.92	35.18
55 Apprc Poten	31.70v	77.05	112.91*	-3.65v	98.77	48.75	51.74	4.02	6.34	17.09	41.88	65.55
56 Inst Hold ✗	32.07	.00	58.77	56.35	74.33	6.15	59.72	28.97	61.38	67.98	85.45	195.67

fundamental information on three stock examples, Chrysler (C), Computer Associates (CA), and Pyro Energy (BTU). Chrysler is a good example of a recommended corporation with an undervalued stock (at the time of this printout). In reviewing the items posted for Chrysler, we will also note certain anomalies and considerations inappropriate to other types of corporations. In order to contrast several criteria, we will also look at Pyro Energy, a stock considered a "hold" on this printout, and Computer Associates, the closest stock to a "sell" on this page. Depending upon your interest, you can cross reference various fundamentals of these stocks with the others on the page, although there are not enough stocks on just one page to draw any statistical inferences.

Note: Since Appendix A was written, Pyro Energy was bought out for $12.00 per share in cash by Costain Holding Co., effective July 26, 1989. As Pyro's buyout price coincided with our high goal price, I think this example of a "hold" is instructive. Computer Associates split its shares 2-for-1 on June 16, 1989, not reflected in Figure A-1.

You will notice three marks to the right of certain figures. The asterisk (*) highlights what I consider to be a very good number, either an undervalued criterion or a superior ratio or percentage. The plus (+) is used to point out a good number, in my estimation, while the v is used to point out a bad number, either an overvalued criterion or a poor ratio or percentage. While these marks are not in themselves sufficient for determining stock selection, they aid us in quickly observing noteworthy conditions. What follows below is the systematic review of each line of our stock analysis printout at the close of April 14, 1989 (see Figure A-1).

1. *Symbol.* Stock ticker symbols. Every issue listed on the New York Stock Exchange, the American Stock Exchange, and the National Association of Securities Dealers Automated Quotation System (NASDAQ) has a unique Cusip number and stock "ticker" symbol. The Cusip number for Chrysler Corp. is 171196108200. You will see Cusip numbers on your stock trade confirmation slips, but normally you will be concerned only with a stock's symbol. You should know your stocks' ticker symbols so as to avoid confusion in ordering stocks. The stock symbol or ticker for Chrysler is C.

Knowing the tickers of the stocks you want to reference is also convenient when asking for current pricing information—accessing quotation machines— or recognizing trades displayed on the moving "tape" shown on daily TV programs, in brokerage houses, and on the various exchanges. Most companies' tickers begin with the initials of their name, like CA for Computer Associates, a computer software company, but once in a while you'll find a symbol like BTU—the standard abbreviation for British thermal units—as a clever symbol for Pyro Energy, a coal, oil, and gas company.

2. *Company.* Abbreviated corporate names. With thousands of tickers in use, and some of them not nearly acronymic, it is easy to confuse or forget which corporation belongs to which symbol. We will be following Chrysler and its numbers in column three, as well as Pyro Energy in column one and CompAssoc in column four.

3. *Exchange.* Where stock trades. The third row displays where a stock is principally traded. You can save time in accessing information or price quotes by being able to tell your broker on which exchange or market a particular stock is traded. NYSE stands for the New York Stock Exchange, OTC shows stocks traded "over-the-counter" on the National Quotation System, ASE refers to the American Stock Exchange, and PSE represents the Pacific Stock Exchange. Some stocks are listed on more than one exchange, such as the New York and the Pacific, and there may be a benefit in trading a particular position in one place or another. With OTC stocks there likely will be more than one market maker so it is up to your broker to shop your trade for the best execution.

Chrysler and Pyro Energy common shares trade principally on the New York Stock Exchange (NYSE), but they also trade on the Boston, Midwest, Pacific, and Philadelphia exchanges. Computer Associates trades on the New York, Boston, and Philadelphia exchanges. It might be of value to know that Chrysler and Pyro Energy also trade on the Pacific Exchange, which stays open for 30 minutes after the NYSE closes. Sometimes stocks can be traded in the "third market" after the regular exchanges are closed. The third market is where listed stocks are traded over-the-counter with special market makers without affecting their exchanges' prices. We have never traded a stock in the third market.

4. *Price.* That date's closing price in dollars and cents, rounded down. Usually this date is for the last trading day of the week, Friday, unless the markets were closed on Friday. Prices are changing by the minute in actively traded stocks, so these prices must be verified at the time any decision to trade is being taken. Even with all the intraday and intraweek fluctuations, some issues will close unchanged for the week as they end trading at the same price they did the preceding week. Such "unchanged" numbers can mask considerable intraweek activity and fluctuation in a stock's price and volume. In Figure A-1, we see that Chrysler closed at $24.50 per share, while BTU closed at $8.375—although it shows only 8.37—and CA closed at $35.75.

5. *Dividend.* Indicated annual dividend in dollars and cents. Most dividends are declared and paid quarterly, but a few represent differing time periods such as semiannual, as well as special or extra dividend declarations. Generally the annual (four-quarter) dividend rate doesn't change often, but some companies have a policy to raise dividends every year (or more frequently) if earnings warrant. During troubled times of low or no profitability, dividends may be reduced or suspended entirely, which often causes a large drop in the market price of that corporation's stock upon release of the presumed bad news. Before making any serious judgments based on the annual indicated dividend, one should check on the corporation's dividend trend, special dividends, stock splits, earnings, retained earnings, or cash flow to see if funds are adequate to support current and likely future dividends.

For many analysts and investors, dividends are a significant determinant of stock selection. Some people are dependent for their everyday needs upon the flow of funds provided by stock dividends. Such people often would be more interested in a seemingly secure and handsome dividend than in a corporation's growth prospects or the potential market price appreciation of its stock. I am more interested in the total return picture, dividends plus appreciation, which results in emphasizing appreciation potentials over indicated dividends. I would be less interested in the stock that yields about 6 percent of its market price in dividend return with a history of appreciating 4 percent to 6 percent per year, for a total return of 10 percent to 12 percent. I would be more interested in the stock that pays no dividend but appreciates 18 percent to 25 percent per year on average.

If one could make consistent choices among high-dividend paying stocks that managed a total return of 12 percent, and non-dividend paying stocks that appreciated 15 percent to 18 percent on average, one would be far ahead of the game giving up dividends (which are taxed in the year they are received) in favor of market price appreciation. Then one could obtain needed cash flows from capital gains sales after allowing a year or so of market price appreciation—or from margin loan withdrawals if cash is needed sooner. Against the more rapidly increasing value of one's "dividendless portfolio," one could borrow the equivalent 6 percent "dividend yield" until the appreciated stock was sold to repay the margin loan. With the additional gains from the higher returns, one could reinvest the difference and see the total portfolio grow and appreciate more than its dividend-paying counterpart.

We have seen in reviewing dividend-adjusted returns (see Figure 3–4) that over the long term dividends actually are a larger part of the total return than price appreciation for blue chip stocks. An excellent and worthwhile, if highly biased, treatise supporting stock selection and portfolio management based on dividends can be found in *Dividends Don't Lie*, by Geraldine Weiss and Janet Lowe (Longman Financial Services Publishing, 1988). Sometimes a dividend reduction that leads to a sharp drop in the market price of a stock can be a wonderful occasion for suggesting an undervalued purchase, even as the dividend players are dumping their shares.

One such a case is ITT, which in July 1984 cut its $2.76 annual dividend to $1.00, causing ITT to drop from the low $30s to $20.625 in a few days, less than half of its January '84 high of $47.375. This dividend-reducing decision to conserve cash clearly made ITT a stronger company while driving its stock into an undervalued buy range. Five years later, ITT traded around $58 per share, was still undervalued (though not a buy candidate), and paid $1.50 in annual dividends.

A more recent example is Union Carbide (UK), which lowered its annual dividend from $1.50 to $.80 per share in May of '88. From a high of $25.875 before the cut, UK dropped to $17, after which we rerecommended it at $19 as of May 27, 1988. At this writing, UK is trading in the low $30s. In our June 2, 1988, newsletter we wrote, "We feel that Carbide took the right steps, inasmuch as the reduced dividend payout allows UK to retain more funds to support expansion during the current favorable industry operating conditions."

Having a preference for non- or low-dividend paying stocks does not bring with it a complete prejudice against dividend paying stocks, especially if they are undervalued bargains in their own right. One may have the best of both worlds, receiving a nice yield while awaiting superior appreciation and a handsome multi-year total return. Chrysler may be such a stock as its indicated dividend is $1.20. Neither BTU nor CA paid indicated dividends at the time of printout.

6. 12 *mo earning*. "Current" after-tax earnings (net income) in dollars and cents per share. Current earnings are usually published as reported quarterly in many places including daily newspapers with substantial financial sections as well as the financial press, electronic data sources, and in quarterly and annual reports. We've already reviewed various definitions of earnings in Chapter 2's review of P/E criteria and considerations of extraordinary earnings and earnings dilution.

For your convenience, we can review some of the principal points about current earnings, which usually refer to trailing earnings or the most recent year's (perhaps last year's) reported earnings. Even trailing earnings of the last four reported quarters are, to a degree, historical, depending upon how long it takes a corporation to close its books for the quarter and publish its financials. It might take a month or two after the end of a quarter to obtain that quarter's results, so that in the immediately preceding four to eight weeks, considerable changes, either positive or negative, could be impacting actual "current" earnings. Still, there are only the "current" published figures with which to work.

Timeliness of reported earnings is only one of our concerns. We must check further to see if these earnings have a significant per share dilution due to rights, warrants, or convertible issues that can increase the number of common shares outstanding. Of course, not all potential dilutions occur. Sometimes rights expire worthless and convertibles are retired without being converted, or stock is bought back on the open market and returned to the corporation's treasury, or new stock is issued at either more or less than current book value. We are also on the lookout for the effects of nonrecurring earnings versus comparisons with continuing earnings from operations.

One of the reasons that we are less concerned than many other analysts about each quarter's earnings is due to our long-term outlook and the significant variations of earnings seen over time. If a company has a down earnings quarter, its stock may sell off much more than is warranted by the temporarily lowered earnings.

Quarterly, six-month, and nine-month trailing earnings are compared to like periods of the previous fiscal year. Sometimes much is made of increases or decreases from the previous quarter (or period), without realizing that the previous period, or the previous year's period, represents unusually depressed or record earnings, so that nominal comparisons distort the longer-term perspective. These distortions could lead the unaware to unreasonable euphoria or illogical disappointment. If significant, undistorted comparative earnings differences do occur, they can signal good buying or selling opportunities.

Chrysler's *12 Mo earn* (last four reported quarters' earnings) is $5.08 per share, while BTU's is $.64 and CA's is $1.79. The meanings of these "current" earnings are found in various comparisons and ratios displayed in Figure A–1 and reviewed in due course. The current earnings figures we use exclude extraordinary gains and losses and are fully diluted. This is the more conservative approach to using current earnings, but it may sometimes mask significant changes in potential future earnings if the extraordinary items are overwhelming or the dilutive effects are mitigated by company actions (such as calling in convertible securities).

7. *3 yr earn.* Average of past three fiscal years' earnings in dollars and cents per share per fiscal year. Often more important than trailing earnings are three-year averaged earnings. This number is generated by adding up the past three fiscal years and dividing by three. Like every fundamental item, this number can stand a bit of further analysis.

On the one hand, the three-years' average earnings can represent a solid earnings trend; on the other, it can cover up highly volatile or unstable earnings over the reported 36 months. For example, a company may have earned $1.00 per share for the first year, $1.50 per share for the second year, and $2.00 per share for the third year. This pattern of earnings shows an average earnings of $1.50 per share for three years, and a nice growth trend. But, the same average earnings could represent the reverse pattern, *viz.*, $2.00, then $1.50, then $1.00, which would be a dismal trend of decreasing earnings though amounting to the same three-year average earnings.

Still, the three-year average earnings figure is a touchstone with which to compare current earnings and projected earnings, showing flat or trending earnings. The three-year average can also give perspective to the longer term P/E ratio of the stock, a topic reviewed in greater detail below.

Chrysler's *3 yr earn* works out to $5.76 per share. We immediately see that Chrysler's three-year average earnings is greater than its current or projected (reviewed next below) earnings. As it happens, Chrysler had record earnings during the past three years so it is not a big negative that both current and projected earnings are below the average of those record years. BTU's three-year average earnings at $.49 are below both current and projected earnings, which suggests a positive earnings trend. CA's three-year average of $.82 sets up an even more positive earnings trend picture than BTU's. This earnings trend pattern becomes a buy consideration later in our analysis.

8. *Proj earn.* Projected or estimated earnings in dollars and cents per share for the upcoming four quarters. Projected earnings are very important and very dangerous, generally representing estimated earnings for the next four quarters to be reported. Our estimates for projected earnings come from several public sources and sometimes our own extrapolations. We study *The Value Line Investment Survey*, and, on occasion, industry sources such as *Institutional Brokerage Estimates Survey* (*IBES*) as well as miscellaneous brokerage and institutional publications to help us determine probable projected earnings.

We know that projected earnings are often notoriously inaccurate. Even chief financial officers of corporations have difficulties projecting earnings for 12 months in advance, given the vagaries of business. Financial analysts, at least one step removed and without as much information at their disposal, may be even more off the mark, or, because they are not so close to the trees, may come up with a better assessment of the forest than the foresters.

However, estimated earnings serve at least two functions. First, they show what others believe a corporation will earn, and much stock is traded on such beliefs. Second, they are a continuing educated guess as to what might happen. It is well known that successive increases or decreases in estimated earnings tend to influence stock prices in similar directions. One can also make interpretations or adjustments based on the fact that in good times earnings estimates tend to become more and more generous, while in bad times earnings estimates tend to become pessimistic.

Corporations which report earnings surprises—compared to ''the Street's'' consensus estimates—often see their stocks move in the direction of the unexpected difference. The April 24, 1989, *Barron's* reviews some of the ramifications of projected earnings in ''The Trader'' feature, written by Lauren R. Rublin. Rublin reports on quantitative research work done by Claudia Mott, who studies earnings surprises. She finds that earnings surprises have a 38 percent chance of being repeated in the next quarter, although there is a 15 percent probability of them going the other way. Why analysts are surprised in the first place, or surprised a second time, is likely based on disbelief and the psychological need to avoid dramatic reassessments.

The actual examples Rublin reports are instructive. Inco, the Canadian nickel producer, earned $1.90 a share in last year's fourth quarter, compared to Street estimates of $1.67. For the first quarter of '89 analysts estimated $2.22, but Inco reported $2.44. ''Seagate, the widely followed disk-drive maker, did the same trick, reporting 15 cents, vs. a projected loss of 10 cents for the December quarter, and 42 cents vs. a consensus 20 cents for the three months ending March.''[2] Rublin gives us two negative earnings surprises, apparently not adjusted for by most analysts.

---

[2]Lauren R. Rublin, ''The Trader,'' in *Barron's*, April 24, 1989, p. 74.

On the negative side, Preston Corp., the trucker, Wednesday reported first-quarter earnings of 19 cents, compared with the 26 cents analysts had expected. In last year's final quarter, the company netted 15 cents, again considerably below the 37 cents analysts had anticipated. And Laclede Steel recently disappointed, with earnings of 69 cents and not the 99 cents the Street had estimated. The guesstimators got it wrong the prior quarter, too, when the company earned 82 cents, hardly the $1.47 the Street had in mind.[3]

While studies show the low level of confidence one should hold in estimated earnings, that does not invalidate their potential usefulness. Better a smoky torch than no torch at all. In a statistical sense, one might expect that the over- and under estimations may have a certain cancelling-out effect over large numbers of stocks and over longer periods of time. Of course, we do not depend upon estimated earnings alone, as other fundamentals must be sufficient to compensate for potential projected earning downgrades and disappointments.

One can select certain earnings estimates from those analysts or publications that seem to have a better handle on a particular corporation's workings. One can also note the variations of earnings estimates and notice significant differences between the mean and modal projections. If three estimates suggest $5.00 per share and one projects $1.00 per share—does the "contrarian" know something the others don't, or vice versa?—then the average estimate for the four is $4.00 per share. Given recent sales, earnings on revenues, cash flow trends, and price/sales ratios, we may have evidence in support of or against the consensus estimated earnings. Then too, we can almost skip the whole subject of quality of projected earnings and merely depend upon recent trends and current fundamental criteria.

Chrysler's *proj earn* are displayed as $5.50 per share, about 8.27 percent greater than current earnings. Combined with the two other earnings figures, we get a picture of a company operating at a high earnings level. Either this would be enough information for us, or we would go to the Chrysler's annual and other reports to try to determine whether Chrysler has peaked as a corporation, still has growth potential, or is an undervalued money-maker at current P/E and projected P/E levels.

Both BTU and, to a larger extent, CA have significantly higher projected earnings percentages than Chrysler. Given the vagaries of projecting earnings, these figures are at least very encouraging signs of the probable health and growth of BTU and CA.

9. *5yr er growth.* Five-year earning growth rate in percentage per year. It is no secret that we would rather own a growing corporation than a stagnant one, unless perhaps the stagnant one had tremendous realizable assets—a so-called

---

[3]Rublin, "The Trader," p. 74.

asset play. Corporations, which have the status of legal entities, have lives of their own in that they are begun, develop, grow, decline, and "die" either through voluntary liquidation, bankruptcy, or merger into another corporation. Ideally, we like to find corporations that are growing nicely, perhaps at 15 percent or more per year on average, with their stock prices not yet reflecting their growth rates. If such a corporation has managed a solid growth rate over a number of years, there is some likelihood that it will continue to do so, although any number of things could go wrong.

Chrysler does not have a meaningful (positive) *5Yr er growth* rate because its current earnings are less than its five-year-ago earnings. For the past five years, from 1984 through 1988, Chrysler's earnings per share from operations have been $5.22, $6.25, $6.31, $5.90, and $5.08 respectively. Its annual rate of change per share for earnings is 31.0 percent according to *The Value Line Investment Survey*. BTU's five-year earnings growth rate of 17.5 percent is above average for all corporations but not enough above average to call it a high growth company. CA's five-year-growth rate works out to 40 percent, a very high growth company to be sure.

10. *P/E norm.* Average price/earnings ratio. The P/E norm or average multiple represents our estimation of what a stock should trade for under normal conditions. It is a key number for estimating present and future potential market price valuations. When we first started determining these average multiples 12 years ago, the P/E norm was calculated as an average of the previous 10 or 15 years of annual P/E ratios. The idea was that if a stock tended to trade, say, at an average 12 times earnings for long periods of time, then that would be a good criterion for estimating current, under-, over-, or fair valuation.

Over the years, this simple approach to using an average P/E ratio has been modified to include the current and anticipated P/E levels of major indices, industry averages, and the current and anticipated returns on equity of each individual stock.

As the general stock market's P/E averages increased, and as certain companies continued to grow and improve their valuation criteria, such as their return on equity percentage, we found it fruitful to modify P/E norms upward, usually above their relatively recent and sometimes historically depressed averages. The rule of thumb that a P/E norm could reasonably equal a stock's return on equity (ROE) percentage seems to be an effective guide or starting criterion, with modification for very high ROEs that are clearly or likely unsustainable. Thus, a stock returning 15 percent on equity (a.k.a. net worth) currently and projecting an equal or greater ROE over the next four quarters could deserve and be expected to trade in the next few years at a P/E of 15, which is to say 15 times earnings.

There are cases where the current P/E ratio is absent, due to losses rather than profits or because of sharp price changes. Though our guideline is to buy relatively low P/E stocks—hopefully at less than 30 percent to 50 percent of the going market or major index level, or the stock's P/E norm—there are times when I will buy stocks with much greater P/Es or stocks having none at all. Usually these candidates are bought on the grounds of tremendous discounts from net worth (so-called asset plays), or in advance of perceived imminent turnarounds where a current short-term profit drop or loss is in the nature of a glitch, the cause of which likely has already been corrected.

I have assigned Chrysler a P/E norm of 10. I believe that in the next three to five years Chrysler's common stock will trade at 10 times its current (or projected) earnings. This is an admittedly high multiple for an automotive company—for instance, *Value Line* displays an average annual P/E ratio of 7.0 in the 1991–93 period. I believe that, given a less cyclical corporate environment for Chrysler, with its massive diversifications into financial services, aerospace, and foreign manufacturers coupled with its 15 percent current return on equity and 15.85 percent projected ROE (both these figures are reviewed below), a P/E 10 is appropriate.

BTU has been assigned a P/E norm of 13.0, based principally on its five-year-earnings growth rate and its projected return on equity *(Proj. ROE)*, reviewed below. Other considerations include its historical P/E average and the overall industry and market earnings multiples. CA has a high P/E norm of 19.00, principally based upon its current return on equity *(Ret equity)* of 23.0 percent and its projected return of equity of 25.81 percent. Other considerations include its strong earnings trend and comparative P/Es with other high-growth computer stocks.

11. *Tang BV.* Tangible book value in dollars and cents per share. Tangible book value is essentially book value less intangible assets. Intangible (nonphysical) assets can include certain deferred charges, copyrights, franchises, goodwill, leaseholds, patents, and trademarks. Goodwill is an asset item on the balance sheet, usually representing the excess of cost basis of an asset (an acquired company) over its own tangible book value at the time of purchase. As Peter Lynch puts it, "If you pay $450 million for a TV station worth $2.5 million on the books, the accountants call the extra $447.5 million 'goodwill.' "[4] In the bad old days with companies overstating assets, goodwill would refer to the "water" (or hot air) on a company's books, something to be very wary of.

While *tangible book value* is meant to disclose a truer picture of the *hard assets minus liabilities value* of a company than mere *book value*—especially if there is a big disparity between the two—we must be careful to investigate the actual values represented by goodwill and other "hidden" assets. The acquired goodwill may well represent a hidden asset bought at bargain levels, which is then written off over many years (often around 10), reducing (penalizing) reported earnings, while the worth of these apparently opaque or intangible assets are actually increasing in value. The franchise cost in the purchase price of acquiring a business is one of these hidden assets, as are trade names,

---

[4]Peter Lynch, *One Up on Wall Street, p. 210.*

proprietary techniques, the customer base, employees and staff, expensed research and development, and the general business franchise itself growing in value. Many companies, like some banks and savings and loans that have acquired branch offices from their competitors, carry large goodwill numbers that substantially represent tangible assets, which are growing in value in terms of replacement or duplication costs.

Our stock analysis sheet shows Chrysler with a tangible book value of $21.00 per share, or $11.53 per share less than book value. The principal reason for this difference is Chrysler's acquisitions of recent years, especially the American Motors-Jeep deal. To the degree that amortizing that goodwill reduces earnings but augments the total going value of Chrysler as a dynamic, growing corporation, I, as a long-term speculator-investor-owner, am happy. Chrysler is becoming more valuable as its amortizing intangible assets are really appreciating over time.

BTU shows tangible book value of $6.05 per share, the same as its intangible book value: CA also shows equivalent tangible and intangible book values at $7.59 per share. At least we don't need to look for the valuations of intangible assets in these corporations.

12. *Book value.* All assets less all liabilities in dollars and cents per share. Book value is essentially assets less liabilities and preferred stock (if any) at liquidating value, or what a corporation is worth from an accounting point of view. Of course, accounting points of view can get very complicated and even contentious. Not all assets or liabilities are created equal. Just as the price of a stock rarely represents the worth of its corporation fairly, so book value frequently overstates or understates the actual worth of its corporation. If you choose not to accept stated book value as an adequate reflection—I do based on my generally statistical approach that overstated book values are compensated for by understated book values in widely diversified portfolios (a thesis that may sound idiotic to security analysts)—then you will want to look for hidden assets and hidden liabilities. I will review more on these subjects when we reach those topics below.

As featured in Chapter 2, we can use book value as one of the basic numbers for a quick analysis of a stock, given the historical relationships of a corporation's stock price to its book value per share. In the case of Chrysler, we see that its book value is $32.53 per share. This number will be used in ratios of fundamental evaluation further down on Figure A-1. The book value of BTU is $6.05 per share, while that of CA is $7.59 per share.

13. *5yr BV growth.* Five-year book value growth in percentage per year. Often it is instructive to see how a corporation's book value has increased over the past few years. In the case of Chrysler, the book value has grown 12 percent per year (although not shown in this analysis), from $18.58 to $32.53. It would seem that Chrysler's book value should increase next year given the difference between after-tax reported earnings and dividends paid, about $3.88 per share, which is about 12 percent. In the case of Pyro Energy (BTU) we see that its book value has grown at 32 percent per year on average for five years, a handsome growth rate. For CA we find an extremely high growth rate of 63 percent. We can observe that, without paying dividends, most or all of the reported after-tax earnings of both BTU and CA should show up in next year's book value as retained earnings and increase shareholders' equity.

14. *BV norm.* Average price/book value multiple (ratio). Just as stocks trade for a multiple on their earnings—as well as other fundamentals such as sales and cash flow—so they trade at multiples of their book values. As previously mentioned, Dow Jones Industrial stocks as an average tend to trade between slightly below one and somewhat above two times book value, with notable exceptions. Heavy industrial corporations with large investments in plant and equipment generally trade at a smaller multiple of their book values than do service industries with smaller amounts of fixed assets.

I have assigned a BV norm of 2.0 for Chrysler and BTU, but a 3.5 for CA. As a computer software company, CA's fixed assets are a much smaller percentage of its total assets, than either Chrysler's or Pyro Energy's, and therefore its book value norm is smaller as well.

15. *Cash flow.* Cash available with which to run a business in dollars and cents per share. We have reviewed cash flow at length in Chapter 2 as one of the principal criteria for stock selection. Generally, cash flow is defined as the net income plus bookkeeping entries such as depreciation and amortization charges. Obviously, different kinds of corporations tend to have different levels of cash flow in general, which also vary in relation to the maturity of their growth cycle. Chrysler's indicated cash flow is $9.45 per share, almost twice its earnings, while BTU's cash flow at $2.00 represents over three time earnings, and CA's cash flow of $2.65 equals 148 percent of earnings.

16. *5yr CF growth.* Five-year cash flow growth rate in percentage per year. We are following the five-year cash flow growth rate much as we follow other five-year growth rates, mostly as confirmation of the overall trend, but also to see if anomalies occur that might indicate a significant change in cash flow production. This sort of monitoring can become pretty esoteric, perhaps not worth the effort, and rarely is sufficient consideration for including or excluding a stock purchase candidate.

Chrysler's five-year cash flow growth rate works out to about 8 percent, while CA's, in keeping with its high-growth profile, is 45 percent, and BTU's is 13 percent.

17. *P/CF norm.* Price to cash flow average multiple (ratio). As cash flow is considered by many a more important measure of a corporation's ongoing health than earnings (net income), the price/cash flow multiple—which works like the price/earnings ratio—gives an instant picture of funds available for current business use in terms of how much "the market" is willing to pay per share for this item. Like all multiples, cash flow averages are based upon historical averages of the stock, perhaps its industry, and to a lesser degree the general market.

Growth stocks such as Computer Associates tend to trade at seemingly too high multiples for P/E, P/BV, and P/CF, as investors expect these three fundamentals to grow rapidly. We have assigned Chrysler a P/CF of 4.0—which sometimes seems low to me in comparison to other corporations, but then Ford and General Motors also carry 4.0's—because of historical precedent and the generally high dollar cash flows generated. BTU has a P/CF of 6.0 (compared to the much larger Texaco oil company's 5.0), but Computer Associates rates a P/CF of 13, given that there's little depreciation or amortization to deduct from its net income and also given its historical and comparative experience.

18. *Revenues.* Total annual sales or revenues in millions of dollars (in $10,000's). It may be intrinsically interesting to see how large a corporation is in terms of its annual sales (revenues). This amount figures prominently in several important ratios—such as price/rev and return on sales, reviewed below—and is yet another measure of year-to-year growth. Chrysler's revenue for the past four quarters (to date of this printout) was approximately $35.472 billion, making it over 211 times larger than BTU in terms of its $168 million in revenues. Computer Associates, perhaps not widely known outside the computer culture and with revenues "only" 1/38th of Chrysler's, is nonetheless a substantial corporation with $925 million in sales.

19. *5yr rv growth.* Five-year revenue growth rate in percentage per year. Just as we would like to see earnings growing at say 15 percent per year, so we would like to see revenues increasing at a similar healthy clip. Both Chrysler and BTU show a mature growth rate—5.5 percent and 6.0 percent, respectively. These rates can be explained in terms of down years near the beginning of the five-year period. CA's growth rate is 32 percent, once again putting it into the growth stock category.

We could have a revenues growth rate average, but that might be unduly misleading due to the volatility of revenues for most corporations over a five-year period. Still, if you are getting into analysis to this degree, you would certainly want to glance at the annual revenues for the past several years, and you should be especially happy to see them having doubled in five years or less, which represents a 15 percent or greater annual growth rate. Well-managed corporations can show improved earnings per share, while revenues remain constant, by cutting costs and improving efficiency, but static or declining sales are usually a bad sign. Sometimes improved earnings—without improved revenues—come at the expense of cutting back on maintenance, upkeep, research, and staff training, thus reducing the corporation's prospects in future years.

20. *Shares comm.* Common shares outstanding in millions and tens of thousands. Knowing how many shares outstanding a corporation has is a basic requirement for calculating many ratios and per-share figures. Several of these relationships are reviewed below in discussing the calculations portion of the stock analysis printout. Shares outstanding can change from time to time as corporations buy back shares—which then become part of their treasury shares—or sell them in the open market.

Many corporations issue shares or rights to buy shares to their executives, which may be exercised later. Sometimes warrants, convertible preferreds, or convertible bonds are converted into common shares and thus increase the pool of shares outstanding. We have mentioned the potential dilutive effect of these pending instruments in terms of book value per share and earnings per share.

Chrysler shows approximately 233.1 million (233,100,000) common shares outstanding. BTU has 13.16 million (13,160,000) common shares outstanding, while CA has 79.6 million (79,600,000) common shares outstanding. Notice that while Chrysler's revenues are over 38 times those of Computer Associates, Chrysler has fewer than 3 times as many shares outstanding. There are no necessary relationships among shares outstanding and revenues or earnings or price per share, etc., although there are meaningful ratios of these and other fundamentals to the shares outstanding amount.

21. *Cur assets*. Current assets in millions of dollars. Current assets are cash or assets that can be converted to cash usually within one year in the normal course of business, such as accounts receivable, inventories, and cash equivalent instruments (e.g., Treasury bills, common stocks of other corporations, and certificates of deposit maturing within one year). Obviously assets can be of higher or lower quality. Uncollectible accounts receivable or inventories that are obsolete, slow-moving, or unsalable are of lower quality than their opposites. We would certainly want to note unusually large or growing receivables and inventories as potential signs of trouble in a corporation's operations.

Inventories should be stated at cost or market value, whichever is lower, based on first-in, first-out (FIFO) or last-in, first-out (LIFO) accounting. FIFO charges sales with the oldest inventory costs; the remaining balance sheet inventory is priced at most recent costs. LIFO charges sales with the most recent costs of inventory; the remaining balance sheet inventory is priced at older costs. During rising prices, LIFO inventory on the balance sheet is usually lower than FIFO. Inventory to sales and inventory turnover ratios may be telling in manufacturing and retail store corporations. These details can usually be gleaned from annual reports, sometimes from their footnotes.

Chrysler's current assets are $33.916 billion ($33 billion, $916 million)— according to *Value Line*—compared to BTU's $37 million and CA's $507 million. Recent accounting rule changes, known as FASB 94, have muddied the analytic waters in requiring corporations to include all assets of their subsidiaries. As *Value Line* puts it,

The adoption of FASB 94 has caused the consolidation of the company's captive finance subsidiary, Chrysler Financial Corp., on the financial statements of the parent. Formerly accounted for on the equity method, CFC necessarily brings with it assets and liabilities that are huge by Chrysler's standards. As a result of the consolidation, some standard financial ratios (return on total capital, interest coverage, etc.) have ceased to be comparable either with Chrysler's historical record, or the FASB ruling. The new reporting method won't affect earnings per share or shareholder equity.[5]

22. *Cur liabs.* Current liabilities in millions of dollars. Current liabilities, the opposite of current assets, are expenses and debts of the corporation that are due and payable within one year (or the normal operating cycle). Liabilities can also involve some esoteric and qualitative considerations, often discussed in the footnotes of annual reports (10-K reports to the Securities and Exchange Commission, which you can request from corporations).

We should be on alert to liability reserves, which represent an unquestioned claim against a corporation, although the exact amount of the claim cannot be determined. Contingent liabilities such as warranties or litigation, and insurance company loss reserves may seriously overstate or understate actual liabilities, although generally estimates are in keeping with historical experience, accounting pronouncements, and IRS guidelines.

Chrysler's current liabilities are reported as $19.650 billion (under FASB 94), with BTU's as $34 million, and CA's as $286 million. Even at a glance, we can see that the relationship (or ratio) of current assets to current liabilities among our three exampled corporations varies greatly. This ratio, called the *current ratio,* is discussed in sequence below.

23. *L/T debt.* Long-term debt (liabilities) in millions of dollars. Those liabilities that normally need not be met within one year are called long-term debt. This is an important basic figure used in several fundamental calculations to determine potential over- and underindebtedness or debt-to-equity trends. Chrysler's long-term debt is $16.6 billion (FASB 94); BTU's is $68 million; and CA's is $177 million.

24. *Tot assets.* All assets in millions of dollars. Short-term and long-term (fixed or capital) assets are combined to yield the total assets figure. Perhaps the first thing to note is that a corporation's total assets are greater than its total liabilities, and to what degree. Then we can see what sorts of relationships exist, such as return on assets, and how they compare to previous years. Chrysler's total assets are $48.567 billion (FASB 94); BTU's are $188 million; and CA's are $1.156 billion.

---

[5]*Value Line Investment Survey*, March 24, 1989. (Copyright © 1989 by Value Line, Inc.; used by permission.)

25. *Pref stock.* Preferred stock outstanding in millions of dollars. Preferred stocks have a prior claim over common stocks on assets in case of a corporate dissolution, and a prior claim on dividends. We common shareholders would rather the corporation had no preferred stock, because we would not like common stock dividends suspended if the current earnings (and perhaps the retained earnings) were insufficient to meet both the required preferred stock payment and payments of the indicated common dividend, which would be "passed" (deleted) in such cases. Also, the fewer priority claims to assets, the better for common shareholders in the case of liquidation or bankruptcy. Happily, BTU and CA have no preferred shares outstanding, while Chrysler has only $300,000 worth. Of course, Chrysler has many bonds outstanding, all of which have a senior claim to assets over common stock.

26. *Yr end cst.* Price per share on 12/31/88 in dollars and cents. This is a marginal item, useful in referencing how the stock's price has fared since the beginning of the year.

27. *Year high.* Highest price per share for the past 52 weeks in dollars and cents. Another marginal item for the convenience of checking the current price and 52-week low price in relation to the stock's 52-week high price.

28. *Year low.* Lowest price per share for the past 52 weeks in dollars and cents. Like the year high, useful only to compare recent price parameters.

29. *15 yr high.* Highest price per share during the past 15 years in dollars and cents. The 15-year high and low prices are probably the least valuable items on this analysis because a corporation can become a significantly or completely different enterprise over one and one half decades. It may be almost idle curiosity to note the stock's price range over the past 15 years, but sometimes there is a clue to historical under -and overvaluations. One must be aware of stock splits that reduce the original cost bases or prices of a stock (or reverse splits that increase said prices) and thus result in split-adjusted figures.

For example, Chrysler split 3-for-2 in both 1986 and 1987, so a share of stock bought before the first split would now be 2.25 shares and the original cost price would be divided by 2.25 to obtain the adjusted cost price. The same process works with the pre-split yearly highs (and lows) so that *Value Line* shows a high for Chrysler of $20.875 in 1985, which means that the shares actually traded as high as $47 per share in 1985, pre-splits.

Pyro Energy split 3-for-2 in 1976, too long ago to make much difference in the overall picture, although long-time shareholders who bought before that split have 1.5 shares and their original cost basis is reduced by 33.3%, as is the high pre-split price figure.

Computer Associates common shares split three times 2-for-1, in 1983, '86, and '87, so a share of stock bought before the first split is now eight shares. CA first traded in 1981 and shows a high for that year of $1.875, but of course the stock traded at eight times that amount, or $15, its actual high price for that year.

The unaware observer might believe that CA could have been bought below $1.875 in 1981, but CA common never actually traded for that dollar amount.

30. *15 yr low.* The lowest price the stock traded during the past 15 years. All the split-adjusted considerations applying to the 15-year high figures (reviewed above) must be applied to the 15-year low figure, thus reducing their pre-split low prices accordingly. Chrysler shows a 15-year low of $1.375 in 1981, split-adjusted, to account for one share becoming 2.25 shares. Of course, Chrysler never actually traded for $1.375—its nominal low was about $3 per share. Even more dramatic is Computer Associates split-adjusted 15-year low of $1.625 for 1981 (when it began trading publicly), which was $13 per share before adjusting for the original share becoming eight shares. Undramatic Pyro Energy, with its single 3-for-2 split in early 1976, can be compared with itself for unadjusted highs and lows for the past 13 years.

Probably long-term highs and lows are most interesting and useful in observing big drops or gains over the period of a few years (although you wouldn't necessarily see this in a single 15-year figure). For instance, according to one "long base" pattern theory, if a corporation's stock loses 80 percent of its price and thereafter trades in a narrow range—say between 20 percent to 25 percent of its former high price—for three years or so, the stock has completed a "long base" and is likely to have a significant advance when it breaks out of its long-base trading range. While I do not search for this pattern, I do appreciate it when it coincides with undervalued fundamental criteria.

31. *VL / S&P.* Value Line's "timeliness" rating, and Standard & Poor's "earnings and dividend rankings for common stocks." *The Value Line Investment Survey* displays a timeliness rating ("relative price performance next 12 months") with *1* highest, *2* above average, *3* average, *4* below average, and *5* lowest. In the early development of this analysis program, I thought it would be nice to see what *Value Line* was projecting for a stock they follow and so included this item. However, several flaws come with this item in that *Value Line* follows only some 1,700 stocks, usually omitting smaller capitalization issues, and one cannot tell from the current ranking the last time a ranking changed and in which direction (if it's not a *1* or a *5*). *Value Line* has demonstrated that its timeliness ranking system works most of the time, with the *1*'s doing better than the *2*'s, etc., if timely switches are made.

I am not a follower of *The Value Line* timeliness rankings because they are heavily based on relative strength and other technical considerations, whereas I am more concerned with fundamental values. I used to joke that, given the choice, I would rather buy *4*'s or *3*'s than *2*'s or *1*'s because the highest ranked issues had already advanced so much in price. Still, it's nice to see whether a recommendable stock is rated by *Value Line* and, if it is rated, to see its current status.

Value Line timeliness rankings at the time of the sample printout give Chrysler a *3* or average year-ahead price appreciation performance, BTU a *2* or above average, and CA a *2* or above average. In following these printouts on a weekly basis, we would have noticed that Chrysler had been recently upgraded from a *4*, while CA had been recently downgraded from a *1*.

In a similar vein, I also have an idle curiosity about Standard & Poor's rankings for common stocks, probably harking back to my desire for so-called safety criteria in stock selection. The bases for these S&P rankings include "a computerized scoring system based on per-share earnings and dividend records of the most recent ten years" and are adjusted "by a set of predetermined modifiers for growth, stability within long-term trend, and cyclicality."[6] For more details, check the monthly S&P *Stock Guide*, widely used by brokers and investors as a quick reference to more than 5,300 common and preferred stocks. The rankings range as follows: *A +* highest, *A* high, *A-* above average, *B +* average, *B* below average, *B-* lower, *C* lowest, *D* in reorganization. To conserve space, we have attributed numerals to the letter rankings with $A+ = 1, A = 2, \ldots D = 8$.

In our printout, Chrysler common has an S&P rank of *B*, which is shown as a *5*. BTU is rated *B-* or *6*, and CA is rated *B +* or *4*. You would want to check the latest S&P *Stock Guide* for current rankings. Chrysler's ranking was recently raised one notch in keeping with its earnings momentum and dividend payout and will probably be raised again if its earnings keep up and its dividend is increased. Obviously, these ratings are based on trailing or historical fundamentals and do not necessarily reflect potential future stock price movements. Still, many investment counselors and money managers will invest only in common stocks with the higher ratings, even as they require similar high ratings for investing in bonds.

The safety factors related to bond prices are probably more reflected in various quality ratings than are those applying to common stocks. It would generally be copping out to place much emphasis on either Value Line's or S&P's rankings, especially in comparison with basic fundamental criteria. Non-dividend paying stocks do not gain good S&P rankings, while the universe of Value Line stocks is too limited.

ANALYZING CALCULATED CRITERIA FROM STOCK ANALYSIS COMPONENTS

Up to now we have been slogging through the basic data for analyzing corporations in terms of their financial fundamentals. The rest of our printout deals with some of the meaningful combinations and ratios derived from the

---

[6]Standard & Poor's, *Stock Guide*, March 1989, p. 5.

"plugged in" data on the top half. The following, then, are the numbers that lead us toward or away from corporations, that suggest undervalued stocks to buy and fully valued to overvalued stocks to sell.

32. *Proj. ROE.* Projected return on equity in percent. Just as we project earnings in an effort to draw a bead on the near future, so we are interested in the probable future returns on equity. ROE, as one of the basic criteria, was reviewed in Chapter 2. We can see at a glance that Chrysler has a "good" projected ROE of 15.85 percent, while BTU's is okay but not as strong at 13.84 percent, and CA's is a robust 25.81 percent, which clearly supports its growth stock status. The formula used is:

$$\text{Proj. ROE} = \text{Proj earn} / (\text{Book Value} + .5 * \text{Proj earn} - .5 * \text{Dividend}) * 100$$

33. *Cur P/E.* Current (trailing four-quarters) price/earnings ratio. By dividing the closing price per share by the current earnings per share, one obtains the price/earnings ratio. The P/E ratio is frequently referred to as the *price earnings' multiple* (or even just *multiple*) because the price of the stock is the P/E multiple times its earnings. Thus, with Chrysler earning $5.08 per share and trading at $24.50 per share, its multiple is 4.82 (4.82 times $5.08 equals $24.50). BTU's P/E is 13.08 and CA's is 19.97. Obviously, Chrysler's P/E is low compared both to the others and to its P/E norm (row 10), while the others are above their P/E norms.

One would also compare the current P/E with the projected return on equity (row 32), the return on equity (row 40), and the internal growth rate (row 41). Comparing these germane figures can give a perspective of the appropriateness of the P/E norm and the relative value of the current P/E in relation to the others.

34. *Div yield percent.* The current indicated annual dividend yield in percent. One obtains a dividend yield by dividing the indicated dividend (row 5) by the current price (row 4). Chrysler pays a slightly better-than-average dividend at 4.89 percent, considering the S&P 500 average dividend is 3.64 percent at this time. Neither BTU nor CA pay a dividend, therefore they have no dividend yield.

For some investors who believe that Chrysler is undervalued, its 4.89 percent yield—getting a $30-per-100-shares check every three months—is a comfort while they await Chrysler's market price appreciation or potential future dividend increases. If we notice the year-end cost (row 26) of our three stock examples, we will see that Chrysler is actually down $1.25 year-to-date, a drop greater than its annual indicated dividend. At the previous year-end, BTU traded for $6.50, so it has gained $1.875 per share or over 28 percent year-to-date, while CA has gained $8.375 per share or over 30 percent year-to-date.

Semidramatic stock price gain examples like these are why I emphasize stock price appreciation over dividend yields. Of course, one could always find a few dramatic examples, and you should understand that my bias is not based on such small samples for such short periods of time. Over very long periods of time, the S&P 500 dividends—as a proxy for large capitalization and blue chip stocks—actually amount to a greater compounded return than price appreciation. However, we will never be buying the S&P 500 or holding it for decades; nor will we be satisfied with its historical total returns of appreciation plus dividends.

Perhaps you can see from my point of view that I could care less about even an 8 percent to 10 percent dividend yield in a stock that also tends to appreciate only 4 percent to 5 percent per year—a total return of 12 percent to 15 percent when I am searching for stocks that can appreciate over 20 percent a year, perhaps doubling in market price in three years.

35. *Pr/tangBV.* Current price to current tangible book value as a ratio. I mentioned my concerns about tangible book values above and in Chapter 2, especially when compared to book values. We certainly like to find companies trading below their tangible book values or at some multiple that is at least 30 percent below their average tangible book value ratios.

In the case of Chrysler—with a tangible book value considerably below its regular book value—we see it trading at 116 percent (1.16) of its tangible book value. We would cross-reference this with Chrysler's book value norm of 2.0 (row 14) and see that it is well below a 30 percent discount from its norm. Of course, there is always the chance that our assigned book value norm is too high (or too low), and perhaps we should also have a tangible book value norm, but in reality such precision is not required as several other fundamental criteria will reinforce each other's indications.

BTU, trading at 138 percent (1.38) of tangible book value, is still nicely below its price to BV norm of 2.0 (row 14), while CA, trading at 471 percent (4.71) of its price to BV norm of 3.5, is well above and therefore overvalued on this criterion. I suspect that future stock price experience will lead us to elevate CA's BV norm, perhaps to 4.5 or higher. After all, these are all estimates and subject to dynamic revision given the growth of corporations and support of their share prices over time by shareholders.

36. *Price/BV.* Current price to current book value per share as a ratio. This criterion is essentially the same as the one above except that it uses book value rather than tangible book value. Actually, in most cases, book value reported by corporations *is* tangible book value, but we make the distinction so as to call attention to special cases. Book value is one of the basic fundamental criteria and was reviewed in Chapter 2. On balance, we like stocks trading below their book values or at least 30 percent below their book value norms, and we consider them potential sell candidates when they trade at or 30 percent above their book value norms.

Chrysler's stock's current price is only 75 percent (.75) of its stated book value, which makes it very undervalued on this criterion, given that its price to

BV norm (row 14) is 2.0 (200 percent). Perhaps 2.0 is too generous a BV norm for Chrysler, but this is my considered valuation level for this criterion. Since BTU and CA have the same book values and tangible book values respectively, there is no difference between their percentages of prices to their book values and their tangible book values.

37. *Cur ratio*. The current ratio of current assets to current liabilities. For a quick check on the current health of a corporation—at least in terms of its balance sheet—we look to see if current assets are sufficiently greater than current liabilities to avoid short-term financial difficulties. For industrial companies, the classic current ratio is 2:1, or twice as many current assets as current liabilities. The current ratio can be misleading if current assets represent disproportionately large accounts receivable with a poor history of collection or huge inventories that are unlikely to be sold at a profit. Very large corporations, especially oil companies, rarely have anything approaching a current ratio of 2:1. You will have to check for industry and company ratios and watch a corporation's current ratio over time—especially noticing deteriorations—to get a feel for this criterion.

Chrysler's current ratio of 1.72 is okay, especially compared to Ford's 1.12 and General Motors' 1.61. BTU's current ratio of 1.08 seems a little thin, but then Exxon shows a current ratio of .84, while Royal Dutch Petroleum's is 1.45. CA's current ratio of 1.77 is not bad but seems a bit anemic compared to IBM's 2.03. We soon see that very large corporations tend to have current ratios of less than 2:1.

38. *Ret sales*. Return (earnings) per dollar of sales as a percent. The return on sales percentage gives a snapshot of how much the corporation is earning per sales dollar. In large corporations you might like to see at least a 3 percent return on sales, but in a supermarket or other high-turnover, low-margin enterprise, you would do well to see 1 percent returns. Each company has its norm and perhaps more important than the actual percentage are the recent and long-term trends.

Chrysler's return on sales at 3.33 percent is okay, but mediocre compared to General Motor's 4.50 percent and Ford's 5.81 percent. Figures like this can be looked at in at least two ways. On the one hand, Chrysler does not get as much per dollar of sales as do its larger American competitors. On the other hand, Chrysler has much room for improvement in this criterion and could conceivably increase its earnings without an increase in sales by finding ways (lowering costs, increasing efficiencies) to improve its return on sales.

BTU, which is mainly a coal producer, shows a nice 5.01 percent return on sales compared to say Exxon's 5.65 percent, but Computer Associates walks away with the plums, recording a 15.40 percent return on sales. Of course, a successful software manufacturer requires less plant and equipment to produce and package its products and should manage a greater return on sales than would an automotive manufacturer or an oil company.

39. *Ret assets*. Return on assets (ROA) as a percent. Return on assets is another principal criterion that was reviewed in Chapter 2. Again, absolute percentages can give a snapshot appraisal, but a securities analyst—even an amateur working with pencil and paper—would want to observe the trend of this criterion to see if the corporation is becoming more or less effective in the profitable use of its assets.

We see that Chrysler's ROA is 2.43 percent compared to BTU's 4.48 percent and CA's 12.32 percent. These comparisons are in keeping with the kinds of corporations we are sampling. Chrysler, with its huge investment in assets (FASB 94) in order to produce cars and trucks and manage its financial subsidiary, is not likely to gain a greater return on assets than would an oil company or a light manufacturer/merchandising/service industry. A glance across the row at the other corporations' figures shows the variability of ROAs. Return on assets is an important criterion for financial companies, especially savings and loans.

40. *Ret equity.* Return on equity (ROE) as a percent. Another of the big seven criteria reviewed in Chapter 2, ROE indicates how well a corporation can turn a profit on its equity or net worth. Traditionally, ROEs of 15 percent or better separate so-called growth stocks from other stocks, but this can be misleading, especially over short periods of time. Again, we would want to be aware of the trend of ROE, hopefully a strong and positive one. Oddly enough, if the ROE of a corporation is too high or unsustainable, that condition is often represented in its stock's high, and therefore vulnerable, overvalued price.

Chrysler shows a handsome 15 percent ROE, which is supported by a projected ROE (row 32) of 15.85 percent. BTU's 10 percent ROE is sub par, but its projected 13.84 percent ROE suggests potential improvement, and one might extrapolate that, with higher average energy prices in the works, BTU might well manage an even better ROE than its currently projected estimate. CA's 23.00 percent ROE is in keeping with its growth stock image and is also supported by its projected ROE of 25.81 percent. This ROE in turn supports the seemingly high 19.0 P/E norm (row 10) assigned to CA.

41. *IntGrowthRt.* The projected internal growth rate (IGR) as a percent. The internal growth rate is an estimate of how much we expect the company to grow in the upcoming year based upon our projection of earnings less dividends. You will notice that if the corporation pays no dividends, then its IGR is the same as its ROE. This criterion is another example of how dividends may be counter-productive to corporate growth as their payout reduces the funds available for reinvestment. Sometimes dividends are actually paid with borrowed funds in a left-pocket-right-pocket routine that weakens the corporation's balance sheet. The formula for computing internal growth rate is

(1 - [dividends / projected earnings]) times ROE where projected earnings are greater than zero

Due to Chrysler's substantial dividend of $1.20 (row 5)—remember dividends come from after-tax profits or retained earnings—its IGR is computed at 11.72 percent, compared to its projected ROE of 15.85 percent (row 32). This is not a bad IRG, especially for a mature, giant corporation, but it's certainly not as encouraging as a 15 percent or better IGR would be. As neither BTU nor CA currently pay dividends, their IGRs are the same as their ROEs, 10.00 percent and 23.00 percent, respectively. IGRs may be easily overlooked by the typical investor in evaluating a corporation's growth characteristics over the years.

42. *Pr/net wkcp.* Current price to net working capital as a percent. This is a filter straight out of Ben Graham's approach, where one looks for a stock trading for less than its net working capital. Since working capital is simply current assets minus current liabilities (net current assets), net working capital is defined as current assets minus all liabilities (current and long-term). When you find a stock trading for less than its net working capital, you are able to buy a company for less than its value plus getting the fixed assets for nothing. Walter Schloss says that Ben Graham got bored with investing when he found that buying stocks for 70 percent of net working capital was all one needed to do to make money in the stock market.

43. *Prj en/pr.* Projected earnings to current price as percent. If we invert the common P/E ratio and make it an E/P ratio, then we obtain an earnings to price ratio, which is to say, what the earnings return is in relation to the price of a stock. A P/E of 5—for example, current price of $10 divided by current earnings of $2—means the stock is trading at five times earnings. But it also means that one is getting a 20 percent return on the stock's price (E/P or $2 earnings divided by $10 price). This little row is just a quick reference identifying the potential projected earnings return based on the current cost basis of a stock.

Chrysler, with projected earnings of $5.50 per share (row 8) turns out to have a projected P/E of 4.45 (current price $24.50 divided by projected earnings 5.50). The reciprocal of the projected P/E 4.45 (that is, 1 over 4.45) equals 22.44 percent, as does the projected earnings divided by the current price (that is, $5.50/-$24.50). This tells us that we may get a 22.44 percent projected return in one year on our investment of $24.50 per share of Chrysler. That is a handsome return, and if it could continue or be realized in the stock's price we would gain an even greater total return. If Chrysler's regular P/E of 4.45 were to advance to 9.0—because the market in its lower–interest-rates bullish thrust valued Chrysler's earnings at that level—even without an increase in earnings in the next year or two, its stock's price would more than double. And with increased earnings for the year, our initial return on investment could return 100 percent in a little over three years, even without a substantial rise in the P/E multiple.

BTU's projected earnings/price of 10.74 percent holds much less promise than Chrysler's, as does Computer Associate's paltry 6.29 percent, which indicates that CA, for all its growth potential, is certainly not undervalued by this criterion.

44. *Price/rev.* Current price per share to current revenues per share (P/R) as a ratio or percent. This is the famous price/sales ratio made popular by Kenneth Fisher, reviewed in Chapter 2 as one of the super seven selectors. Chrysler sports an undervalued P/R of 16 percent (.16)—which means that its stock trades for only 16 cents per dollar of sales—and could easily triple from this level when "the market" looks more favorably on the auto industry and Chrysler in particular. BTU's P/R also seems slightly undervalued at 65 percent (.65), its stock trading for 65 cents per $1 of sales. But CA, with a P/R of 307 percent (3.07), is in the fully valued to overvalued area with its stock trading for $3.07 per $1.00 of revenue.

45. *Price/CF.* Current price to cash flow (P/CF) as a ratio. P/CF is also one of the super seven criteria explicated in Chapter 2. Obviously, different corporations tend toward different ratios, and the long-term trend is an important consideration. We look at a corporation's P/CF in the light of its P/CF norm (row 17), which represents historical perspective, as well as in the light of its recent trend.

With Chrysler trading at 2.59 times cash flow, we have a very undervalued reading, even though its P/CF norm is only 4.0, currently reflecting the low esteem in which automotive companies are held and probably a tad low in relation to future norms. When I tell you that some of our norms may be too high or too low, I am expressing my intuitions or gut feelings, but that doesn't permit me to change them willy nilly. I expect that in a year or two we might be carrying Chrysler's P/CF norm at 5.0. Meanwhile, BTU is also undervalued with a P/CF of 4.18 compared to its P/CF norm of 6.0, but CA, trading at 13.49 times its cash flow, must be considered overvalued on this criterion.

46. *MV Change percent.* Market value (price) change since year-end in percent. Sometimes it's convenient to see at a glance how a stock's price has performed during the year. This row shows that Chrysler's stock price is down 4.85 percent for the year, while BTU's stock price has advanced 28.84 percent and CA's stock price has advanced 30.59 percent. We made reference to this relationship when commenting upon year-end cost above (row 26).

47. *Mkt value.* Market value or capitalization in millions of dollars. An important and interesting factor is a stock's market capitalization, computed by multiplying the number of shares outstanding (row 20) by the current price per share (row 4). We have commented on market capitalization elsewhere, especially in reference to studies that show that small "cap" stocks tend to appreciate significantly more over time than large cap stocks. We also use market value to consider other criteria such as price-to-revenues ratios (P/R, row 44) as different-sized corporations have different P/R criterion levels (see Chapter 2).

Chrysler is definitely a very large cap stock with a market value of over $5.7 billion (approximately $5,710,950,000)—233.1 million shares outstanding (row 20) times $24.50 (row 4)—but, surprisingly, Computer Associates has a market cap of about $2.85 billion ($2,845,700,000). I write *surprisingly* because Chrysler's total assets are 42 times larger than CA's (row 21) and Chrysler's revenues are 38 times larger than CA's (row 18), while Chrysler's market cap is barely twice as large as CA's. Although there is no necessary relationship, these disparities could give a clue as to how undervalued Chrysler is and how fully valued CA might be. BTU weighs in with a market cap of $110.21 million ($110,210,000), which qualifies it as a small cap stock by most criteria.

VALUATION COMPUTATIONS

The first 31 rows consist of input data, some of which is intrinsically interesting and useful individually as well as in comparison with each other. Rows 32 through 47 consist of computations yielding basic ratios and percentages that indicate various levels of fundamental valuation. Now we turn to the bottom lines, rows 48 through 56, which actually give us our high and low goal prices as well as a few other convenient figures and keys. Each of these items is simple—sometimes embarrassingly so—but they add up to a fairly representative picture of an undervalued corporation, especially given the limited amount of time that we want to spend on such analysis.

After wading through all these items, you may feel that the whole thing is just too complicated to even begin tracking on your own. I can tell you again that, once you have gained the least facility for the subject, you can probably analyze a corporation in an hour or less, initially, and thereafter keep up with it by spending about 5 to 10 minutes a week using a computer and database. Of course, you needn't follow nearly as many stocks as we do nor go into such detailed analysis.

You can do computer screens rather rapidly—selecting those stocks that meet certain specified criteria—to find only the most promising candidates and then follow up on them. If a criterion, whether checked manually or by computer, doesn't satisfy your guideline, you can quit working on that stock and move on to the next one. Perhaps you will save those stocks that showed some promise in an "almost qualified" file and review them at a later date when they might have become more undervalued and thus satisfy your standards.

48. *P/CF goal.* Price cash flow goal in dollars. This is merely multiplying the current cash flow (row 15) by the price/cash flow norm (row 17) to arrive at the cash flow goal figure. For some corporations such as financial institutions, cash flow is not a meaningful figure, which explains the blank spaces for CalFed, etc. Chrysler has a cash flow goal of $37.80 ($9.45 times 4.0). BTU's P/CF goal is $12.00, nicely above its current price, while CA's P/CF goal of $34.45 is just below its current price. These goal prices will be combined with other goal prices to arrive at a low and high goal range, reviewed below.

49. *P/E goal.* Current price/earnings goal in dollars. By multiplying the current earnings (row 6) times the P/E norm (row 10), we arrive at a normal price/earnings goal. In theory, this is the price the stock should be trading at today given its average (fair) P/E multiple and its current price. Thus, Chrysler's P/E goal is $50.80, or more than twice its current price. BTU's P/E goal is $8.32, which is less than its current price, as is Computer Associates's P/E goal of $34.01. Obviously, a corporation may be worth far more than its current earnings would indicate, so while this is an important consideration, it is neither necessary nor sufficient for recommending or not recommending a stock. Of course, that could be said about every criterion being reviewed.

50. *ProjE goal.* Projected earnings price goal (PEG) in dollars. By multiplying the projected earnings (row 8) times the P/E norm (row 10), we obtain the projected earnings price goal. Although it has been pointed out more than once that projected (estimated) earnings are notoriously unreliable in general, we still would like to see what a stock might reasonably trade for, given that its projected earnings were realized. Working with a large number of stocks, we can be slightly cavalier that over estimations and underestimations will tend to cancel each other out, and, besides, we are not merely relying on just this one criterion.

Chrysler's PEG amounts to $55.00, again more than twice its current price. BTU's PEG is $11.70, comfortably above its current price. CA's PEG is $42.75, still above its current price and one of the few reasons to continue holding this otherwise fairly valued stock.

51. *BV goal.* Book value price goal (BVG) in dollars. We have already considered that corporations trade at a multiple of their book values and thus we derive book value norms (*BV norm,* row 14). By multiplying the book value norm against the book value (row 12), we obtain a book value price goal. We use book value because in takeover situations buyouts usually occur at a multiple of book value, and it's easier to compare book values since so many companies' tangible book values are identical to their book values.

Chrysler's BVG is $65.06, again more than twice its current price. BTU's BVG is $12.10, about the same as its P/CF goal. CA's BVG is only $26.56, well below its current price. This could mean that CA's BV norm is too low, or else this is a little warning that CA is overvalued, at least by this criterion.

52. *2 x price.* Two times the current price in dollars. This is just a ready reference item to show what twice the current price is, so that we can quickly see the relationships of the goal prices to twice the current market prices. Of course, the asterisks point out when goal prices are greater than twice the current price—that is, when the current price is less than 50 percent of the goal price—since asterisks point out undervalued criteria.

We see that twice Chrysler's current price is $49, which is below four of our goal price amounts. BTU's goal prices are well below twice its current price, while CA's goal prices are far away from twice its current price (generally less than its current price).

THREE SUMMARY KEYS GIVE A SNAPSHOT

53. *Recommends.* A quick key for noticing undervalued conditions. Every day our stock analysis data base is updated with any revised fundamental information obtained. We print out daily recommended buy and sell candidates, and every week the stock analysis "booklet" is printed. In order to quickly notice buy candidates or a general snapshot of a few of the more telling undervalued relationships, we use a priority system consisting of a number combined with a letter.

The first key gives indication that a stock

1 Is undervalued by one or more of its goal prices.
A Has three or more goal prices greater than twice its current price— sufficient to consider a stock undervalued.
B Has two goal prices greater than twice its current price.
C Has one goal price greater than twice its current price.

Thus Chrysler's *1A* signals a highly probable undervalued buy candidate. Neither BTU nor CA has any *1* rating, so they clearly are not buy candidates.
The second key refers to a stock's

2 Earning's trend, the relationships among current earnings (row 6), three-year average earnings (row 7), and projected earnings (row 8).
A Earning's pattern when projected earnings are higher than current earnings, which are higher than three-year average earnings.
B Earning's pattern when the current or projected earnings are greater than both of the other earnings figures.
C Earning's pattern when either the current or the projected earnings are greater than the three-year average.

This is a crude "trend," given that the earnings momentum or percentage change is not indicated, nor can we tell the actual trend of the three-year average figure. Still, a positive pattern is supportive of a positive goal-price ranking and other items.

With our current examples we see that Chrysler has a *2C* because its projected earnings are greater than its current earnings only. This can help explain Chrysler's poor price action year-to-date and suggests that the market's apparent antipathy toward Chrysler (and the auto stocks) is based upon current and anticipated earnings trends. Even as these paragraphs are being written, Chrysler has reported better-than-expected earnings. I was tempted to substitute another example that looks stronger than Chrysler, say Ford, but I want to show that undervalued stocks will outperform the market over the years, so I will stay with Chrysler to see if over the next few years our analysis proves predictive of its long-term under-valuedness being superior to its short-term "out of favoredness."

Both BTU and CA carry *2A*, which indicates each has some earnings momentum and apparently a rising earnings trend. When you are trying to decide which stocks to hold—because you need to liquidate some issues or to replace some issues with other, more promising stocks—a strong earnings trend is a strong plus in the "keep 'em" column. BTU's current earnings are almost 31 percent greater than its three-year average, and its projected earnings are over 40 percent greater than its current earnings. Even though other BTU criteria are mediocre, this earnings potential makes BTU a strong hold. Similarly, CA's current earnings are 118 percent greater than its three-year average earnings, and its projected earnings are almost 26 percent greater than its current earnings. Because of this powerful earnings trend, otherwise slightly overvalued CA is still a hold at this time based on its earnings and growth potential.

The third key refers to a few fundamental relationships.

3 Each stock is checked to see if its price is less than two thirds of its book value, if its price is less than $15 per share, if it has a dividend greater than 4.0 percent, and if its market cap is less than $200 million.

A Means that all four conditions are met.

B Indicates that three of the four conditions are satisfied.

C Refers to two conditions being present.

D Is assigned when any one of the four conditions exists.

These third-key parameters are neither that meaningful nor critical, but they do suggest certain positives for a stock, based upon several historical market studies. We do not pay very much attention to them in practice, unless they strongly augment a marginally undervalued set of other criteria.

Chrysler has a *3D* because its dividend is greater than 4.0 percent. BTU's *3C* represents a stock trading for less than $15 per share with a market cap of less than $200 million. CA does not meet any of these fundamental relationships.

54. *Goal price.* An average of the meaningful goal prices in rows 48 through 51 in dollars. In an effort to include cash flow, earnings, projected earnings, and book value into a more encompassing goal price, we add them together and divide by four. In cases where cash flow is not a significant criterion, we add the remaining three goal prices together and divide by three. Clearly this system tends to overemphasize earnings, but we have not found that to be a terrible flaw, especially when other criteria are reviewed. For example, inferior returns on sales, assets, and equity could be a bar to recommending an otherwise undervalued buy candidate based on its earning goal prices alone. If the current earnings are negative, we eliminate earnings goal price from the average goal price calculation.

Chrysler's average goal price is $52.16, again more than twice its current price. As a technique, we take the high and low goal prices from the calculated five—usually focusing on the average goal price (row 54) and the projected earnings goal price (row 50)—as a suggested minimum and maximum buy or sell limits. In the case of Chrysler, its current goal price range is $52.16 to $55.00, and it is therefore a currently recommended stock.

BTU's average goal price is $11.03, and its goal price range is $11.00 to $12.00—we usually round up to the nearest dollar— based on its average goal price and its projected earnings goal price. Notice how nicely BTU's cash flow and book value goal prices agree with its goal price range. (As noted on p. 273, BTU was bought out for $12.00 per share on July 26, 1989.)

CA's average goal price is $34.44, just below its current price. CA's goal price range is $34 to $43, based upon its average and projected earnings goal prices. Notice how CA's lower goal price range is echoed in its cash flow and current earnings goals but is significantly above its book value goal. This would indicate that a conservative investor might want to take profits in Computer Associates at its current price level. However, the very strong earnings trend and high returns on equity, sales, and assets would keep the aggressive speculator holding CA shares for their high goal price and possibly beyond as increased earnings continue over the quarters and years to make CA an ever more fundamentally valuable corporation.

55. *Apprc poten.* Appreciation potential from current levels expressed in percent. This is another convenience figure showing the relationship of the average goal price (row 54) to the current price (row 4). We could see that Chrysler's average goal price was above twice its current price (row 52), but now we know that Chrysler's current price has a 112.91 percent appreciation potential to reach its average price goal. BTU's appreciation potential is 31.70 percent, while CA's potential appreciation is negative, a -3.65 percent, signifying its valuation condition (according to various criteria) reviewed above.

When reviewing potential buy candidates, one could use this figure to compare undervalue—how much appreciation potential these candidates have according to this system of evaluation. The appreciation potential number can also be the beginning of a search for fairly or overvalued stocks to be trimmed out. If we were convinced that we were entering an extended and severe bear market, the appreciation potential percentages could be a guide for short selling. We have never engaged in short selling.

56. *Inst hold percent.* Percent of shares held by institutions. As studies show that stocks widely followed by analysts and held by institutions tend not to appreciate over long periods of time as much as those not widely followed or held—the so-called neglected stock effect—we like to see at a glance this criterion on our stock analysis printout. Both Chrysler and Computer Associates, with 58.77 percent and 56.35 percent respectively of their shares, in institutional hands, are widely held by institutions; while BTU, with 32.07 percent of its shares in institutional hands, is less widely held by institutions but not at all in the neglected stock category. On this printout, Cannon Express, with 6.15

percent institutional ownership, and Bay View Federal, with no institutional ownership, are examples of stocks with low or negligible institutional interest.

WHAT DOES IT ALL MEAN?

I wish I could say that it means water runs downhill and seeks its lowest level. That would be a neat conclusion, but we wouldn't have to go through all the steps above to agree on water's tendencies. In one sense, it means that corporations can be evaluated, estimated—as an estimator might value your house or private business—and their stocks selected for purchase or sale on the outcomes of these analyzed fundamentals.

It means that, when a corporation's stock—such as Chrysler's—is out of favor today yet has a sufficient configuration of undervalued fundamental criteria, there is a good chance that it is trading for less than half its probable market price in the next three to five years. It means that Pyro Energy at the time of this analysis has a good chance of advancing another 30 percent or more over the next few years (which it did in a few months) and that Computer Associates, although it has great historical appreciation, considerable potential, and a great growth pattern, nevertheless may be getting a little expensive in terms of fundamental valuations. It means buy Chrysler, hold Pyro Energy, and be prepared to sell Computer Associates in the near future.

Additionally, by slowly becoming familiar with such numbers and relationships, we can build our knowledge and expertise and develop intuition about stock picking in general, based on the limited number of stocks that have come to our attention. As the quarters and years go by we can see how Chrysler, and Computer Associates—as just two of many examples—develop as corporations and how their stocks fare in relation to that development and to market conditions. Perhaps Chrysler will continue to disappoint and Computer Associates will advance beyond our "reasonable" fundamental analysis. Still, over a long period of time and with a large number of stocks, my experience has shown that such analysis leads to a considerable majority of winners that far overcome the sizeable number of unavoidable losers.

APPENDIX B

TPS PORTFOLIO AT
JUNE 30, 1989

Appendix B

TPS Portfolio at June 30, 1989

Quantity	Security	Unit Cost	Total Cost	Price	Market Value	Pct. Assets	Cur. Yield
1,000.00	AM International	4.22	4,224.43	5.25	5,250.00	0.6	0.0
300.00	Ahmanson Co	20.58	6,175.50	22.00	6,600.00	0.7	4.0
1,000.00	Allied Research	5.43	5,429.00	2.50	2,500.00	0.3	0.0
150.00	Allied-Sig'l Cp.	29.49	4,423.80	33.00	4,950.00	0.6	5.5
500.00	Am. Fructose Cp.	13.74	6,872.10	14.50	7,250.00	0.8	0.0
1,200.00	Am. Integrity In	5.96	7,148.00	5.00	6,000.00	0.7	0.0
305.00	Am. President	21.84	6,661.87	31.12	9,493.12	1.1	1.9
400.00	Ambase Corp.	15.71	6,282.42	13.75	5,500.00	0.6	1.5
627.00	Anthony Indstrs.	6.72	4,213.83	17.12	10,737.37	1.2	2.6
200.00	Arvin Industries	15.16	3,031.26	23.87	4,775.00	0.5	2.8
300.00	Bank of New York	20.24	6,072.50	48.75	14,625.00	1.6	3.9
175.00	Boatmen's Banc.	15.70	2,747.50	36.37	6,365.62	0.7	5.5
550.00	Broad Inc.	15.87	8,729.00	10.37	5,706.25	0.6	1.0
200.00	Brown Group	31.99	6,398.32	33.75	6,750.00	0.8	4.7
350.00	CalFed Inc.	18.51	6,477.49	24.25	8,487.50	1.0	5.8
300.00	Carriage Inds.	5.71	1,713.50	5.25	1,575.00	0.2	1.9
100.00	Chelsea Ind's	10.15	1,014.98	28.87	2,887.50	0.3	2.5
750.00	Chrysler Corp.	17.20	12,903.13	24.75	18,562.50	2.1	4.8
100.00	City Inv. Liq.	2.52	251.75	2.12	212.50	0.0	0.0
2,000.00	Clabir B Wrt	0.78	1,563.78	0.02	32.00	0.0	0.0
200.00	Cont'l III Hold	10.73	2,145.93	0.08	15.62	0.0	0.0
1,000.00	Cooper Tire	6.93	6,927.27	29.00	29,000.00	3.2	1.2
200.00	Cubic Corp.	18.15	3,631.00	14.25	2,850.00	0.3	2.9
2,100.00	DH Technology	5.29	11,108.00	10.12	21,262.50	2.4	0.0
67.00	Delta Airlines	3.16	211.58	67.87	4,547.62	0.5	1.8
4.00	Diamond Sham Off	7.20	28.81	8.62	34.50	0.0	32.5
50.00	Diamond Sham R&M	15.78	788.77	21.75	1,087.50	0.1	2.0
150.00	Downey S&L	18.79	2,818.50	26.12	3,918.75	0.4	1.4
800.00	Elco Industries	9.04	7,230.00	15.00	12,000.00	1.3	3.2
700.00	Far West Fin'l	10.58	7,406.41	10.37	7,262.50	0.8	0.0
400.00	Fed Nat'l Mortg.	27.05	10,819.60	89.12	35,650.00	4.0	1.4
100.00	Figgie Int'l "A"	29.43	2,942.80	77.00	7,700.00	0.9	1.6
100.00	Figgie Int'l "B"	29.43	2,942.79	85.00	8,500.00	1.0	1.4
200.00	First Chicago	22.64	4,528.12	41.12	8,225.00	0.9	4.4
880.00	First Fin'l Cp.	8.82	7,762.06	17.00	14,960.00	1.7	3.8
200.00	Firstar Corp.	9.86	1,972.50	26.62	5,325.00	0.6	4.2
400.00	Fleet/Norstar	12.79	5,117.70	27.00	10,800.00	1.2	4.7
600.00	Ford Motor Co.	13.01	7,803.65	48.50	29,100.00	3.3	6.2
100.00	Forest Cty Ent.A	8.18	817.61	54.00	5,400.00	0.6	0.8
100.00	Forest Cty Ent.B	8.18	817.61	55.50	5,550.00	0.6	0.8
400.00	Fuqua Inds	13.89	5,557.50	30.00	12,000.00	1.3	1.1
200.00	General Dev'ment	18.88	3,776.00	12.50	2,500.00	0.3	0.0
250.00	General Dynamics	63.77	15,941.50	58.25	14,562.50	1.6	1.7
400.00	General Motors	33.42	13,366.59	41.75	16,700.00	1.9	7.2
20.00	General Motors H	35.18	703.51	28.12	562.50	0.1	2.6
700.00	GlenFed S&L	13.16	9,211.17	22.00	15,400.00	1.7	5.5
100.00	Golden West Fin.	37.00	3,700.00	46.12	4,612.50	0.5	0.6
100.00	Great Am. Saving	15.53	1,553.00	12.50	1,250.00	0.1	4.8
1,250.00	Great Western	17.03	21,289.50	20.00	25,000.00	2.8	4.0
20.00	Green A.P. Inds	8.88	177.55	27.25	545.00	0.1	1.5

Appendix B—*Continued*

Quantity	Security	Unit Cost	Total Cost	Price	Market Value	Pct. Assets	Cur. Yield
16.00	Henley Group	29.00	463.94	61.75	988.00	0.1	0.0
800.00	Heritage Ent	3.73	2,983.87	1.50	1,200.00	0.1	0.0
361.00	Hibernia Cp. "A"	12.24	4,417.44	20.75	7,490.75	0.8	4.4
450.00	HomeFed Corp	24.62	11,078.50	38.75	17,437.50	2.0	0.5
1,000.00	Humana Corp	19.95	19,954.00	34.00	34,000.00	3.8	3.1
200.00	ITT Corp.	33.04	6,608.88	56.87	11,375.00	1.3	2.6
620.00	Imperial Cp Am.	11.91	7,383.50	5.75	3,565.00	0.4	0.0
50.00	Intgrat'd Res.	30.06	1,503.00	4.00	200.00	0.0	0.0
1,200.00	Johnston Inds	8.46	10,148.25	14.12	16,950.00	1.9	0.0
100.00	Katy Industries	17.24	1,723.82	23.12	2,312.50	0.3	0.0
403.00	Kaufman & Broad Home	0.00	0.00	17.00	6,851.00	0.8	1.8
800.00	Kysor Inds.	9.61	7,691.74	15.62	12,500.00	1.4	3.8
300.00	Lockheed Corp	44.84	13,451.00	47.87	14,362.50	1.6	3.8
200.00	MAXXAM Inc	12.99	2,597.76	30.87	6,175.00	0.7	0.0
200.00	Maxus Energy	11.63	2,326.08	8.37	1,675.00	0.2	0.0
501.00	Maytag	9.57	4,793.63	22.25	11,147.25	1.2	4.5
595.00	Mercury S&L	5.49	3,267.17	4.87	2,900.63	0.3	0.0
200.00	Modine Mfg.	11.16	2,231.54	19.12	3,825.00	0.4	3.1
300.00	NBD Bancorp	6.58	1,973.90	43.87	13,162.50	1.5	3.8
549.00	Nortek Corp	11.77	6,459.19	8.00	4,392.00	0.5	1.2
100.00	Occidental Pete	23.57	2,356.73	27.37	2,737.50	0.3	9.1
100.00	Orient Exp Htls	3.68	367.53	4.75	475.00	0.1	0.0
400.00	Oxford Inds	13.11	5,243.19	12.25	4,900.00	0.5	4.1
300.00	P & F Inds "A"	4.63	1,390.50	3.19	956.25	0.1	0.0
500.00	P.R. Cement	6.75	3,375.00	46.75	23,375.00	2.6	1.4
100.00	PS Group	20.79	2,079.12	35.00	3,500.00	0.4	1.7
468.00	Pacific G & E	11.15	5,219.99	20.25	9,477.00	1.1	6.9
1,000.00	Pan American	4.69	4,686.06	3.87	3,875.00	0.4	0.0
200.00	Paramount Commun.	7.95	1,589.13	59.25	11,850.00	1.3	1.2
242.00	Phillips-Van Heu	2.10	507.72	19.12	4,628.25	0.5	1.5
400.00	PinWest Corp.	27.25	10,899.13	11.87	4,750.00	0.5	13.5
500.00	Pyro Energy	6.03	3,012.66	12.00	6,000.00	0.7	0.0
1,600.00	Richton Int'l	5.92	9,470.00	3.75	6,000.00	0.7	0.0
2,712.00	Robeson Inds	3.46	9,371.54	3.37	9,153.00	1.0	0.0
200.00	Royal Dutch	22.89	4,578.63	62.75	12,550.00	1.4	5.8
300.00	Rymer Foods	16.54	4,962.35	11.00	3,300.00	0.4	0.0
100.00	Ryser Foods	10.53	1,052.95	7.37	737.50	0.1	0.0
500.00	Salomon Inc	29.50	14,748.59	24.37	12,187.50	1.4	2.6
217.00	Sara Lee	21.48	4,660.24	53.87	11,690.87	1.3	2.7
300.00	Sea Containers	22.34	6,700.80	67.50	20,250.00	2.3	0.9
200.00	Security Pacific	22.17	4,435.00	44.50	8,900.00	1.0	5.1
400.00	Shell Transport	19.05	7,619.49	39.62	15,850.00	1.8	6.4
200.00	Signal Apparel	6.55	1,310.00	7.00	1,400.00	0.2	0.0
400.00	Smith, A.O. "A"	13.36	5,343.12	18.75	7,500.00	0.8	4.3
1,000.00	Smithfield Foods	5.90	5,896.50	15.00	15,000.00	1.7	0.0
432.00	Snyder Oil	10.11	4,365.97	4.00	1,728.00	0.2	15.0
1,479.00	Southmark Corp.	6.64	9,820.59	0.34	508.41	0.1	0.0
200.00	Std. Motor Prod.	17.86	3,571.88	16.87	3,375.00	0.4	1.9
200.00	Tesoro Petroleum	14.57	2,914.19	9.12	1,825.00	0.2	0.0
200.00	Texaco Inc.	36.21	7,241.52	50.37	10,075.00	1.1	6.0

Appendix B—*Concluded*

Quantity	Security	Unit Cost	Total Cost	Price	Market Value	Pct. Assets	Cur. Yield
1,760.00	Transcisco Ind A	4.84	8,520.26	7.50	13,200.00	1.5	4.0
1,760.00	Transcisco Ind B	4.84	8,520.28	7.25	12,760.00	1.4	1.4
1,000.00	Wellco Entrprs.	13.18	13,181.93	16.12	16,125.00	1.8	1.6
75.00	Wheelabrator Group	0.53	39.50	7.37	553.12	0.1	0.0
8.00	Wickes Cos. Wts.	3.75	30.00	0.12	1.00	0.0	0.0
700.00	Z-Seven Fund	21.35	14,946.00	14.12	9,887.50	1.1	0.0
			570,516.48		878,171.41	98.4	2.8
PREFERRED STOCK							
720	Clabir Pfd	16.47	11,859.22	7.75	5,580.00	0.6	0.0
120	Eastern Air Pd D 2.84	0.00	0.00	15.75	1,890.00	0.2	18.0
1	WCI Hldings Pfd	5.75	5.75	13.75	13.75	0.0	0.0
			11,864.97		7,483.75	0.8	4.6
CORPORATE BONDS							
4,000	MAXXAM Reset Note 13.500% Due 03-01-00	70.36	2,814.24	96.00	3,840.00	0.4	14.1
4,500	Sheller Globe Bond 13.750% Due 06-01-01	0.00	0.00	71.50	3,217.50	0.4	19.2
			2,814.24		7,057.50	0.8	16.4
GRAND TOTAL			585,195.68		892,712.65	100.0	2.9

APPENDIX C

ALL FORMERLY RECOMMENDED STOCKS WHICH HAVE NOT BEEN CLOSED OUT AS OF MAY 17, 1989

All Formerly Recommended Stocks Which Have Not Been Closed Out

	Date 1st Recommend	TPS	Symbol	Common Stock	1st Rec. Price	Price 5/17/89	Percent Change
1	10/ 9/87	227	ABIG	Am. Bankers Ins	11.875	10.250	-13.68%
2	9/28/84	175	ACT	Amer. Century Corp.	10.000	0.250	-97.50%
3	6/ 5/87	221	AEPI	AEP Industries	7.750	16.000	106.45%
4	4/11/86	201	AFC.A	American Fructose	9.500	13.500	42.11%
5	3/ 7/80	79	AFL	Amer. Family Corp.*	1.705	17.875	948.39%
6	9/26/86	209	AHM	Ahmanson (H.F.)	20.750	20.250	-2.41%
7	4/24/87	219	AIIC	American Integrity	5.875	4.500	-23.40%
8	11/11/88	246	AL	Alcan Aluminum	29.250	33.750	15.38%
9	2/19/82	128	ALD	Allied-Signal*	16.576	33.875	104.36%
10	10/30/87	228	ALW	Williams (A.L.)*	15.125	15.375	1.65%
11	3/ 1/85	182	AM	AM International	4.750	6.000	26.32%
12	7/ 9/82	136	AMN	Ameron Inc.*	10.188	36.000	253.36%
13	12/11/87	230	AMSWA	Amer. Software "A"*	4.917	15.875	222.88%
14	2/24/89	251	AMX	Amax, Inc	25.500	26.000	1.96%
15	12/28/84	179	ANT	Anthony Industries*	6.167	17.750	187.81%
16	9/11/78	40	APGI	Green, A.P. Inds.	3.691	27.500	645.06%
17	10/30/87	228	APK	Apple Bank*	21.875	35.625	62.86%
18	10/ 9/81	120	APS	Am. President Cos.*	12.000	37.000	208.33%
19	1/17/86	197	ARAI	Allied Research	5.125	3.000	-41.46%
20	4/ 3/87	218	ARB	Amer. Realty Trust	4.875	4.250	-12.82%
21	2/ 7/86	198	ARC	Atlantic Richfield	52.125	90.250	73.14%
22	8/19/88	242	ARDNA	Arden Group A	44.000	49.000	11.36%
23	2/19/82	128	ARV	Arvin Industries*	6.500	24.125	271.15%
24	10/30/87	228	ARX	ARX Inc.	6.591	3.875	-41.21%
25	10/30/87	228	ASAL	BankAtlantic S&L	12.500	9.250	-26.00%
26	12/02/88	247	AVX	AVX Corp.	15.250	21.375	40.16%
27	12/11/87	230	AXP	American Express	21.750	33.875	55.75%
28	6/15/84	170	BAC	Bank of America	15.625	25.250	61.60%
29	11/20/87	229	BC	Brunswick Corp.	15.250	20.625	35.25%
30	11/11/88	246	BCO	Blessings Corp	14.000	19.000	35.71%
31	3/26/82	130	BK	Bank of New York*	12.792	44.750	249.83%
32	5/29/81	111	BOAT	Boatmen's Banc.*	10.429	34.500	230.81%
33	3/ 7/80	79	BRO	Broad Inc.*	3.722	8.000	114.94%
34	5/27/88	238	BS	Bethlehem Steel	19.125	23.000	20.26%
35	10/30/87	228	BSC	Bear Stearns*	11.429	15.000	31.25%
36	3/22/85	183	BTU	Pyro Energy	8.625	8.375	-2.90%
37	5/27/88	238	BVFS	Bay View Fed S&L	17.000	21.375	25.74%
38	12/30/83	162	C	Chrysler Corp.*	12.278	24.375	98.53%
39	5/25/84	169	CAL	CalFed Inc.	12.625	22.750	80.20%
40	3/17/89	252	CANX	Cannon Express	6.375	6.750	5.88%
41	5/16/80	84	CAO	Carolina Freight*	3.813	23.250	509.76%
42	12/12/80	99	CBK	Continental Bank*	42.800	23.875	-44.22%
43	5/25/84	169	CBU	Commodore Int'l	27.250	18.000	-33.94%
44	10/30/87	228	CCI	Citicorp	20.250	30.375	50.00%
45	10/30/87	228	CCTC	CCT Corp.	7.125	2.500	-64.91%
46	9/25/81	119	CCX	CCX Inc.*	5.625	3.500	-37.78%
47	2/ 9/79	51	CDA	Control Data*	16.438	20.000	21.67%
48	10/30/87	228	CDO	Comdisco	16.875	26.500	57.04%
49	6/14/85	187	CGE	Carriage Industries	4.875	5.000	2.56%
50	8/28/87	225	CHCR	Chancellor Corp.	7.750	5.500	-29.03%

	Date 1st Recommend	TPS Symbol	Common Stock	1st Rec. Price	Price 5/17/89	Percent Change
51	1/12/79	49 CHD	Chelsea Industries*	9.318	28.500	205.86%
52	10/19/84	176 CHRZ	Computer Horizons	5.750	7.750	34.78%
53	3/26/82	130 CI	CIGNA Corp.	50.375	53.500	6.20%
54	11/20/87	229 CIS	Concord Fabrics*	3.750	4.000	6.67%
55	11/20/87	229 CIS.B	Concord Fabrics B*	3.750	3.875	3.33%
56	11/30/79	72 CNK	Crompton & Knowles	4.959	40.500	716.70%
57	9/ 8/78	40 CNV	City Investing*		1.750	
58	10/ 9/87	227 COFD	Collective Bancorp*	10.875	8.750	-19.54%
59	1/13/78	23 CP	Canadian Pacific*	5.000	18.375	267.50%
60	11/28/80	98 CPH	Capital Holding*	8.938	38.625	332.14%
61	9/18/87	226 CSA	Coast Savings	18.375	16.000	-12.93%
62	5/ 5/78	31 CSX	CSX Inc.*	7.710	32.875	326.39%
63	10/21/77	17 CTB	Cooper Tire*	1.547	27.750	1693.79%
64	3/21/80	80 CTR	Constar Int'l.*	6.500	26.375	305.77%
65	8/17/84	173 CUB	Cubic Corp.	17.250	17.125	-0.72%
66	12/16/77	21 CUM	Cummins Engine	38.375	69.500	81.11%
67	10/ 9/81	120 D	Dominion Resources*	16.313	44.625	173.55%
68	1/12/79	49 DAL	Delta Air Lines*	24.092	67.875	181.73%
69	8/27/82	139 DBRSY	DeBeers Consolidated	4.125	14.500	251.52%
70	5/27/88	238 DEC	Digital Equipment	100.125	96.625	-3.50%
71	1/ 9/87	214 DHTK	DH Technology	5.000	10.250	105.00%
72	10/31/80	96 DNA	Diana Corp.*	5.227	6.875	31.53%
73	9/18/87	226 DPT	Datapoint	8.000	3.750	-53.13%
74	11/11/88	246 DRM	Diamond Sham R&M	15.000	26.000	73.33%
75	8/ 7/87	224 DSL	Downey Savings	19.250	18.750	-2.60%
76	9/ 8/78	40 DSO	DeSoto Inc.	15.250	40.500	165.57%
77	2/28/86	199 DTM	Dataram Corp.	11.625	8.500	-26.88%
78	11/20/87	229 DXT	Dixon Ticonderoga	5.938	18.375	209.47%
79	10/30/87	228 DYTC	Dynatech	17.000	17.625	3.68%
80	12/ 2/77	20 EAL	Eastern Air*	6.250		-100.00%
81	12/11/87	230 ECOL	American Ecology	9.750	9.500	-2.56%
82	9/26/86	209 ELCN	Elco Industries*	9.500	16.500	73.68%
83	9/28/84	175 ELK	Elcor Corp.*	5.625	9.500	68.89%
84	1/17/86	197 ESCA	Escalade Corp.*	2.985	11.000	268.57%
85	10/19/79	69 ETN	Eaton Corp.*	17.250	60.500	250.72%
86	3/22/85	183 EXC	Excel Industries*	5.867	11.125	89.61%
87	9/13/85	191 EXCG	Exchange Bancorp*	3.667	14.625	298.81%
88	12/ 9/83	161 F	Ford Motor Corp.*	13.834	49.750	259.62%
89	10/21/88	245 FBO	Federal Paper Board	19.500	25.000	28.21%
90	11/30/79	72 FCA	Fabri-Centers*	3.167	14.250	349.95%
91	8/28/87	225 FED	1st Fed. Fin. Corp.*	13.600	17.500	28.68%
92	2/12/88	233 FEXC	First Exec Corp.*	11.111	15.875	42.87%
93	7/29/88	241 FFA	First Fed America	14.625	21.375	46.15%
94	9/28/84	175 FFHC	First Financial Cp.*	7.500	16.500	120.00%
95	2/08/85	181 FFOM	First Fed'l Michigan	11.000	14.500	31.82%
96	12/11/87	230 FG	USF&G Corp.	29.500	32.625	10.59%
97	2/22/80	78 FIGI	Figgie Int'l "B"*	11.500	89.000	673.91%
98	2/22/80	78 FIGIA	Figgie Int'l "A"*	11.500	74.000	543.48%
99	3/21/80	80 FLD	Fieldcrest-Cannon*	12.000	26.500	120.83%
100	3/23/84	166 FNB	First Chicago Corp.	24.250	39.750	63.92%

	Date 1st Recommend	TPS	Symbol	Common Stock	1st Rec. Price	Price 5/17/89	Percent Change
101	10/03/80	94	FNG	Fleet/Norstar Fin'l*	2.406	29.000	1105.32%
102	8/16/85	190	FNM	Fed'l Nat'l. Mortgag	20.250	77.375	282.10%
103	8/11/78	38	FQA	Fuqua Industries*	3.063	29.875	875.35%
104	11/30/84	178	FRA	Farah Manufacturing	17.500	11.625	-33.57%
105	8/ 8/80	90	FSR	Firstar Corp*	6.313	27.500	335.61%
106	8/28/87	225	FWES	First Western Fin'l	11.250	8.000	-28.89%
107	1/27/78	24	FWF	Far West Financial*	2.958	10.500	254.97%
108	4/24/87	219	GD	General Dynamics	66.625	57.000	-14.45%
109	12/27/85	196	GDV	General Development	15.500	13.875	-10.48%
110	5/ 5/78	31	GDW	Golden West Fin'l*	4.278	45.625	966.50%
111	10/30/87	228	GDYN	Geodynamics	8.250	13.500	63.64%
112	2/10/84	164	GLN	GlenFed Corporation	9.000	18.125	101.39%
113	2/08/85	181	GM	General Motors*	38.803	41.500	6.95%
114	2/08/85	181	GMH	General Motors "H"*	1.072	26.750	2395.34%
115	8/ 7/87	224	GNT	Green Tree Accpt.	25.625	6.375	-75.12%
116	11/09/84	177	GRR	G.R.I. Corp.	5.375	7.875	46.51%
117	10/30/87	228	GT	Goodyear Tire	47.875	52.500	9.66%
118	9/28/84	175	GTA	Great Amer. Savings*	7.083	13.250	87.07%
119	5/ 5/78	31	GWF	Great Western Fin'l*	6.233	19.125	206.83%
120	7/ 9/82	136	HC	Helene Curtis*	6.000	56.500	841.67%
121	9/18/87	226	HEI	HEICO Corp.*	18.750	12.250	-34.67%
122	10/30/87	228	HELE	Helen of Troy	5.500	21.750	295.45%
123	2/19/82	128	HENG	Henley Group*		68.750	
124	3/23/84	166	HFD	HomeFed Corp*	13.750	39.250	185.45%
125	8/19/88	242	HGIC	Harleysville Group	15.625	22.000	40.80%
126	9/13/85	191	HHH	Heritage Entertain.	3.750	1.750	-53.33%
127	2/28/86	199	HIBCA	Hibernia Corp.*	12.908	24.750	91.74%
128	9/ 8/78	40	HME	Home Group Inc.*	18.375	13.250	-27.89%
129	1/13/78	23	HMX	Hartmarx Inc.*	4.945	26.250	430.84%
130	12/30/88	248	HOC	Holly Corp	19.500	32.000	64.10%
131	10/30/87	228	HOF	Hofmann Inds.	2.125	4.750	123.53%
132	8/ 7/87	224	HTHR	Hawthorne Fin.	26.000	26.250	0.96%
133	6/13/86	204	HUM	Humana Corp.	25.375	32.325	27.59%
134	7/ 5/85	188	HWG	Hallwood Group*	19.250	4.750	-75.32%
135	5/24/85	186	HYDE	Hyde Athletic	5.250	7.500	42.86%
136	10/23/81	121	IAD	Inland Steel	23.250	40.875	75.81%
137	1/13/78	23	ICA	Imperial Corp.*	8.173	5.000	-38.82%
138	8/28/87	225	ICH	I.C.H. Corp.	13.125	4.625	-64.76%
139	8/16/85	190	IDCC	Intek Diversified	2.375	1.625	-31.58%
140	9/ 5/86	208	IFG	Inter-Reg. Fin'l	13.750	7.125	-48.18%
141	12/02/88	247	INDB	Independent Bank Cor	11.250	10.750	-4.44%
142	9/18/87	226	IRE	Integ. Resources	29.375	17.000	-42.13%
143	8/ 3/84	172	ITT	ITT Corp.	25.000	57.750	131.00%
144	11/20/87	229	IV	Mark IV Indus.	10.250	14.125	37.80%
145	1/17/86	197	JII	Johnston Industries	9.500	20.250	113.16%
146	10/30/87	228	JMY	Jamesway Corp.	6.625	10.375	56.60%
147	11/20/87	229	JPM	Morgan (J.P.)	34.375	37.750	9.82%
148	3/ 7/80	79	KBH	Kaufman&Broad Home*		13.250	
149	3/12/82	129	KGM	Kerr Glass	10.750	9.750	-9.30%
150	9/18/87	226	KLM	KLM Royal Dutch	25.625	20.625	-19.51%

	Date 1st Recommend	TPS	Symbol	Common Stock	1st Rec. Price	Price 5/17/89	Percent Change
151	3/21/80	80	KM	K-Mart Inc.*	12.500	38.125	205.00%
152	12/28/79	74	KZ	Kysor Industrial	5.813	16.625	186.00%
153	11/20/87	229	LADF	LADD Furniture	12.375	16.125	30.30%
154	2/ 9/79	51	LEN	Lennar Corp.*	2.958	21.125	614.16%
155	10/ 2/86	209	LK	Lockheed Corp.	45.625	47.125	3.29%
156	10/30/87	228	LMS	Lamson & Sessions	5.375	14.625	172.09%
157	10/30/87	228	LNDL	Lindal Cedar Homes*	4.132	7.750	87.55%
158	4/15/88	236	LUR	Luria(L) & Son	10.125	9.875	-2.47%
159	5/25/84	169	LZB	La-Z-Boy*	7.000	18.375	162.50%
160	2/ 3/89	250	MASX	Masco Inds	9.375	9.875	5.33%
161	11/20/87	229	MCN	MCN Corp.*	13.973	19.125	36.87%
162	4/ 7/89	253	MCU	Magma Copper	5.875	5.875	0.00%
163	7/ 9/82	136	MDR	McDermott Int'l	17.875	19.375	8.39%
164	7/ 8/88	240	MO	Philip Morris	85.375	135.500	58.71%
165	10/ 9/81	120	MOB	Mobil Corp.	27.375	50.375	84.02%
166	10/19/84	176	MODI	Modine Mfg.*	6.850	19.500	184.67%
167	7/17/87	223	MRI.A	McRae Industries	6.250	5.625	-10.00%
168	5/ 4/84	168	MSL	Mercury Savings*	6.632	4.750	-28.38%
169	10/19/84	176	MXM	MAXXAM Inc.*	15.000	30.250	101.67%
170	12/ 2/77	20	MYG	Maytag Corp.*	2.880	20.875	624.83%
171	10/21/88	245	N	Inco Ltd*	20.125	31.750	57.76%
172	11/18/77	19	NAV	Navistar Int'l*	29.125	5.250	-81.97%
173	4/ 9/82	131	NBD	NBD Bancorp*	7.208	44.500	517.37%
174	12/11/87	230	NME	Nat'l Medical Ent.	16.625	31.250	87.97%
175	11/30/79	72	NSD	National Standard	14.125	7.250	-48.67%
176	8/21/81	117	NSH	Nashua Corp.*	9.500	38.375	303.95%
177	9/28/84	175	NTK	Nortek Corp.*	10.500	8.875	-15.48%
178	10/30/87	228	NUVI	NUVision	7.750	6.750	-12.90%
179	2/19/82	128	OLN	Olin Corp.	19.875	51.625	159.75%
180	9/25/81	119	OM	Outboard Marine*	6.563	42.000	539.95%
181	12/11/87	230	OMM	OMI Corp*	3.250	8.625	165.38%
182	10/ 9/81	120	OSG	Overseas Shipping*	13.929	20.250	45.38%
183	11/ 4/77	18	OXM	Oxford Industries*	2.406	11.375	372.78%
184	2/19/82	128	PC	Penn Central Corp.*	6.808	24.875	265.38%
185	4/ 1/83	149	PCG	Pacific G&E*	9.602	19.625	104.38%
186	2/ 3/89	250	PD	Phelps Dodge	57.875	58.500	1.08%
187	10/ 9/81	120	PET	Pacific Enterprises*	22.149	43.500	96.40%
188	12/19/86	213	PFINA	P&F Industries	3.125	3.125	0.00%
189	10/30/87	228	PGI	Ply-Gem Inds.	10.375	14.250	37.35%
190	8/19/88	242	PICN	Pic'n'Save	12.875	14.500	12.62%
191	11/20/87	229	PMK	Primark*	3.750	8.250	120.00%
192	10/30/87	228	PMSI	Prime Med. Serv.	2.000	0.750	-62.50%
193	9/ 8/78	40	PN	Pan American	10.375	4.500	-56.63%
194	10/ 9/87	227	PNRE	Pan Atlantic Insur	8.250	6.750	-18.18%
195	12/27/85	196	PNW	Pinnacle West Cap.	27.250	12.125	-55.50%
196	10/30/87	228	POP	Pope & Talbot	12.750	22.625	77.45%
197	1/12/79	49	PRN	Puerto Rican Cement	4.625	45.750	889.19%
198	3/12/82	129	PSG	PS Group*	22.750	35.750	57.14%
199	12/11/87	230	PSX	Pacific Scientific	10.000	12.250	22.50%
200	3/25/77	2	PVH	Phillips Van-Heusen*	2.075	17.875	761.45%

	Date 1st Recommend	TPS	Symbol	Common Stock	1st Rec. Price	Price 5/17/89	Percent Change
201	10/30/87	228	PWJ	Paine Webber	17.000	19.000	11.76%
202	5/ 5/78	31	R	Ryder Systems*	6.708	25.250	276.42%
203	11/ 7/86	211	RAY	Raytech Corp.	5.000	1.750	-65.00%
204	11/ 9/84	177	RBSN	Robeson Ind.*	6.364	3.375	-46.97%
205	7/24/81	115	RD	Royal Dutch Petro.*	16.688	61.750	270.04%
206	10/30/87	228	REGB	Regional Bancorp	11.250	19.250	71.11%
207	10/ 9/87	227	RGB	Barry(R.G.)	8.000	8.875	10.94%
208	4/11/86	201	RIHL	Richton Int'l	6.250	3.625	-42.00%
209	10/ 9/87	227	RLI	RLI Corp.	12.500	7.875	-37.00%
210	9/28/84	175	RLM	Reynolds Metals*	14.375	56.125	290.43%
211	11/20/87	229	ROK	Rockwell	18.500	22.000	18.92%
212	3/12/82	129	RSR	Riser Foods*	11.375	6.750	-40.66%
213	10/30/87	228	RTN	Raytheon	69.250	70.125	1.26%
214	11/20/87	229	S	Sears	35.500	46.875	32.04%
215	4/18/80	82	SB	Salomon Brothers*	10.138	25.375	150.30%
216	10/30/87	228	SBIG	Seibels Bruce	11.750	11.250	-4.26%
217	10/30/87	228	SBOS	Boston Bancorp.	14.250	15.125	6.14%
218	8/ 3/84	172	SC	Shell Transport*	15.750	39.375	150.00%
219	11/ 6/81	122	SCR	Sea Containers*	14.786	46.000	211.11%
220	2/28/86	199	SEQP	Supreme Equipment	7.750	3.250	-58.06%
221	2/28/86	199	SFDS	Smithfield Foods*	5.625	16.500	193.33%
222	2/19/82	128	SFX	Santa Fe Pacific*	15.500	21.625	39.52%
223	10/30/87	228	SGAT	Seagate	13.000	14.000	7.69%
224	1/12/79	49	SGI	Slattery Group*	16.125	40.000	148.06%
225	5/25/84	169	SHG	Sheller-Globe*			
226	10/23/81	121	SHW	Sherwin Williams*	2.313	28.875	1148.38%
227	12/ 4/81	124	SIA	Signal Apparel*	4.563	5.500	20.53%
228	1/12/79	49	SLE	Sara Lee*	6.925	53.875	677.98%
229	4/13/84	167	SM	Southmark Corp.*	6.324	0.500	-92.09%
230	1/13/78	23	SMC.A	Smith (A.O.) "A"*	9.917	20.375	105.46%
231	3/ 1/85	182	SOI	Snyder Oil Partners*	14.815	3.750	-74.69%
232	10/30/87	228	SP	Spelling Prods.	5.500	9.250	68.18%
233	7/ 9/82	136	SPC	Security Pacific*	10.729	44.375	313.60%
234	8/ 7/87	224	SPF	Standard Pacific	12.125	15.250	25.77%
235	2/19/82	128	SPG	Sprague Technologies	1.801	11.750	552.42%
236	9/ 8/78	40	SQA.A	Sequa Corp. "A"*	57.721	67.000	16.08%
237	10/30/87	228	SSIAA	Stockholder Sys.	6.750	11.000	62.96%
238	8/19/88	242	SSM	SSMC Inc.	22.875	27.875	21.86%
239	11/20/87	229	STO	Stone Cont.*	20.417	29.125	42.65%
240	7/17/87	223	SUPD	Supradur Cos.	9.750	12.000	23.08%
241	10/19/84	176	TCL	Transcon Int'l	10.000	2.375	-76.25%
242	10/30/87	228	THMP	Thermal Inds.	4.750	4.000	-15.79%
243	12/11/87	230	TMK	Torchmark Corp	22.625	38.750	71.27%
244	11/15/85	194	TNI.A	Transcisco Inds "A"*	3.466	7.625	119.99%
245	11/15/85	194	TNI.B	Transcisco Inds "B"*	3.466	7.250	109.17%
246	4/13/84	167	TOD	Todd Shipyards	32.125	2.750	-91.44%
247	10/29/82	142	TOS	Tosco	15.000	5.125	-65.83%
248	9/25/81	119	TSO	Tesoro Petroleum	14.625	10.125	-30.77%
249	10/30/87	228	TT	TransTechnology	16.500	18.750	13.64%
250	12/27/85	196	TUR	Turner Corporation	25.750	17.000	-33.98%

Appendix C—*Concluded*

	Date 1st Recommend	TPS	Symbol	Common Stock	1st Rec. Price	Price 5/17/89	Percent Change
251	4/17/81	108	TX	Texaco Inc.	35.875	54.000	50.52%
252	12/31/81	126	TYC	Tyco Laboratories*	3.094	37.875	1124.14%
253	9/28/84	175	U	USAir Group.	28.000	45.250	61.61%
254	7/26/85	189	UAC	Unicorp-American	11.125	5.750	-48.31%
255	11/11/88	246	UCC	Union Camp	32.000	37.375	16.80%
256	11/28/80	98	UK	Union Carbide*	5.683	27.875	390.50%
257	12/31/87	231	USH	USLIFE Corp	28.500	43.125	51.32%
258	11/20/87	229	UTDMK	Utd Investment Mgt*	6.750	16.250	140.74%
259	11/14/80	97	VAT	Varity Corp*	5.125	2.875	-43.90%
260	5/25/84	169	VFC	VF Corporation*	11.938	33.000	176.43%
261	10/ 9/81	120	VO	Seagram Co.*	16.833	74.875	344.81%
262	9/ 8/78	40	WCH.P	WCI Preferred*	180.489	14.000	-92.24%
263	10/30/87	228	WDC	Western Digital	16.500	11.375	-31.06%
264	4/23/82	132	WFC	Wells Fargo Bank*	11.313	77.750	587.26%
265	10/30/87	228	WGO	Winnebago	8.000	8.000	0.00%
266	2/19/82	128	WHGP	Wheelabrator Group*		8.375	
267	12/27/85	196	WLC	Wellco Enterprises*	7.938	16.875	112.59%
268	10/30/87	228	WLD	Weldotron	4.750	5.750	21.05%
269	5/28/82	134	WN	Wynn's International	13.000	27.125	108.65%
270	6/16/78	34	WNT	Washington National*	16.500	25.250	53.03%
271	1/27/78	24	WWW	Wolverine World Wide	3.250	13.250	307.69%
272	9/11/81	118	X	USX Corp.	29.250	35.125	20.09%
273	5/19/78	32	Z	Woolworth (F.W.)*	10.125	52.000	413.58%
274	6/26/87	222	ZSEV	Z-Seven Fund	23.000	14.000	-39.13%

Note: Stocks without recommended prices (1st Rec. Price) and percent change reflect spinoffs with bonds or partial liquidations resulting in no meaningful figures until the liquidations are completed or the bonds or original stocks are sold.

APPENDIX D

ALL FORMERLY RECOMMENDED STOCKS WHICH HAVE BEEN CLOSED OUT THROUGH JUNE 30, 1989

All Formerly Recommended Stocks Which Have Been Closed Out

	Date 1st Recommend	TPS Symbol	Common Stock	1st Rec. Price	Price Closed	Percent Change	CLOSED
1	7/11/80	88 AAE	Amerace Corp.	20.375	47.500	133.13	10/84
2	12/ 4/81	124 ABZ	Arkansas Best	4.000	26.000	550.00	7/88
3	7/ 5/85	188 ACF	ACI Holdings	9.875	15.000	51.90	4/87
4	10/30/87	228 ADVN	Advanta Corp.	7.250	9.500	31.03	5/89
5	3/12/82	129 AGM	Amalgamated Sugar	42.500	66.000	55.29	11/82
6	10/21/77	17 AH	Allis-Chalmers	23.625	3.625	-84.66	12/85
7	3/22/85	183 AINC	American Income Life	10.375	19.000	83.13	5/89
8	9/25/81	119 AMA	Amfac Corp.	20.250	32.250	59.26	6/87
9	4/22/77	4 AMI*	Amer. Medical Int'l*	9.636	39.500	309.92	6/80
10	9/21/79	67 AMT	Acme-Cleveland	22.250	12.875	-42.13	6/87
11	11/ 6/81	122 AMZ	Amer. Seating	11.875	29.250	146.32	1/83
12	2/ 7/86	198 ARC	Atlantic Richfield	52.125	86.000	64.99	4/87
13	9/23/77	15 ARM	Armtek*	6.532	46.000	604.23	10/88
14	9/11/81	118 ASR	Amstar Corp.	21.875	47.000	114.86	2/84
15	9/23/77	15 AV	Avco Corp.	15.000	50.000	233.33	1/85
16	11/20/87	229 AWCSA	AW Computer	1.375	0.750	-45.45	6/88
17	4/18/80	82 BCH	Bache Group*	7.875	32.000	306.35	6/81
18	2/19/82	128 BE	Benguet	3.750	5.500	46.67	3/85
19	11/18/77	19 BF	Budd Corp.	23.625	34.000	43.92	4/78
20	7/28/78	37 BG	Brown Group*	8.583	43.625	408.27	6/87
21	4/ 6/79	55 BHW	Bell & Howell*	8.063	53.750	566.63	6/87
22	9/28/84	175 BIRD	Bird Inc.	5.500	10.500	90.91	4/86
23	12/ 4/81	124 BNK	Bangor Punta	19.875	27.500	38.36	2/84
24	8/24/79	65 BRF	Borman's Inc.	5.875	27.000	359.57	1/89
25	6/ 2/78	33 CAL*	Continental Airlines	13.875	6.125	-55.86	?/82
26	3/28/80	81 CAN	Cannon Mills	21.375	50.000	133.92	3/82
27	1/13/78	23 CCF	Cook United*	2.519	1.250	-50.38	3/85
28	10/ 9/87	227 CFG	Copelco Fin Svc.	8.000	8.750	9.38	11/88
29	12/12/80	99 CIH	Cont'l Illinois Hld	17.170	0.125	-99.27	3/88
30	5/ 5/78	31 CKE	Castle & Cooke*	6.200	18.750	202.42	11/86
31	12/27/85	196 CLG.P	Clabir Pfd.*	11.375	7.625	-32.97	3/88
32	12/27/85	196 CLG.X	Clabir "B" Wt.*	1.500	0.063	-95.83	3/88
33	3/ 7/80	79 CPG	Colonial Penn Gp.	17.250	35.000	102.90	1/86
34	7/28/78	37 CPS	Columbia Pictures	22.125	73.000	229.94	6/82
35	9/28/84	175 CSA	Caressa Inc.	10.500	15.750	50.00	11/84
36	4/12/85	184 CVRS	Converse Inc.	16.250	28.000	72.31	9/86
37	10/30/87	228 CWCC	Capital Wire	7.500	13.750	83.33	7/88
38	3/26/77	2 DML	Dan River	8.625	22.500	160.87	6/83
39	12/28/84	179 DUCK	Duckwall-Alco	13.500	17.750	31.48	9/85
40	8/12/77	12 DWR	Dean Witter*	10.000	50.000	400.00	1/82
41	11/20/81	123 DYN	DynCorp.	8.500	24.250	185.29	2/88
42	4/18/80	82 EC	Englehard Corp.*	19.107	37.500	96.26	2/87
43	11/30/84	178 ECOL	American Ecology	7.125	22.625	217.54	6/87
44	11/ 9/84	177 EFG	Equitec Financial	10.625	3.000	-71.76	11/88
45	11/ 9/84	177 EMLX	Emulex Corp.	7.125	9.750	36.84	4/86
46	12/11/87	230 ENVR	Envirodyne Indus.	15.750	40.000	153.97	5/89
47	2/ 7/86	198 EQUI	Equion Corp.	7.500	9.750	30.00	4/89
48	11/30/84	178 ETX	Entex Inc.	20.250	22.500	11.11	2/88
49	12/16/77	21 EXR	Elixir Industries	4.875	10.000	105.13	2/82
50	2/19/82	128 EY	Ethyl Corp.*	2.406	30.500	1167.66	4/87

Appendix D—*Continued*

	Date 1st Recommend	TPS	Symbol	Common Stock	1st Rec. Price	Price Closed	Percent Change	CLOSED
51	10/30/87	228	FBC	First Boston	25.375	52.500	106.90	1/89
52	6/17/77	8	FBG	Faberge Inc.	8.625	32.000	271.01	3/84
53	12/28/84	179	FBT	Fst City Banc Tex*	1462.500	22.250	-98.48	8/88
54	3/12/82	129	FEN	Fairchild	12.125	9.125	-24.74	3/86
55	3/23/84	166	FIN	Financial Corp Amer.	17.000	0.875	-94.85	8/88
56	7/15/77	10	FM	Franklin Mint	11.125	27.000	142.70	3/81
57	7/28/78	37	FMC	FMC Corp.*	24.000	112.750	369.79	2/87
58	3/ 7/80	79	FS	Fisher Scientific*	15.625	55.000	252.00	8/81
59	7/28/78	37	GDV*	GDV Inc.	9.875	20.000	102.53	10/81
60	7/25/86	206	GEMH	Gemcraft Inc.	9.000	0.875	-90.28	8/88
61	7/ 1/77	9	GFC	Gibraltar Financial*	6.917	2.875	-58.44	8/88
62	3/12/82	129	GH	General Host*	6.960	17.625	153.23	12/84
63	3/26/82	130	GLM	Global Marine	12.250	1.125	-90.82	6/88
64	8/21/81	117	GNO	Gino's Inc.	7.875	18.000	128.57	5/82
65	9/ 8/78	40	GOR.A	Gordon Jewelry*	10.188	36.750	260.72	6/89
66	7/24/81	115	GOTLF	Gotaas Larsen*	6.000	48.000	700.00	12/88
67	1/13/78	23	GR	Goodrich	19.750	51.000	158.23	2/87
68	10/31/80	96	GRX	Gen'l Refract	7.750	22.500	190.32	8/88
69	3/22/85	183	GST	Genstar Corp.	21.500	41.823	94.53	5/86
70	3/28/80	81	GT	Goodyear Tire	11.875	48.000	304.21	11/86
71	8/11/78	38	GW	Gulf + Western*	12.800	65.625	412.70	8/86
72	7/ 9/82	136	GX	GEO International	10.000	5.500	-45.00	6/87
73	10/30/87	228	GXY	Galaxy Carpet	12.750	14.000	9.80	6/89
74	10/ 4/85	192	HASR	Hauserman Inc.	14.750	5.000	-66.10	11/88
75	4/ 8/77	3	HGH	Hughes & Hatcher	7.000	11.730	67.57	11/77
76	9/25/81	119	HLY	Holly Sugar	30.125	121.875	304.56	5/86
77	11/28/80	98	HML	Hammermill Paper*	17.667	64.500	265.09	10/86
78	6/14/85	187	HYO	Husky Oil, Ltd.	7.250	8.750	20.69	4/87
79	1/13/78	23	HZ	Hazeltine*	3.417	18.000	426.78	8/86
80	3/26/82	130	ICX	IC Industries*	7.407	34.000	359.03	6/87
81	6/11/82	135	ID	Ideal Toy	11.000	14.850	35.00	8/82
82	10/31/80	96	INA	INA Corp.	38.625	45.375	17.48	4/82
83	5/ 2/80	83	INR	Insilco Corp.*	7.817	31.750	306.17	10/88
84	9/ 8/78	40	IU	IU International*	12.000	16.375	36.46	12/84
85	10/30/87	228	JAC	Johnstown Amer.	2.500	0.313	-87.50	8/88
86	1/12/79	49	JAN	Jantzen Inc.	17.250	30.000	73.91	1/80
87	1/13/78	23	JOL	Jonathan Logan*	7.417	28.000	277.51	10/84
88	3/12/82	129	KAB	Kaneb Services	13.750	2.250	-83.64	11/88
89	1/12/79	49	KCC	Kaiser Cement	22.750	27.500	20.88	12/86
90	7/ 9/82	136	KEN	Kenai Corp.	6.625	0.090	-98.64	4/86
91	5/ 5/78	31	KES	Keystone Corp.*	7.083	18.000	154.13	6/87
92	9/11/81	118	KML	Kane Miller	10.750	21.000	95.35	2/84
93	4/20/79	56	KOE	Koehring	17.125	37.000	116.06	9/80
94	3/ 7/80	79	KT	Katy Industries	12.000	18.500	54.17	4/86
95	11/30/79	72	LES	Leslie Fay	6.875	16.000	132.73	6/82
96	7/28/78	37	LEV	Levitz Furniture*	9.813	39.000	297.43	4/85
97	5/ 4/79	57	LST	Lowenstein M.	11.200	63.000	462.50	10/85
98	9/11/81	118	LTV	LTV Corp.	17.875	9.125	-48.95	4/86
99	4/21/78	30	MCC	Mesta Machinery	21.500	2.875	-86.63	12/84
100	7/30/82	137	MCN	Midcon Corp.	21.000	80.039	281.14	6/87

Appendix D—*Continued*

	Date 1st Recommend	TPS Symbol	Common Stock	1st Rec. Price	Price Closed	Percent Change	CLOSED
101	1/13/78	23 MG	Monogram Ind.	14.000	57.750	312.50	8/83
102	9/11/81	118 MGU	Michigan Sugar	14.125	43.500	207.96	5/84
103	5/ 4/79	57 MHT	Manhattan Ind.*	9.557	18.000	88.34	2/88
104	9/25/81	119 MM	Marine Midland	17.875	83.510	367.19	10/87
105	5/ 6/77	5 MME	McNeil Corp.	12.125	39.000	221.65	8/86
106	11/30/79	72 MMO	Monarch Mach. Tool*	10.063	20.000	98.75	6/87
107	1/12/79	49 MOH	Mohasco Corp.	5.111	35.000	584.80	6/88
108	7/29/77	11 MRS	Morse Shoe*	7.800	30.500	291.03	4/86
109	1/13/78	23 MRX	Memorex Corp.	27.375	14.000	-48.86	12/81
110	5/ 6/77	5 MTM	Marathon Mfg.	8.125	47.250	481.54	12/79
111	10/19/84	176 MTN	Mountain Medical	3.750	6.000	60.00	6/88
112	10/ 3/80	94 MWK	Mohawk Rubber*	13.875	40.000	188.29	1/84
113	10/ 9/81	120 MXS	Maxus Energy Corp.*	3.125	7.625	144.00	8/88
114	11/28/80	98 NAC	National Can	23.250	42.000	80.65	4/85
115	11/30/84	178 NIN	NI Industries	15.500	22.000	41.94	2/85
116	3/24/78	28 NPH	North Amer. Phillips	12.563	56.000	345.75	10/87
117	11/ 9/84	177 NSO	New American Shoe*	11.500	1.375	-88.04	11/88
118	6/27/80	87 NTY	National Tea	4.125	8.000	93.94	1/82
119	2/ 8/80	77 OI	Owens-Illinois*	12.063	60.500	401.53	3/87
120	1/11/80	75 OPKM	Opelika Ind.	39.000	8.250	-78.85	12/84
121	4/17/81	108 OXY	Occidental Petroleum	29.625	38.250	29.11	6/87
122	10/23/81	121 P	Phillips Petroleum*	12.875	16.625	29.13	4/87
123	8/22/80	91 PCF	PennCorp Financial	8.125	14.000	72.31	1/83
124	1/12/79	49 PHL	Philips Industries*	2.500	35.250	1310.00	4/86
125	6/27/80	87 PII	Pueblo International	3.000	26.000	766.67	6/88
126	10/ 7/77	16 PIR	Pier One*	6.125	16.500	169.39	11/79
127	9/25/81	119 PLA	Playboy Enterprises	8.500	11.250	32.35	12/84
128	9/25/81	119 POR	Portec Inc.	11.375	18.250	60.44	12/84
129	11/20/81	123 R	Uniroyal	7.375	22.000	198.31	9/85
130	1/13/78	23 RAY	Raymark*	24.382	9.375	-61.55	12/85
131	9/25/81	119 RC	Research-Cottrell	10.750	43.000	300.00	7/87
132	10/23/81	121 RCI	Reichold Chemicals	12.500	33.625	169.00	4/86
133	1/12/79	49 REP	Republic Corp.*	14.479	43.000	196.98	2/85
134	7/30/82	137 RHH	Robertson (H.H.)	23.875	38.750	62.30	12/84
135	9/28/84	175 RI	Radice	8.875	0.750	-91.55	6/88
136	10/ 7/77	16 ROC	Rockower Bros.	11.500	21.000	82.61	12/80
137	3/ 7/80	79 ROP	Roper Corp.*	2.375	54.000	2173.68	4/88
138	7/11/80	88 RVB	Revere Copper	13.500	22.500	66.67	12/86
139	4/ 8/77	3 RYR	Rymer Corp.*	10.593	19.375	82.90	11/86
140	4/13/84	167 SA	Safeway Stores	23.750	67.044	182.29	11/86
141	9/23/77	15 SBI	Sterchi Bros.	9.125	33.000	261.64	2/86
142	3/21/80	80 SCM	SCM Corp.	20.875	75.000	259.28	4/86
143	6/ 2/78	33 SHA	Shapell Industries	24.625	65.000	163.96	7/84
144	11/16/79	71 SHC	Shaklee Corp.	6.813	18.375	169.70	4/86
145	6/ 2/78	33 SHP	Stop & Shop*	3.000	39.000	1200.00	2/88
146	7/ 9/82	136 SII	Smith International	22.375	8.125	-63.69	6/87
147	4/21/78	30 SKC	Skil Corp.	13.000	30.000	130.77	4/79
148	6/17/77	8 SLT	Salant Corp.	7.125	12.000	68.42	6/87
149	9/ 8/78	40 SMB	Sunbeam Corp.	22.500	27.750	23.33	1/82
150	7/ 1/77	9 SMI	Springs Industries	6.125	34.500	463.27	6/87

Appendix D—*Concluded*

	Date 1st Recommend	TPS	Symbol	Common Stock	1st Rec. Price	Price Closed	Percent Change	CLOSED
151	3/28/80	81	SMP	Standard Mtr. Prod.*	2.000	16.750	737.50	4/86
152	1/18/85	180	SSSI	Servamatic Systems	1.875	0.020	-98.93	8/86
153	2/10/78	25	SVN	Sav-On-Drugs	7.125	18.750	163.16	11/80
154	9/25/81	119	SVS	Sav-A-Stop	7.875	16.000	103.17	3/82
155	3/23/79	54	SWS	Sargent-Welch Sci.	13.375	33.000	146.73	12/84
156	7/14/78	36	TA	Transamerica	15.750	37.125	135.71	4/86
157	5/18/79	58	TAN	Tandy Corp.	19.750	42.500	115.19	6/80
158	10/20/78	43	TF	20th Century Fox*	23.910	68.000	184.40	6/81
159	9/25/81	119	TK	Technicolor	16.625	23.000	38.35	11/82
160	5/ 5/78	31	TKA	Tonka Corp.*	9.875	14.625	48.10	3/85
161	12/27/85	196	TKA	Tonka Corp.	18.333	12.000	-34.54	8/88
162	5/20/77	6	TRI	Triangle Industries*	2.375	32.625	1273.68	7/88
163	4/13/84	167	TWA	Trans World Airlines	8.750	26.750	205.71	3/88
164	12/24/81	125	UER	United Energy Res.	40.500	41.000	1.23	9/85
165	4/22/77	4	UFL	United Financial*	11.700	33.600	187.18	1/80
166	9/ 8/78	40	USG	USG Corp.*	7.657	48.000	526.88	7/88
167	3/ 7/80	79	USI	US Industries	7.875	23.000	192.06	5/84
168	6/ 2/78	33	USL	US Leasing Int'l	15.000	68.000	353.33	11/87
169	4/13/84	167	VRO	Varo Inc.	10.250	15.750	53.66	4/86
170	8/10/79	64	WHMCG	White Motor	6.750	1.900	-71.85	4/80
171	2/ 9/79	51	WHX	Wheeling-Pittsburgh	15.750	22.000	39.68	8/88
172	6/13/86	204	WILF	Wilson Foods	9.250	14.500	56.76	3/89
173	4/ 1/83	149	WMS	Williams Electronics	11.750	7.125	-39.36	6/87
174	8/12/77	12	WPI	Western Pac. Ind.*	20.750	186.000	796.39	11/86
175	3/21/80	80	WPM	West Point-Pepperell	5.908	58.000	881.72	5/89
176	1/12/79	49	WRC	Warnaco Ind.*	5.188	46.500	796.30	5/86
177	7/30/82	137	WSN	Western Co. No. Amer	9.000	0.500	-94.44	6/88
178	5/20/77	6	WUR	Wurlitzer Co.	8.750	3.125	-64.29	12/85
179	1/13/78	23	YES	Yates Industries*	5.250	40.000	661.90	7/80
180	10/19/84	176	YNK	Yankee Companies	6.750	0.750	-88.89	6/88
181	7/29/77	11	ZAL	Zale Corp.	14.750	50.000	238.98	12/86
182	7/ 9/82	136	ZOS	Zapata Corp.	15.250	2.750	-81.97	6/88
183	11/ 4/77	18	ZY	Zayre Corp.*	0.959	24.000	2402.61	4/88
							195.39	

INDEX